the
Photography Storytelling Workshop

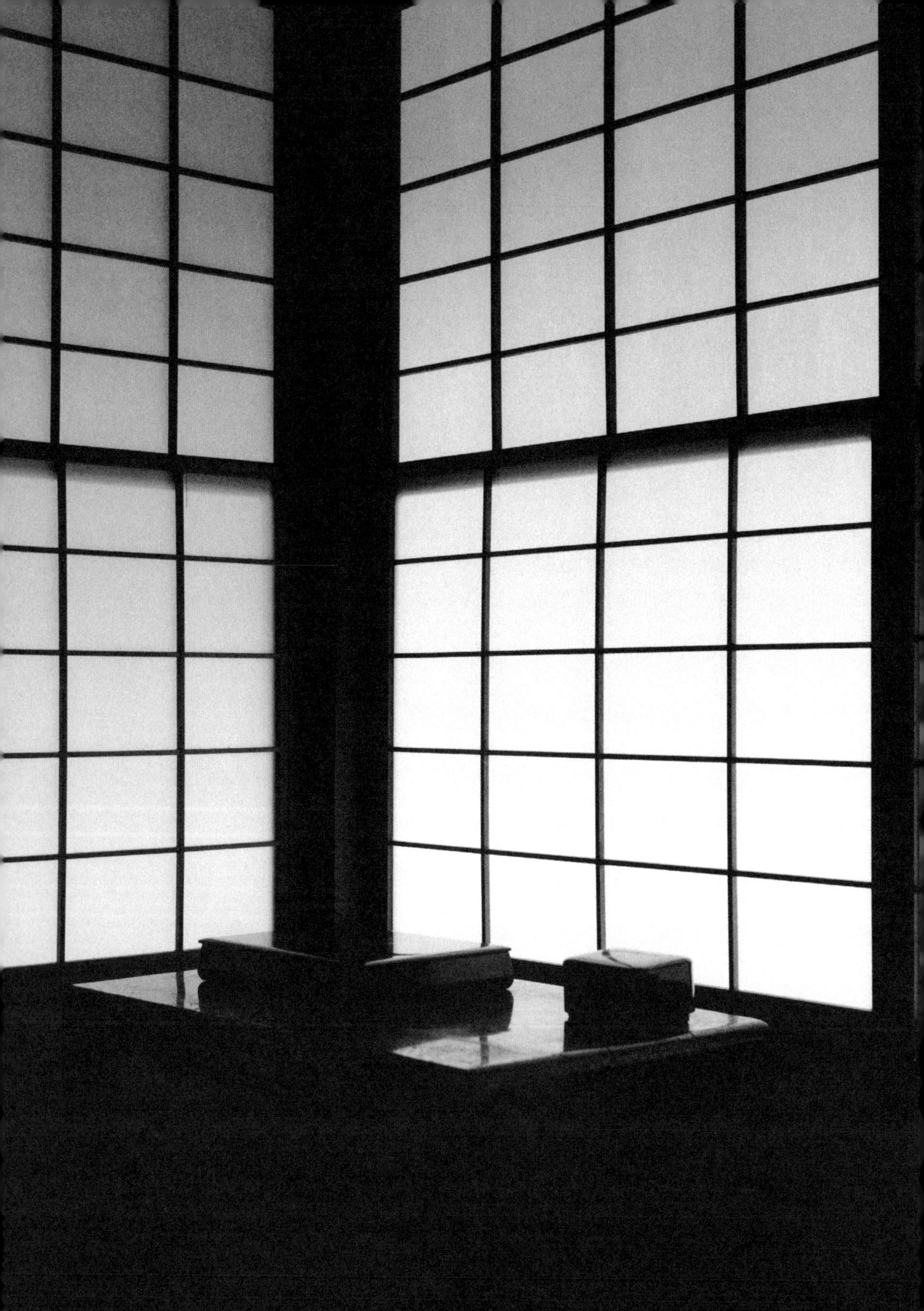

the Photography Storytelling Workshop

FINN BEALES

Foreword by **Alex Strohl**

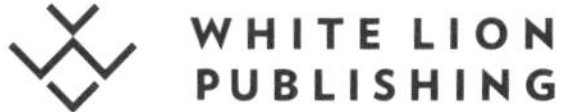

WHITE LION PUBLISHING

First published in 2020 by White Lion Publishing,
an imprint of The Quarto Group.
1 Triptych Place, 2nd Floor,
London, SE1 9SH,
United Kingdom
T (0)20 7700 9000
www.Quarto.com

A catalogue record for this book is available from
the British Library.

ISBN 978 0 7112 5470 1
Ebook ISBN 978 0 7112 5471 8

10 9

Commissioning Editor   Zara Anvari
Project Editor   Ellie Wilson
Editor   Charlotte Frost
Designer   Isabel Eeles

Typeset in Garamond Pro and Akzidenz Grotesk

Printed in China

Contents

6   Foreword
8   Introduction
11   The Power of Images
13   Sparking the Imagination
14   Where to Start?
17   What You Will Need
18   Gear: DSLR or Mirrorless
20   Gear: Phone Apps
21   **Exercise / Image Editing on
       a Smartphone**

22 | Storytelling 101

24   What is a Story?
26   Location
28   Character
30   Event
32   Environmental Portraiture
34   **Project / Capture an Environmental
       Portrait**
38   The Importance of Shot Type
40   Shot Types: Extreme Long & Long
42   Shot Types: Medium & Medium Close
44   Shot Types: Close-Up & Cutaway
46   **Project / One Subject, Ten Ways**
50   Creating a Body of Work
52   **Project / Everyday Cinematic**

| 56 | **Step 1: Pitch** |

58 Website
60 Instagram
64 Ask the Right Questions
66 The Creative Call
68 Project / Develop a Treatment
72 Pricing
74 Selling the Estimate

| 76 | **Step 2: Prep** |

78 Developing a Mood Board
80 Mood-boarding for Colour
84 Combining Colour Palettes
86 Developing Your Own Colour
Palette for Image Grading
86 Exercise / Making the Grade
88 Project / Edit Like a Painter
90 The Location Recce
92 Mission Control

| 96 | **Step 3: Shoot** |

98 Meeting Your Subjects
100 See the Light
102 Types of Sunlight
**104 Project / Capturing Mystery:
Shooting Silhouettes**
108 Camera Settings
110 Shooting with Prime Lenses
112 Exercise / Phone Portraits
114 Shooting Technique: Rembrandt
115 Exercise / Rembrandt Lighting
116 Shooting Technique: Catchlights
**117 Exercise / Experimenting with
Catchlights**

118 Shooting Technique: 50 & Stitch
(The Brenizer Method)
119 Exercise / Stitching
120 Shooting Technique: Beginner Panning Shot
121 Exercise / Panning with a Smartphone
122 Project / Keep Moving: Motion Blur
126 Shooting Technique: Advanced Tracking Shot
127 Exercise / Tracking
128 Shooting Technique: Cinematic
130 Project / Dreamlike Scenes with Lens Flare
134 Shooting Technique: Dirty Foreground

| 136 | **Step 4: Edit** |

138 Save Time: Organise Your Images
140 Making Your Selects
142 Lightroom Collections
143 Exercise / Making Collections
144 Grading: Basic Adjustments
**148 Project / Shoot with Film to Influence
Your Grade**
150 Introducing Film Grain & Effects
150 Exercise / Adding Light Leaks
152 Building a Story
158 Backup, Backup, Backup

| 162 | **Step 5: Deliver** |

164 File Formats
166 Sharpening
168 Project / Finalising Your File
172 Delivering Your Selects

174 Index
176 There is No Finish Line

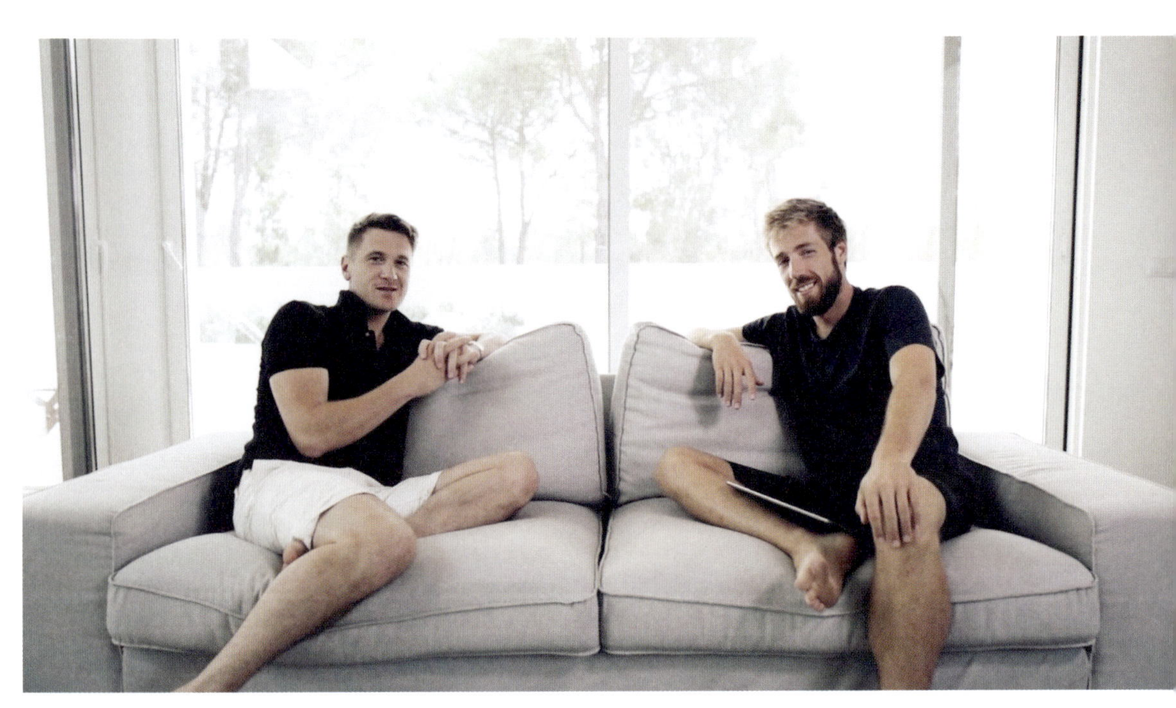

Foreword

by Alex Strohl

I started out as a graphic design major and ended up getting into photography at university. One of my classes, 'Introduction to Photography', was taught by a veteran of documentary photography who encouraged us to use film cameras and taught us a host of old-school techniques including how to go from negative to print and how to dodge and burn as Ansel Adams famously did. This new world was thrilling, and I was just following my curiosity with no clear plan in sight until somehow, I ended up shooting advertising campaigns for some of the world's largest brands and carving a niche in the competitive adventure photography world. Never did I imagine I'd be running a thriving photography studio with a full-time team all from the woods of Montana.

Among the talented people I've met on this journey, Finn is the one who has inspired me to use stories within my work. This, in turn, led me to create a workshop focusing on his approach to visual storytelling. After I'd finished filming it, I remember being so excited to get home and view it in a whole new way – following his process and looking for stories in the everyday. His method for building a narrative using the three impactful prompts: 1. Character, 2. Location, 3. Event (covered in this book) has encouraged me to rethink my own approach to my photographic projects.

Finn and I are part of a new generation of creatives who have built careers out of living in remote places. With the advent of the internet and more specifically, social media, gone are the days were photographers had to be based in Paris, New York, or any large city to 'make it'. The age where if you wanted to become a photographer you had to take an internship at your local newspapers are gone. All you need is a camera, a phone and internet access. And some damn good stories to tell. This is exciting because it puts the control back in the hands of the creatives, it has levelled the field as we all have the same tools and only the stories and ideas make the difference. You can see this in Finn's photography throughout the book, in the way that he uses his home surroundings in Wales as a backdrop to his shoots.

Finn and I have both walked the same squiggly line, sometimes falling off but always getting back on and carrying on. He has been bold and chosen his own path and as a result, he's become a world-class photographer who deserves every one of his achievements. This book shares the practices that have helped him get there, together with the knowledge that he's picked up working with just about every brand you'd dream of shooting. There are only a handful of people who could write this book and Finn sits at the top of this list.

Introduction

Today's world is awash with images, but what makes people stop scrolling or walking by? What makes them remember an image or a photographer's work? In my mind, it's the stories they tell. Stories are the real 'influencers'. From fairy tales and legends, to religious texts and political campaigns, it's the stories that capture us and the emotions they elicit that make the messages last. The aim of this book is to help you create lasting photographs, the sort Dorothea Lange called 'second lookers'. using a tried-and-tested approach that puts the story at the heart of everything you do.

How to Use this Book

We'll start with the basics, including what equipment you need and the essence of a great photograph. Then we'll examine the craft of storytelling and how this can be applied to photography. From there, the book follows the process of making a photo story. I cover pitching for work and doing your prep, the actual shoot, the edit and the final collation of your images. In each section you will find step-by-step exercises illustrating fundamental techniques and projects to challenge your creativity and broaden your skill set. You'll also find tips, creative briefs and plenty of real-world examples.

The Workshop

This book was inspired by a photo story I created for a company called Cool & Vintage, based in Portugal. Cool & Vintage specialise in the restoration of vintage Land Rovers, but don't think of this as an automotive shoot. I want to show you how to incorporate a product (like a car) into a broader story that makes for a more entertaining set of images.

With the rise of influencer-based marketing, this is especially useful when developing branded content for platforms like Instagram. Straightforward product placement is a lazy way to market anything, in my opinion. It is much better to build a story around a product and entertain your audience along the way.

So, following my process in this workshop we will pitch, prepare, shoot, edit and deliver.

By the end of this book you will be able to pitch for jobs, win contracts and craft a shoot from start to finish. We'll look at shoot preparation, including working with mood boards and call sheets, directing models, and post production and editing. We'll even touch on the tricky topic of pricing your work.

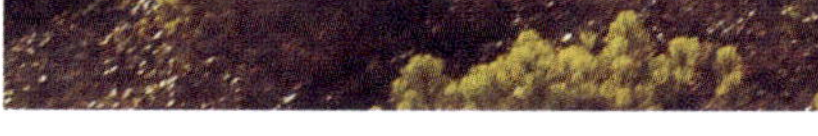

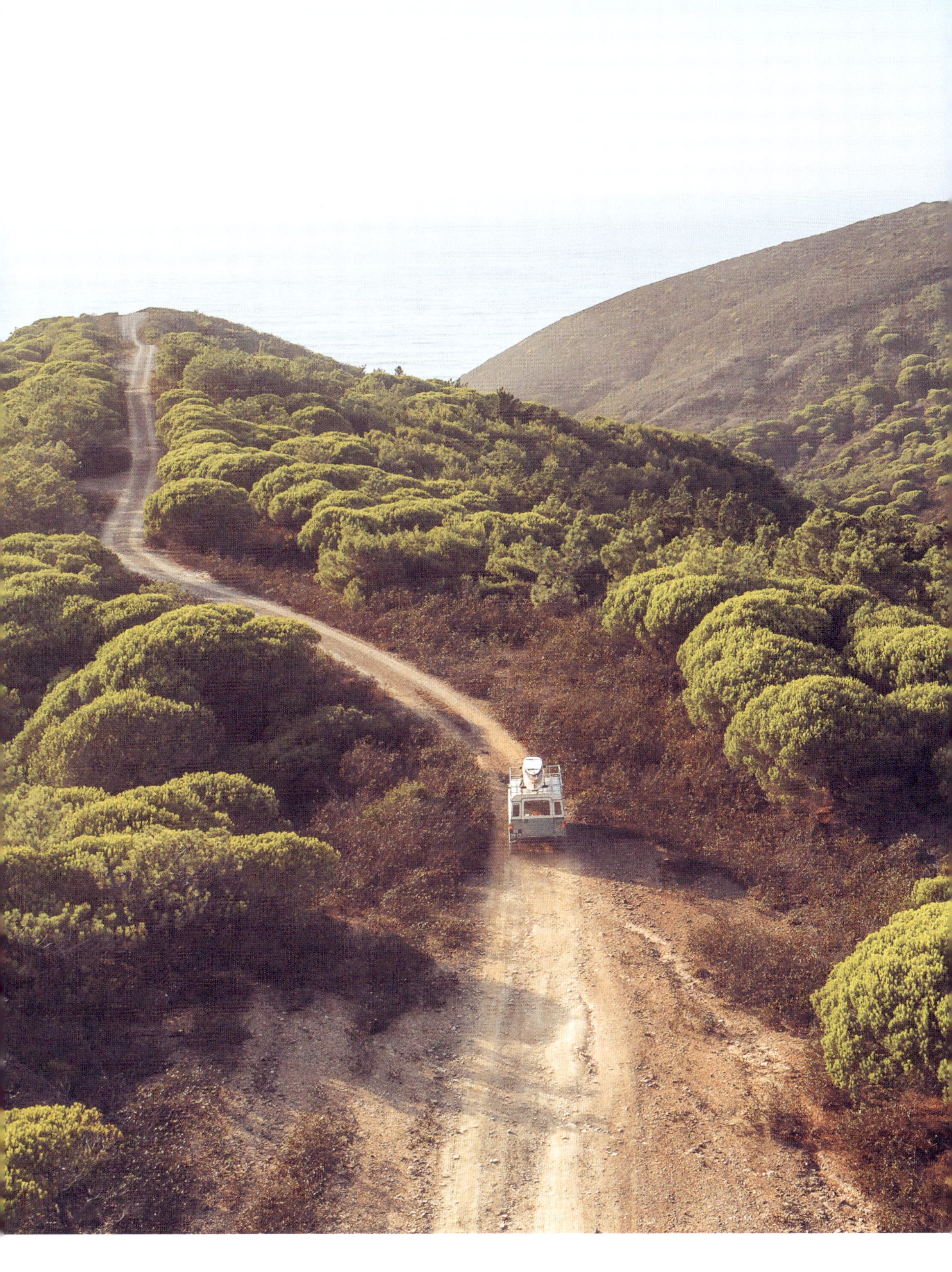

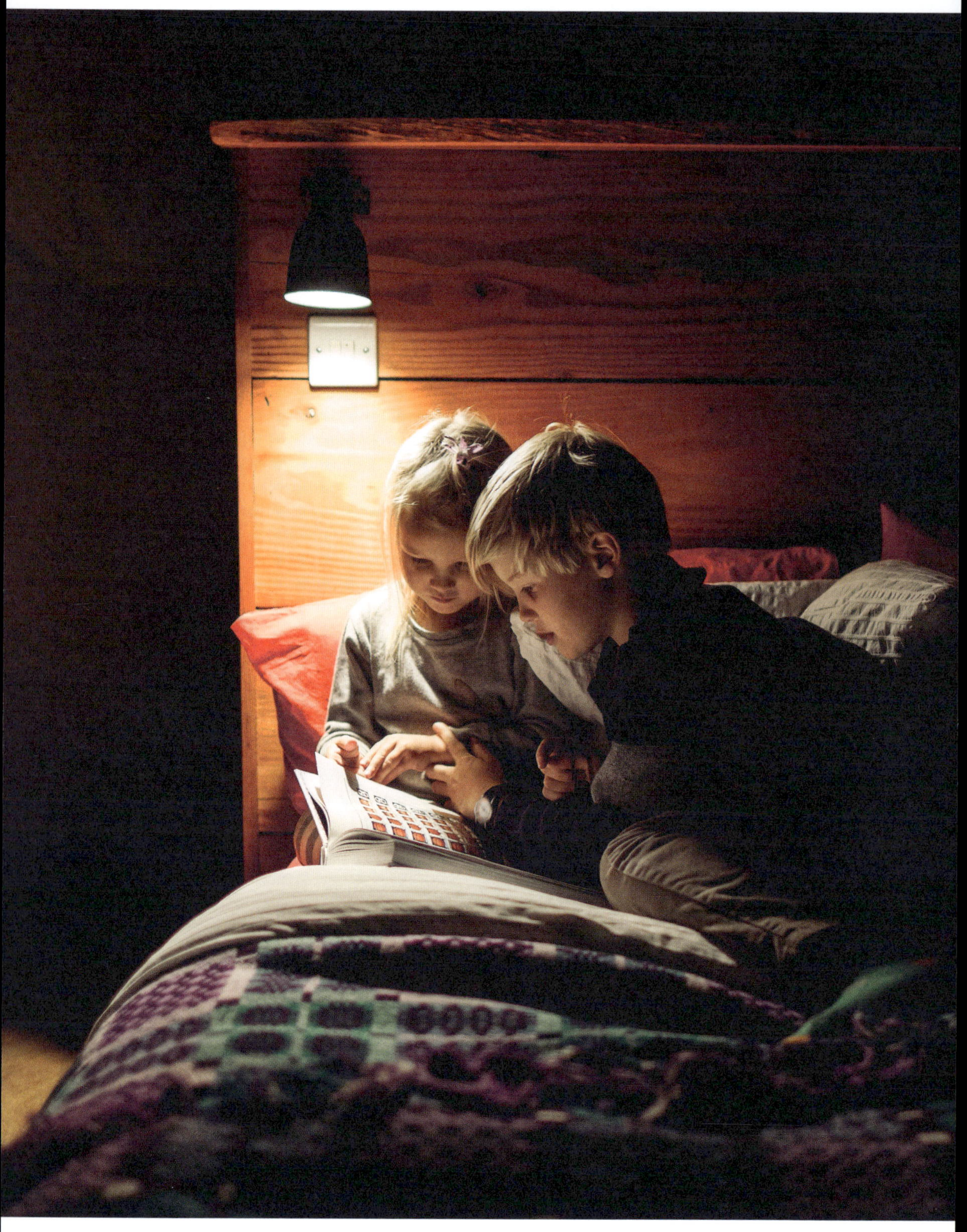

THE POWER OF IMAGES

The thing I love most about photography, over other mediums, is that something is always left to the viewer's imagination. I liken it to the difference between a movie and a book: I love both, but I'm sometimes disappointed if I watch a movie after I've read the same story. That's because a book allows me to bring my own imagination to the table. The story feels richer because my mind is working on a deeper level. I feel the same way about photographs.

What are my kids reading here? Where are they?

These questions are posed to a stranger viewing the image, piquing their interest.

Photographs leave gaps in the narrative that viewers can fill with their own imagination. There's always something left unanswered; there's no verbal communication, sound or music adding atmosphere. These feelings must be present in the images alone and the photograph should tell you just enough to activate your desire to know more. This might come from lighting or maybe a close-up of a character's face or hands. An image should provoke an intuitive, visceral feeling – there might not be a rational explanation for it, but you know when you feel it.

TIP / Pose questions to your audience and compose your image in a way that leaves something to the viewer's own imagination. Don't give too much away.

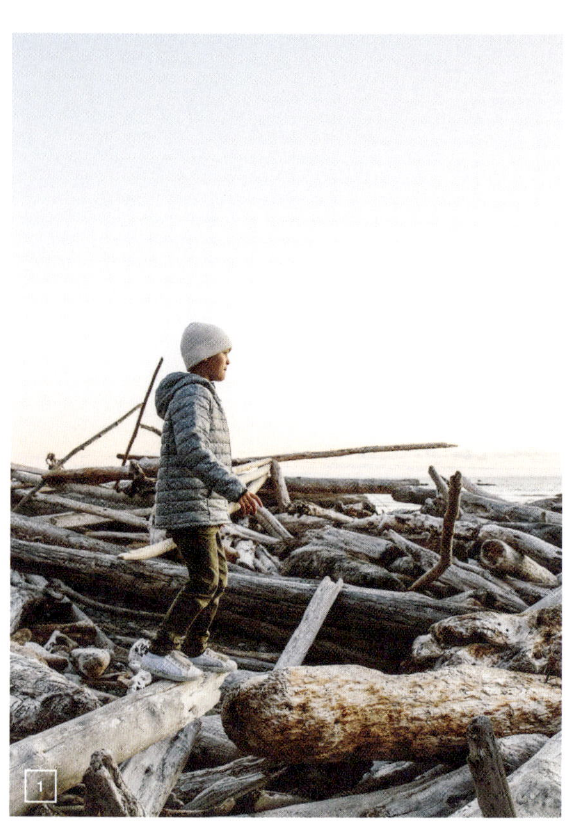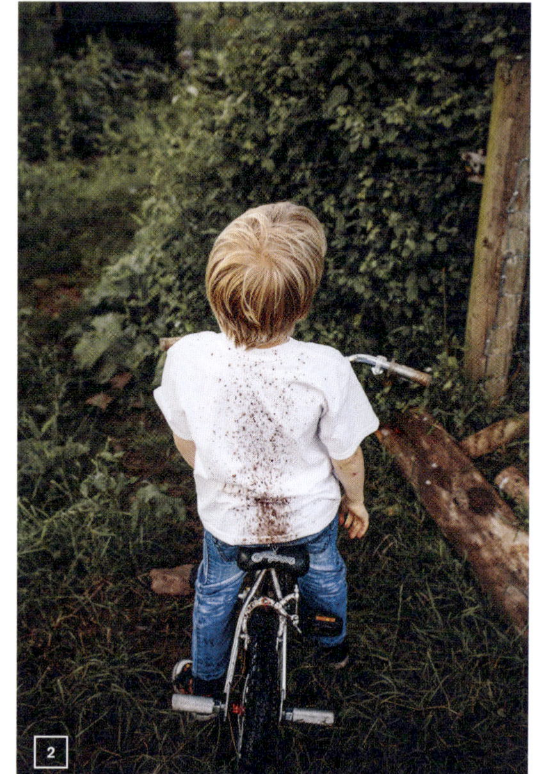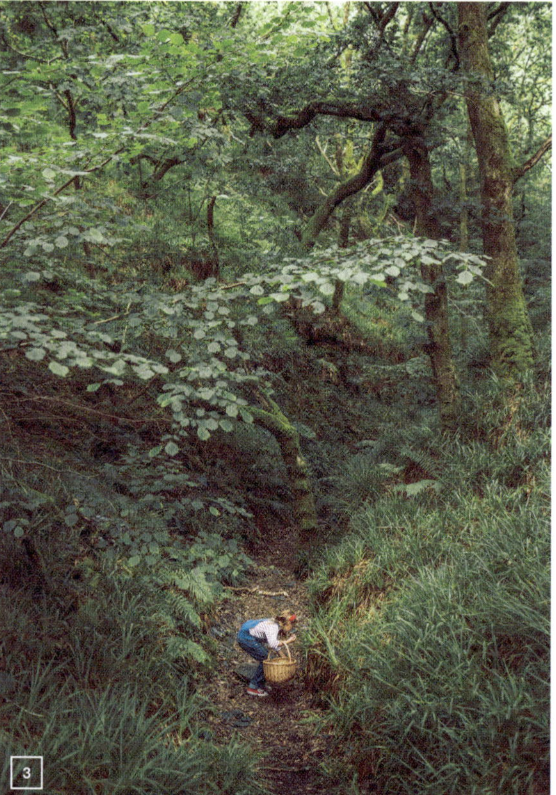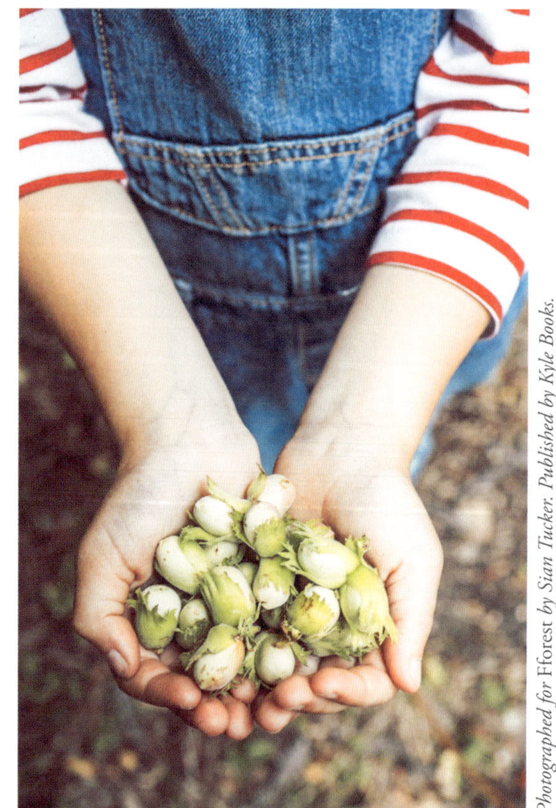

Photographed for Fforest by Sian Tucker. Published by Kyle Books.

SPARKING THE IMAGINATION

Photographs that leave gaps in the narrative allow a viewer to fill it with their own imagination, but how do you go about making pictures along these lines?

1 POSE A QUESTION TO YOUR AUDIENCE

There is a pleasure in not knowing. It activates the mind. Frame your images in a way that poses a question to your audience and engages them in your work.

Consider this image: there is a story here but it isn't evident. *What is my son looking at? Why is he standing on so much driftwood? Is he in danger?* Compose your shots so your subjects are looking at something outside of the frame to add intrigue to the image.

2 A REASON TO PRESS THE SHUTTER

When you make a photograph you are essentially preserving a memory. Use your own memories as a trigger to press the shutter. Think about your own childhood: fun times, sad times, exciting times and so on.

Another image of H here. Learning to ride a bike is a strong memory for most people… the freedom, the speed and the thrill of exploring on two wheels. When I saw H's T-shirt sprayed with mud from his BMX, it brought back a flood of memories from my own childhood. I wanted to preserve this memory. I had a reason to press the shutter.

3 REDEFINE YOUR UNDERSTANDING OF EMOTION

Emotion doesn't just mean laughing or crying. It is an instinctive feeling related to the human condition. Think about this as much as the environment you are working in. Motivate your subjects to do something that your audience can relate to.

See the examples of my daughter collecting hazelnuts – the first image in particular. I have a lovely portrait of her standing with the basket that I could have included, but I prefer this one. Bending down, basket over her arm to pick a nut from the forest floor – this is a picture about the human condition and not just a girl in the forest. It has more emotion. The audience can relate to it.

WHERE TO START?

It can be hard to know where to start. There are a million ways to talk yourself out of making work, and saying that it's already been done is an easy excuse. But everyone is different, which means everyone's take is different, even if the subjects being photographed are the same.

FOLLOW YOUR INTERESTS

You shouldn't look at what's popular and simply repeat. I see this time and time again on platforms like Instagram, which are driven by popularity. Following a trend is a recipe for empty art, and by chasing the trend you are being influenced, as opposed to being the influencer. If you want to stand out from the pack, you need to hone your storytelling and follow your heart.

Regarding subject matter for your photographs, only you know what makes you curious, what sparks your interest, what gets you out of the chair to shoot. I can teach you techniques to improve your storytelling capabilities, but I can't make you somebody you're not. I can't stress this enough.

TELL STORIES LOCALLY

As much as it is inspiring, perusing endless streams of epic, location-based imagery on platforms like Instagram can sometimes be a little debilitating to your creative process. If you feel like this, close the app for a week. Don't be influenced by it. Slow down and take notice of your own surroundings. You'll be amazed what comes to mind when you're free from distraction.

You don't need to travel to exotic locations to make great photographs. Some of my favourite pictures (and incidentally most liked images on Instagram) were made at home. The use of light, subjects and the stories inferred are doing the heavy lifting. These images could have been photographed anywhere.

George Tice, the famous American photographer noted for his work documenting everyday life in his hometown of New Jersey, said:

'As I progressed further with my project, it became obvious that it was really unimportant where I chose to photograph. The particular place simply provided an excuse to produce work... you can only see what you are ready to see – what mirrors your mind at that particular time.'

Technologies change, trends change, fashions change, but the fundamentals of good storytelling haven't changed in millennia.

TIP / We are all individuals, so trust your instincts and follow your gut. Make work that interests you and see how it fits once it's made. If work is made for the right reasons it will more than likely prevail.

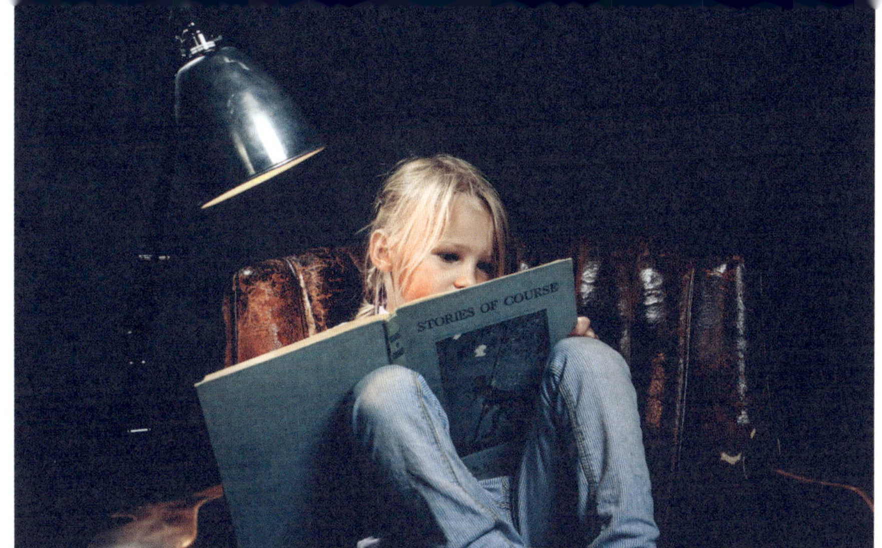

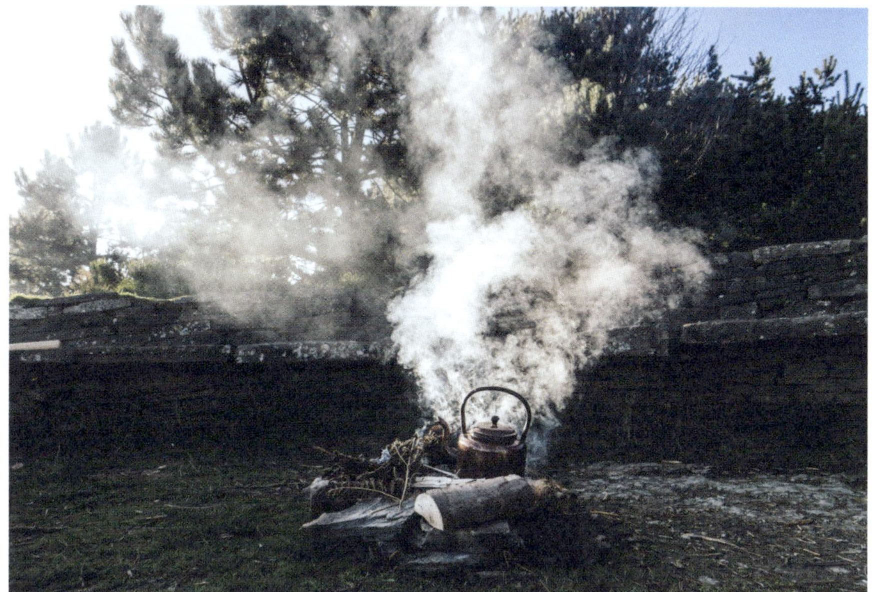

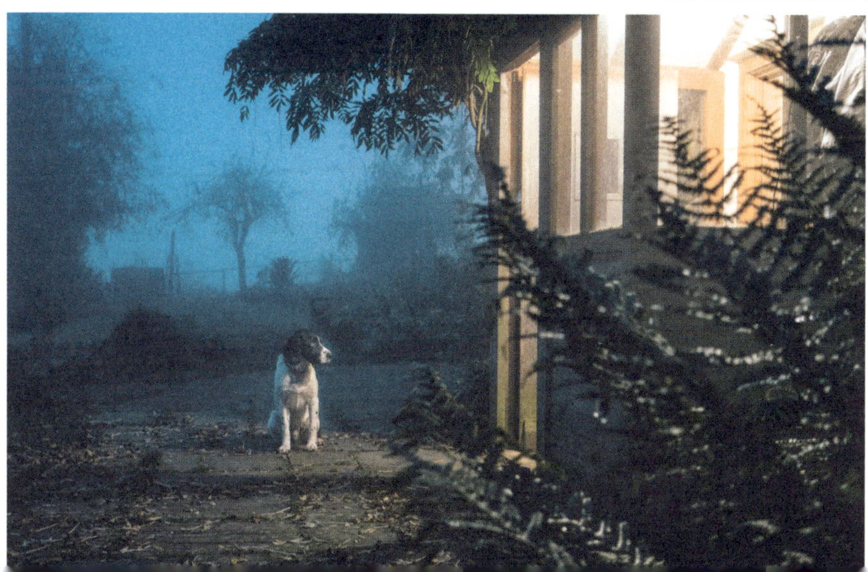

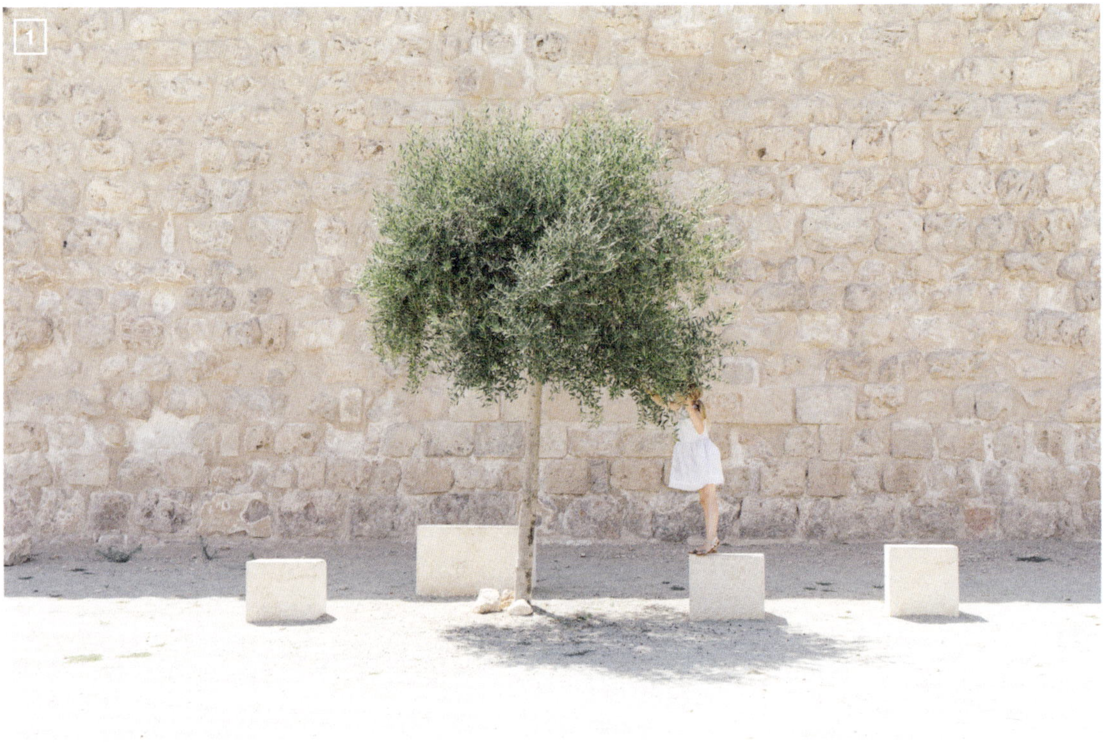

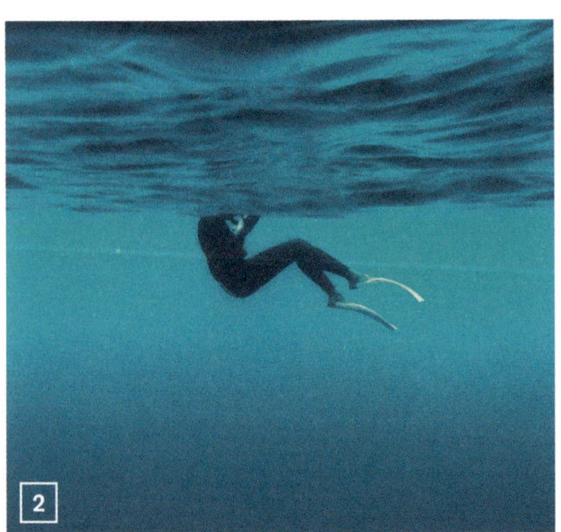

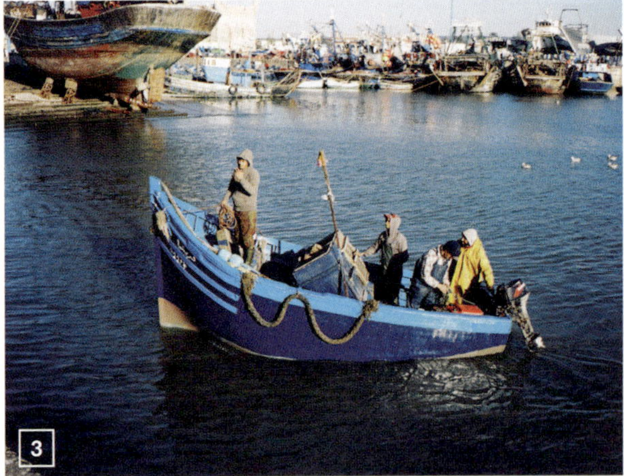

WHAT YOU WILL NEED

You don't need to spend a huge amount on equipment to make good images. For example, one of the photos opposite was shot on an iPhone, one on a standard DSLR and one on a cheap film camera. It's essential to realise it's not the camera that makes the picture – you do.

Below is a list of what you need to get started and to complete the exercises in this book.

CAMERA

You will need a DSLR camera with an interchangeable lens. Don't worry about spending big money on this – the lenses you shoot with are more important and a better use of your cash.

LENSES

Invest in your glass. A good quality lens will stand the test of time and travel with you from camera to camera. I'm still using lenses I bought 10 years ago. If you were to buy just one, opt for my 'desert island' lens, the humble 50mm prime. I guarantee you'll still be using it in a decade.

SPARE BATTERIES

A camera stops working when it runs out of power. This is a boring item to spend money on, but it's so frustrating to get stopped in your tracks for the sake of something so simple. Remember: if you're flying, check with the airline whether you can carry batteries in the cabin or if you need to check them in.

EDITING SOFTWARE

You will need a computer and some editing software to process your images. I use Adobe Lightroom for storing, rating and editing photographs; Adobe Photoshop for advanced photo manipulation (not necessary for the processes covered in this book);

and a plugin called Exposure for emulating real-world film effects like grain, dust and light leaks, all sourced from old film stock.

REFLECTOR

A reflector is a highly underrated piece of equipment that can have a massive impact on the quality of your images. A reflector *reflects* light and allows you to bounce it into the right places and create a more dynamic environment. They are inexpensive and lightweight, they don't require batteries and they will last for years. Invaluable.

SMARTPHONE

A smartphone is useful for shooting pictures, but also for the myriad photo apps available today – see page 20 for some of my favourites.

DRONE

Not an essential item, but a drone is a superb way of upping the production value of a shoot. Until they were invented, you'd need to spend tens of thousands on a helicopter to get those spellbinding aerial shots. Now you can take them with an inexpensive camera drone – you'll just need to master the controls.

1 *Shot with a Canon DSLR.*

2 *Shot with an iPhone in an underwater case.*

3 *Shot with a 35mm Contax film camera.*

GEAR:
DSLR OR MIRRORLESS

Don't get hung up on expensive gear – many of the images in this book were shot on my iPhone. Light and composition are more important. However, I do receive a ton of questions relating to my equipment, so here is a quick list of what's in my camera bag.

CAMERA

CANON EOS 5D MARK IV

My weapon of choice, 99 per cent of the time. Weather-sealed, reliable and tough. I love it.

LENSES

50MM F/1.2

My desert island lens. I love, love, love this focal length. If you're just starting out with a DSLR, ditch the kit zoom that was inevitably bundled with your camera body and pick up an f/1.4 or f/1.8 version of this lens. Learn to love the constraints associated with shooting at a fixed focal length. It will make you a better photographer. Fact.

24MM F/1.4

Tack sharp between f/4 and f/8 with good colour and contrast. This is a great lens for landscape work and even some portraiture. It provides an ample stage for your subject, though it's important to step back from them to prevent any distorted limbs!

24–70MM F/2.8

A useful (if a touch boring) zoom lens for shooting a variety of different situations. This lens can even compete with some primes in terms of sharpness.

70–200MM F/2.8

Heavy and expensive, but super useful and always in my bag. Far reaching and fast, it also delivers dreamy looking portraits.

100–400MM F/4.5–5.6

A recent addition, but deserving of a place here, this lens is amazing for picking out details in the distance and compressing the landscape.

ACCESSORIES

SANDISK 64GB EXTREME PRO MEMORY CARDS

I have a few of these and they work just as well next to an erupting volcano as they do in a blizzard.

SPARE BATTERIES

As mentioned on the previous page, these are boring but essential, especially if you're shooting all day. You don't want to have to stop shooting when your camera runs out of power.

GIOTTOS SILK ROAD YTL TRIPOD

Lightweight, carbon-fibre tripod. This model has a cool Y-shaped folding mechanism so that it takes up less space when collapsed.

KIRK ENTERPRISE SOLUTIONS BH-1 BALL HEAD

Lightweight and silky smooth, this is a quick-release ball head.

DAY BAG

DOMKE F-2

Designed so you can get at equipment instantly without having to take the bag from your shoulder,

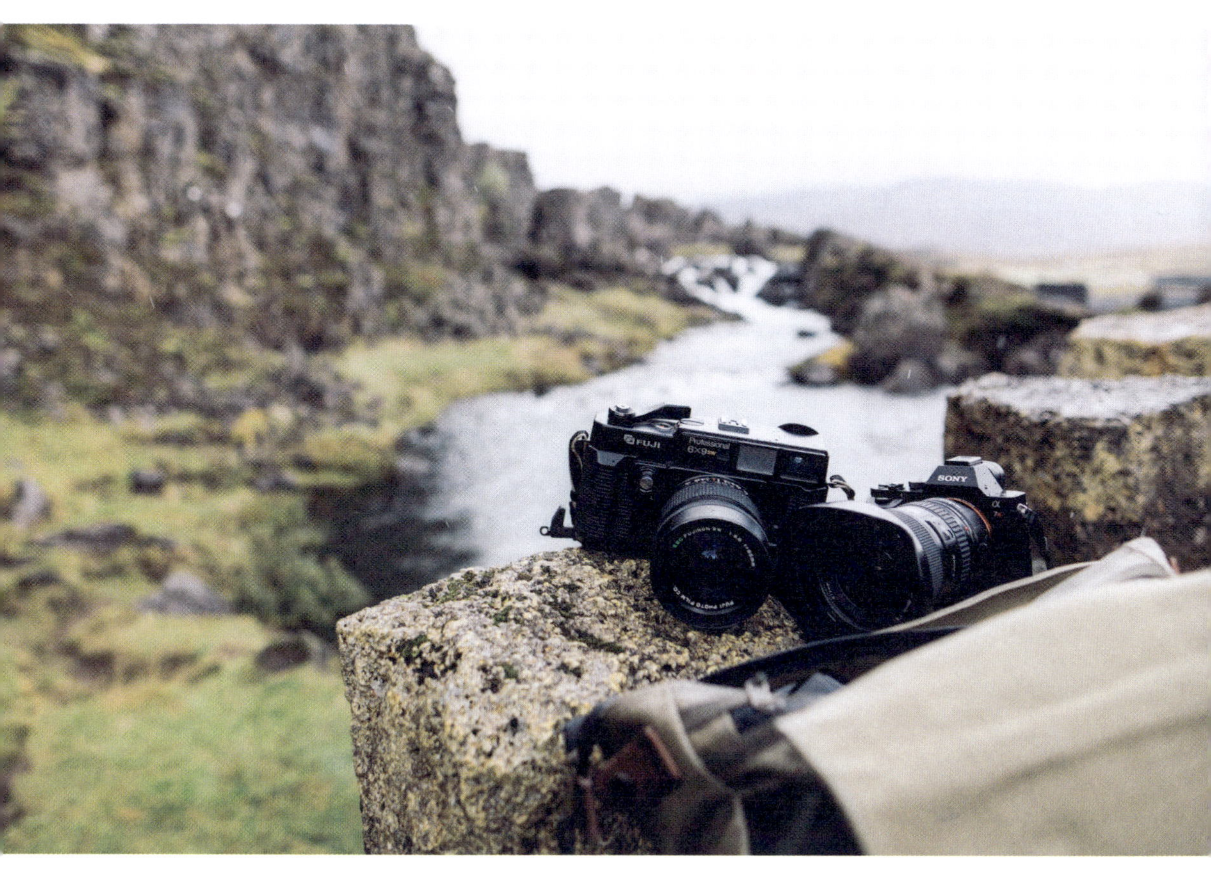

nothing compares to the Domke F-2 in the field. I also love the 'low profile' look to this bag – it doesn't scream, *'I'm carrying a ton of expensive gear!'* I flat-pack this bag in my checked luggage and use a ThinkTank Roller to transfer all my (heavy) gear through the airport. Two bags are better than one.

TRANSFER BAG

THINKTANK AIRPORT INTERNATIONAL ROLLER

This is very nearly my favourite piece of equipment out of everything listed here. Lenses are heavy! Add a laptop, batteries, hard drives, camera bodies and it won't be long before your body starts to complain if you load it all onto your shoulders. Aside from its solid design and plethora of security features, I simply love the mobility this thing gives me through an airport. Once you experience wheeling a heavy bag versus carrying one, there really is no going back.

I decant gear from my ThinkTank Roller into my Domke once I reach my destination. The roller then stays in my hotel room, locked via its built-in cable to a solid object, securing all the gear I don't require on location each day.

GEAR:
PHONE APPS

There are thousands of photography apps available for iOS and Android devices. Some help you plan shoots, while others are for editing and post production. Many of the very best photography apps are totally free. I've listed a few of my favourites below.

PLANNING APPS

SUN SURVEYOR

A smartphone app that calculates the location of the sun and therefore the direction of light for any location on earth, at any date and time. Using augmented reality overlays, the app can show you where the sun will be and when, so you can visualise the lighting environment ahead of your shoot. An invaluable app for a location recce (see page 90).

PHOTOPILLS

A Swiss Army knife of an app. It can be a little overwhelming when you first open it, but spend some time getting to know the interface and you'll find it feature rich and great for planning shoots.

CADRAGE

A superb app for recceing locations. Cadrage allows you to simulate any camera and lens combination using your phone. It also allows you to build detailed shotlists (see page 92) to share with your team.

SHOOTING APPS

8MM

A fun app for simulating 8mm cine footage. Vintage camera effects are applied in real time so it is easy to see what your are shooting. Record video in the app and it saves directly to your mobile phone's camera roll.

HYPERLAPSE

My favourite app for recording timelapse footage. It's better than the native camera apps because you can vary the length of the timelapse after recording the event by adjusting the speed.

EDITING APPS

AFTERLIGHT 2

A fast and intuitive filtering and editing app. I particularly like the 'touch tools' for dodging and burning areas of an image using my finger.

SNAPSEED

Age old (in the world of phone apps) and powerful. Google backing means it has some impressive features. Check out the Head Pose and Portrait tools. Black magic!

VSCO

A classic film emulation app with some of the best filters available today. The built-in camera is pretty solid too, with manual exposure controls, Raw functionality and separate focus/metering controls.

TOUCHRETOUCH

An easy-to-use object removal and cloning app. Remove small imperfections from your photos by tapping them. Only blemishes, and not the content around them, are marked and taken away. (See the example opposite.)

LAYOUT APPS

UNFOLD

Described as a toolkit for storytellers, Unfold allows you to create a more curated editorial look in your Instagram Stories. Drag and drop photographs into aesthetically pleasing pre-built templates.

SCRL

Similar to Unfold, but designed for grid posts as opposed to Stories, SCRL allows you to create a seamless carousel with Instagram's multi-photo feature.

CONTINUAL

Split long videos into 15 second clips for posting to Instagram Stories.

Here's an example of how to 'dodge' and 'burn' a digital image using the smartphone app Snapseed. Dodging and burning are based on traditional darkroom techniques for regulating exposure on specific areas of a print. In plain English, they let you emphasise parts of your image by lightening or darkening them. The technique was elevated to an art form by the famous American landscape photographer Ansel Adams, although he used darkroom techniques to get the effect as opposed to a swipe of the finger.

1 Look for a strong focal point. A roadway, tree or person that draws the viewer's eye into the picture.

2 Shoot with the native camera app and try to expose to a midtone, an area that's inbetween the darkest (shadows) and lightest (often sky) parts of your image. There's often a lot of detail in the sky and shadows, and it's a shame to lose this. Double-tap an area on the screen that is closest to the midpoint between black and white (i.e. grey). This will give you the best exposure for all the elements in the frame.

Exercise /

Image Editing on a Smartphone

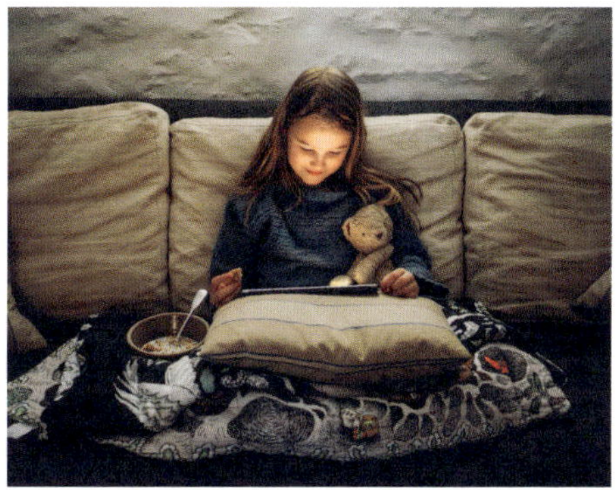

3 First, use Tune Image and set the Ambiance to about 30% to put some life back into the picture. Next, choose the Selective Adjust tool and add points to areas of the image that you want to enhance. I generally work with the light already in the picture. It's a simple process of brightening the highlights and darkening the shadows, always working to isolate the subject in your frame.

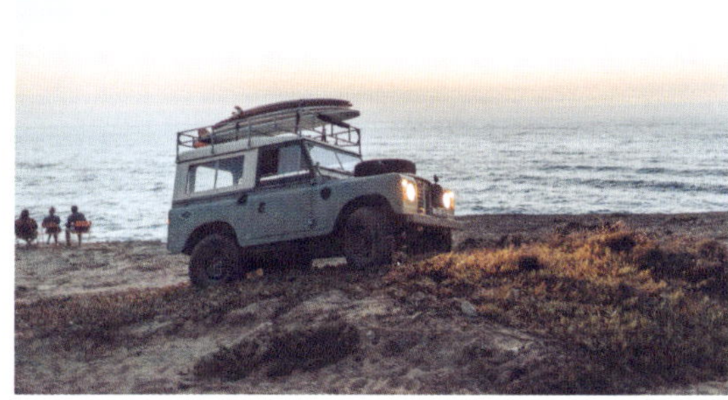

TouchRetouch – *Now you see them...*

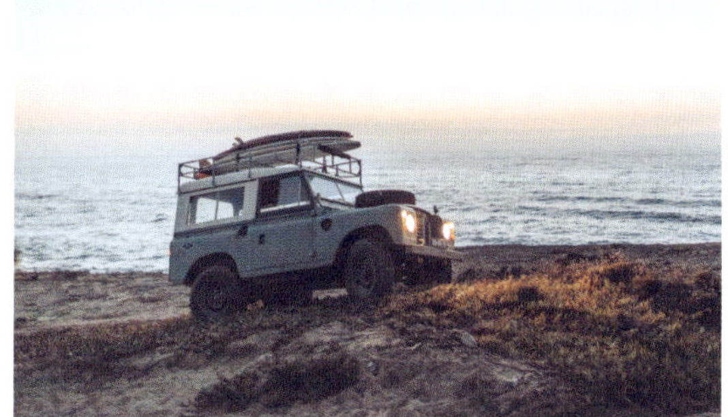

Now you don't!

Storytelling 101

Great leaders tell great stories. They know how to spin a good yarn and it's these tales that capture and direct our attention. Thanks to social media platforms like Instagram, anyone can share their stories quickly, allowing others to live vicariously through their experiences.

In this chapter, I'm going to break down the process behind telling stories and look at how we can apply these techniques to photography. By the end, you'll have learned an easy-to-follow method for creating compelling photo stories from your own experiences and ideas.

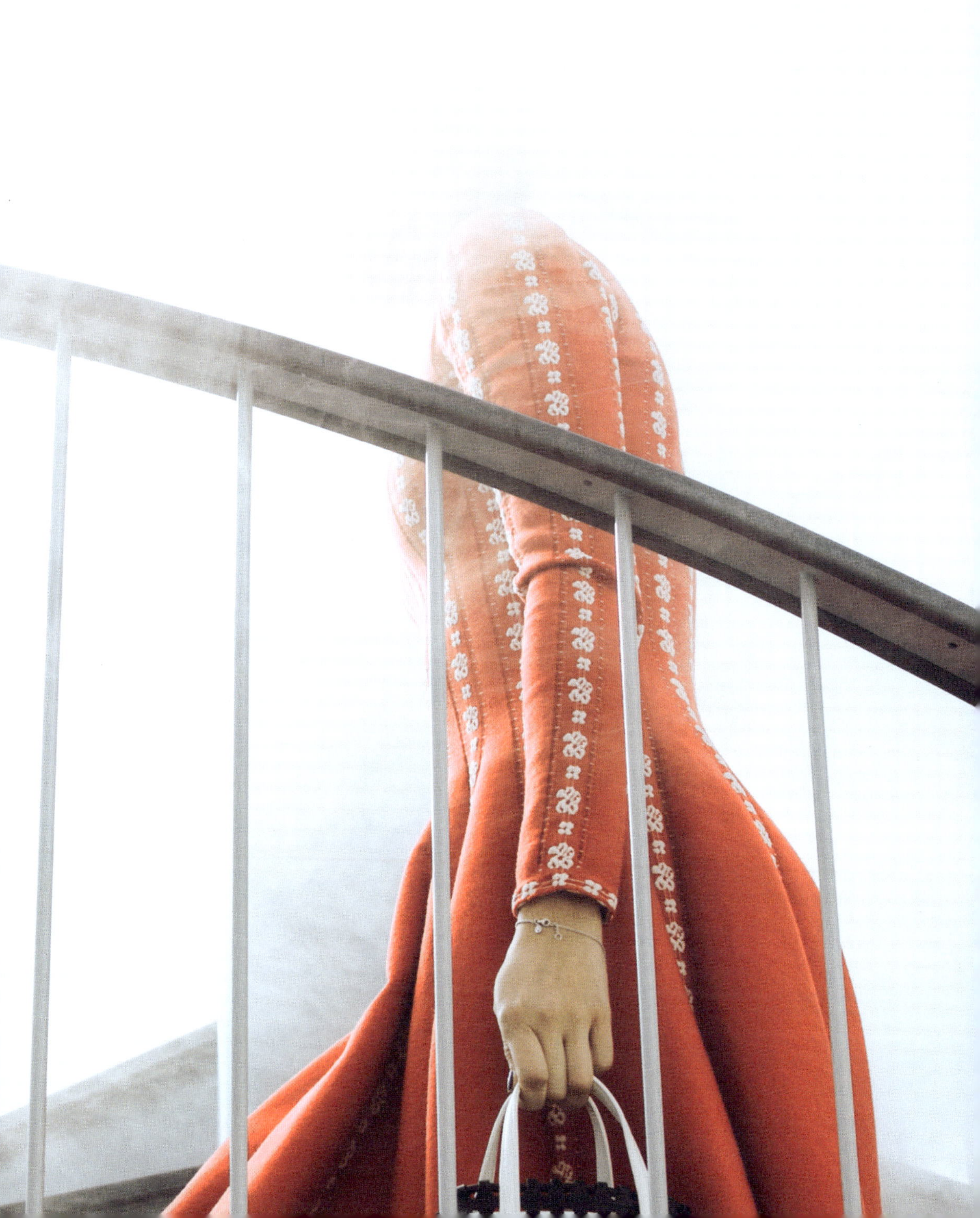

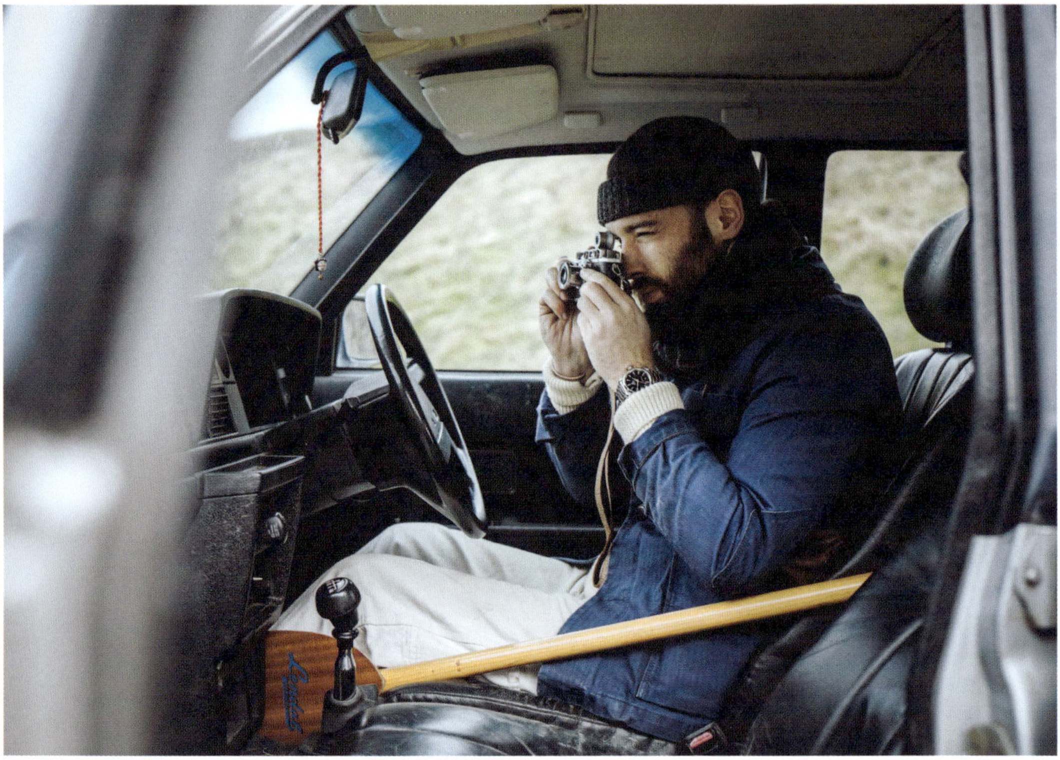

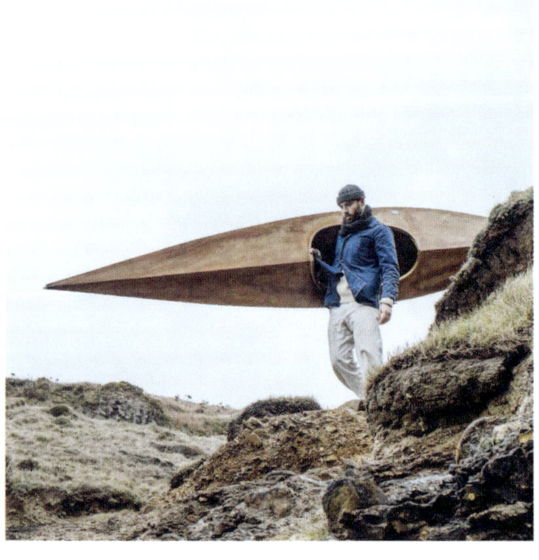

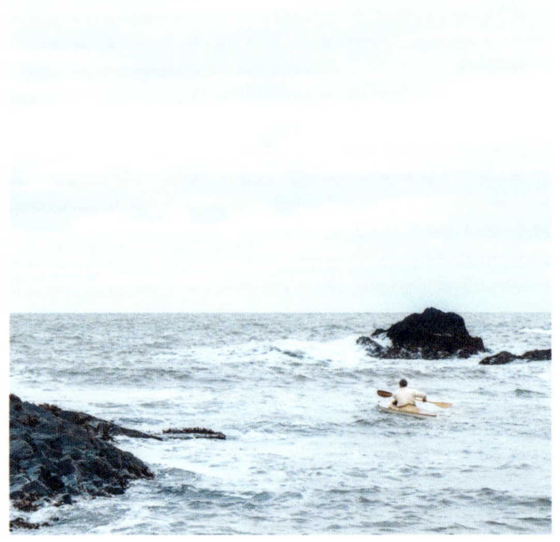

WHAT IS A STORY?

This seems like a good place to start, considering this is a book about storytelling, but it's a puzzling question. We all know what a story is, right? You've read stories, watched them, listened to your friends regaling you with tales about their antics – but have you ever considered what makes a good story? What keeps you turning the page, sitting in the seat, or listening? Is there a method we can follow to improve how we tell our own?

STRUCTURE

A relative of mine is a Hollywood scriptwriter, and I love talking to him about the art of storytelling. His take is that a good story needs structure, as opposed to pure narrative, which is a simple sequence of events: I did this, then I did that, then I went here.

A story has a beginning, a middle and an end, and ideally this ending ties up a plotline, or perhaps answers questions that are posed at the beginning. Structure adds a level of satisfaction to the experience – there's a payoff.

THEME

So we've established it needs structure, but what else? A good story has a theme, a central idea, and this is something you should be able to summarise in one or two words: betrayal, romance, mystery, escape, etc. The theme should also correspond with the ending. While not necessarily explicit, it should grow out of the story and ideally your audience will enjoy discovering it themselves. A strong theme makes the discovery even more gripping.

In the example opposite, a theme slowly unfolds. I depict a photographer in his car, then I introduce his canoe, then I finish with him setting out over a cold winter sea. The theme here is discovery or adventure. Note how I plant a seed in the first image – his paddle.

ATMOSPHERE

Closely related to theme is atmosphere. The style and tone has to be right for the type of story you want to tell. It provides the ambience and is achieved by casting the characters correctly and appropriate art direction, which includes the choice of props, wardrobe, vehicles and so on. All of these things work together to generate the right atmosphere and make your story more convincing.

SIMPLICITY

Lastly, keeping it simple is vital. A good story doesn't overcomplicate matters. A common flaw when relaying any type of information is saying too much. An account with too much detail that weighs too heavily on your structure is a boring story!

So where do you start? Simple: you need a plot. And for that you need three main elements:

1 Location
2 Character
3 Event

If you're a wedding or a documentary photographer, you already have those three things in place. You have your characters (the bride and groom); you have your location (the venue); and you have your event (the wedding ceremony).

But if you're shooting lifestyle or brand photography, you're going to need to do a little more legwork to get those elements in place. The magic lies in what happens when those three elements collide – when they interact. Let's explore each one individually.

Opposite: Ad campaign for Omega Seamaster.

LOCATION

The location not only gives a story context, it also gives you real opportunities to embellish a story. It is the stage for your characters and your event, so recceing sites ahead of the shoot day is critical. Pour effort into establishing scenes and ensure the props you are using suit the vibe of your story.

SCENE SETTING

Presenting your viewers with a sense of when and where events are taking place helps to anchor your story. If a viewer can see and, more importantly, *believe* the environment in which events are taking place, your story becomes all the more immersive. Your setting also helps establish the tone of your story. Here are two of my favourite techniques for setting the tone using location details.

GETTING UP CLOSE

Capturing a location isn't just about taking an epic landscape shot. Shoot the wide scenes, but remember to get intimate. There's a great Robert Capa quote: *'If your photographs aren't good enough, you're not close enough.'* Images shot in close proximity to subjects often create a more intriguing and intimate photograph. However, don't rely on your zoom. Learn to compose with your feet, as opposed to the turn of a zoom ring – it will lead to more creative results. Try capturing the action up close: crops of eyes, hands, even feet! Focus on textures, such as close crops of rocks and trees, furniture if you're inside and signposts if you're in a city – all of these things are visual clues that will help orientate your audience, keeping them interested and connected. These photographs bring your audience into your story and help enrich the narrative.

PERIOD DETAILS

Nostalgia is that warm, fuzzy feeling we feel when we think about memories from our past, and leaning on it helps create emotion. Some subtle propping or styling can help achieve this, even if you wish to keep events in the present. Ensure these details match the time period of your setting, as this will help make your story more believable.

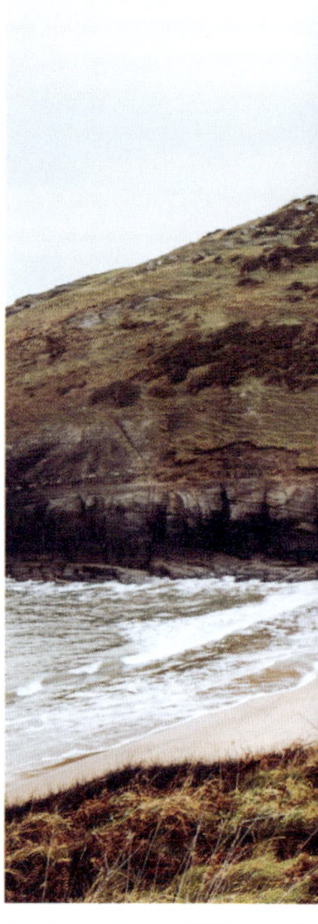

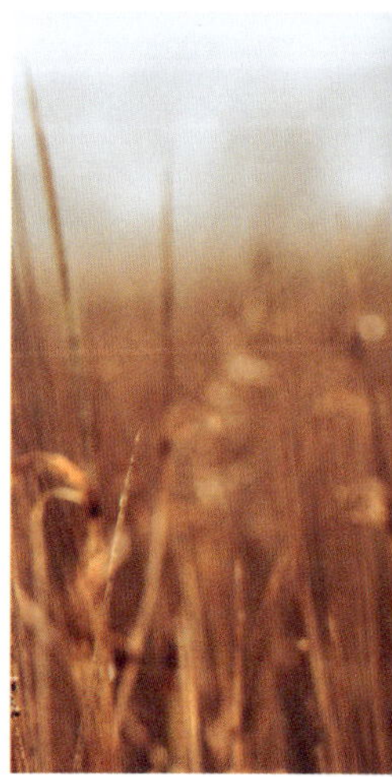

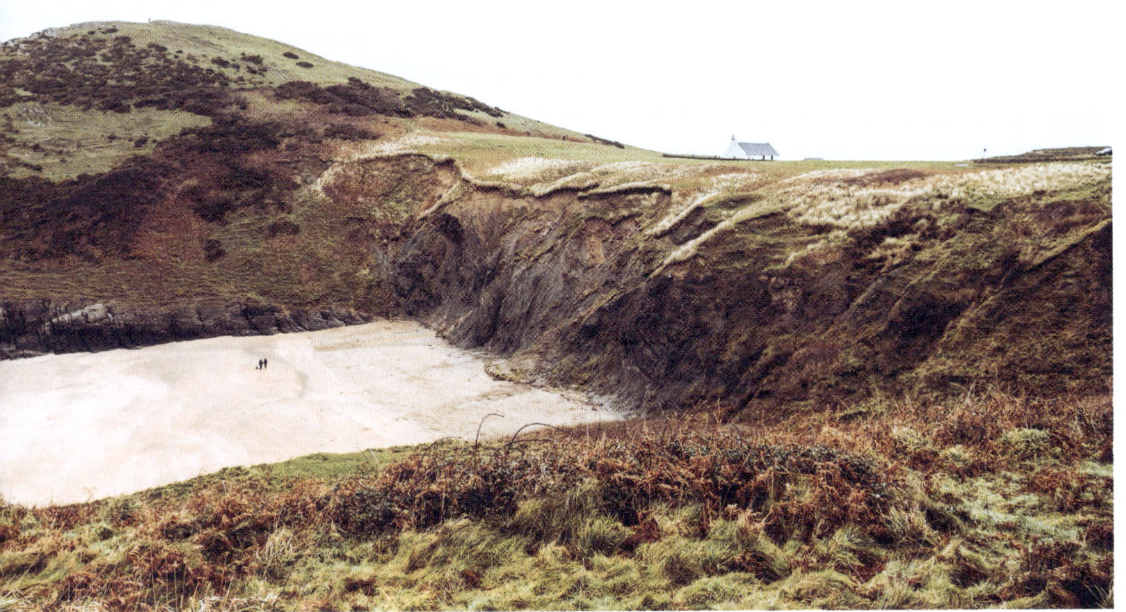

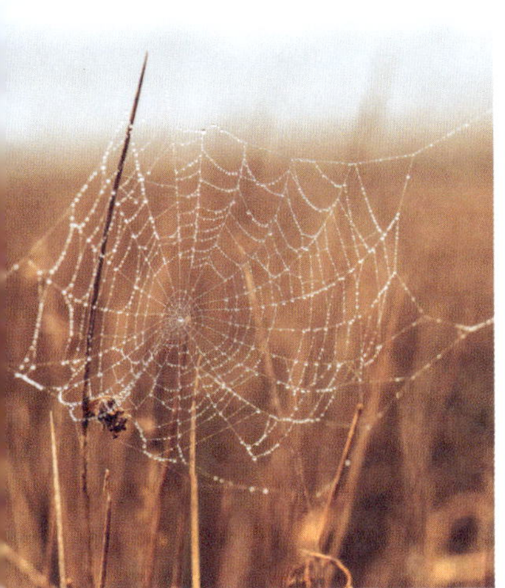

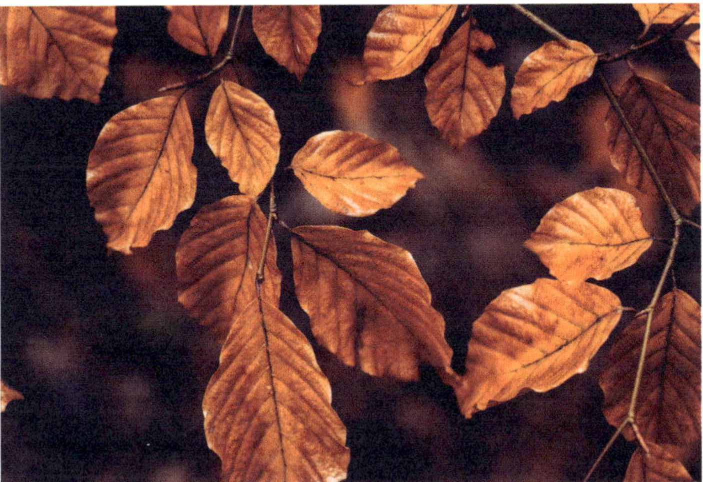

CHARACTER

Casting can be a fairly lengthy process in the commercial world of photography, but I don't really want to dig too deep into the aesthetic aspect. I'm more interested in how you can use characters to craft events in your story.

MOTIVATIONS

It might sound strange, but a good way to drive events within your story is to start with your character's desires. Desire is at the heart of everything we do and identifying that in your character and relaying it to your audience is a great way to get them to connect with your story on an emotional level.

By identifying these aspirations we can craft events. Once we know what our character wants most, we can start thinking about obstacles and setbacks that prevent them from achieving their goals. Setbacks or reversals in fortune are ultimately events. Someone relaying a disaster story is pretty exciting to listen to!

CASTING CHARACTER

Think about your character and whether they suit the client brief and the wider narrative of your story. They should match your product or story in terms of age, appearance and experience. Consider how these factors relate to the activity or situation you are shooting. Think about clothing and styling – these elements are a huge part of creating a realistic and believable narrative. The wardrobe you choose can also help deliver that feeling of nostalgia referred to on the previous page. Think about appropriate props (watches, accessories, and so on) and how you might capture your character interacting with them.

REAL CHARACTER

For this shoot, I wanted to focus on a surfer using a vintage Land Rover to access his greatest desire: surfing the perfect wave. I chose a board-shaper in his mid-forties who was local to the area. He looks cool, but he's also a touch vintage; he's well suited to my brief and my story.

As a bonus, this person knew the local surfing scene inside out, as well as the location. I was able to look to him to help craft my story. He was comfortable in his board-shaping room and also on the beach, so I didn't have to direct him too much. It's much easier working with a real person doing their actual job or hobby than with a model, and it can often lead to more natural-looking images.

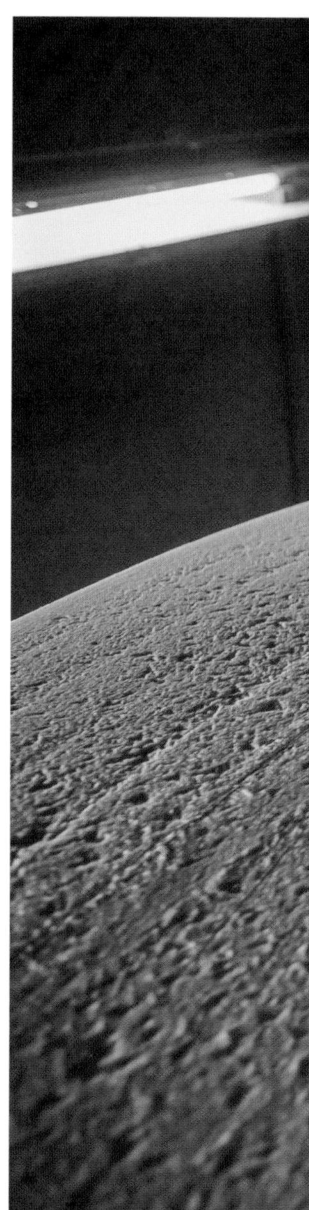

Shoot authentic stories by casting
realistic characters. Start to build
events by understanding your
character's needs or desires. Events
are the obstacles or setbacks that
might prevent them from achieving
these goals.

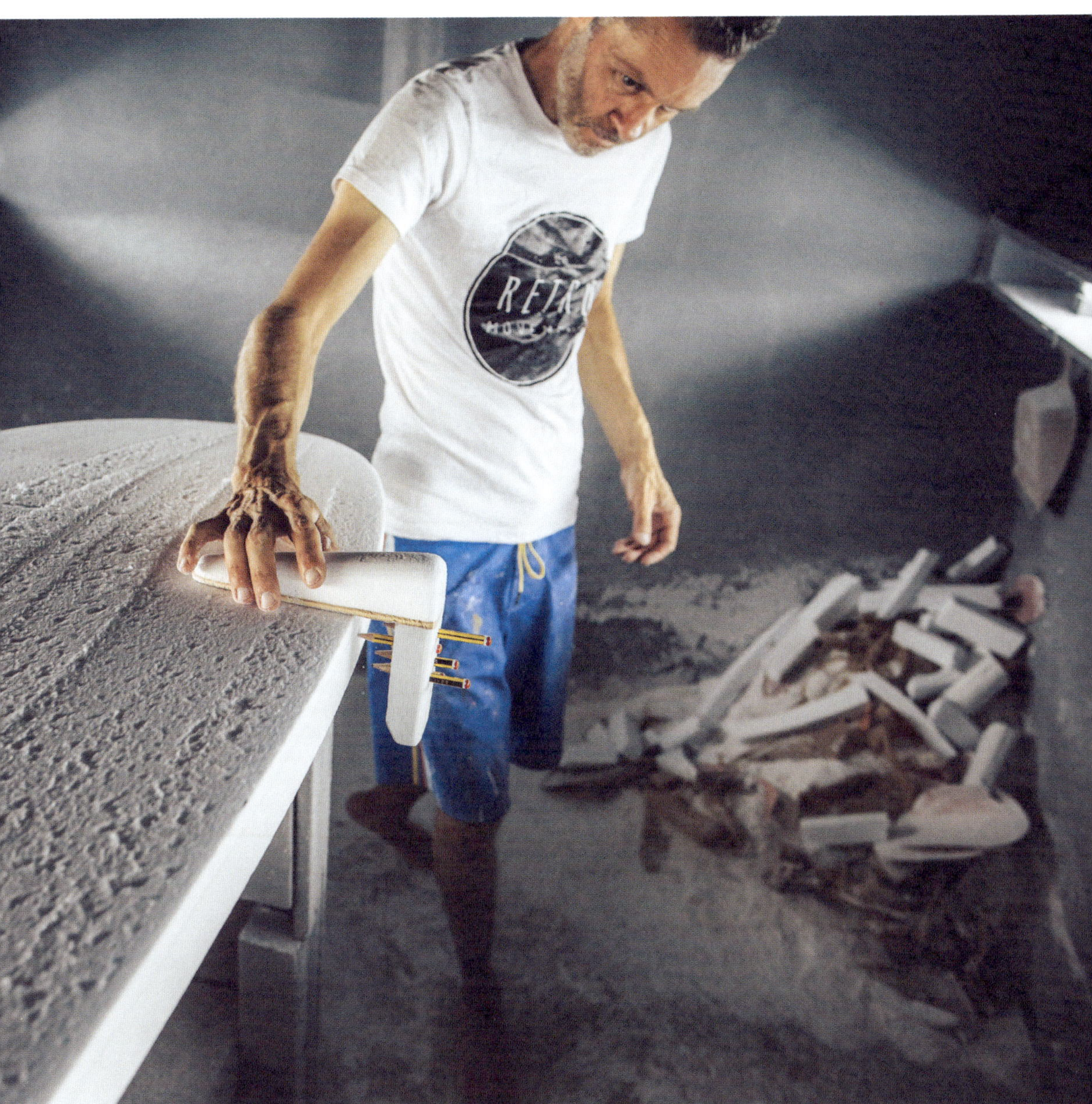

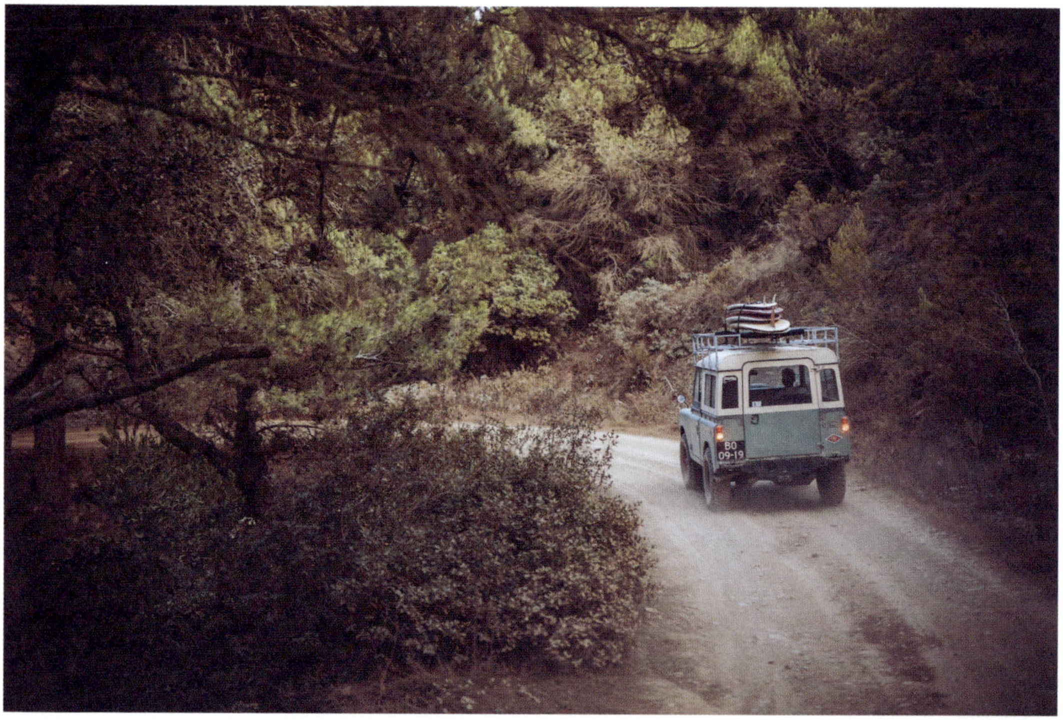

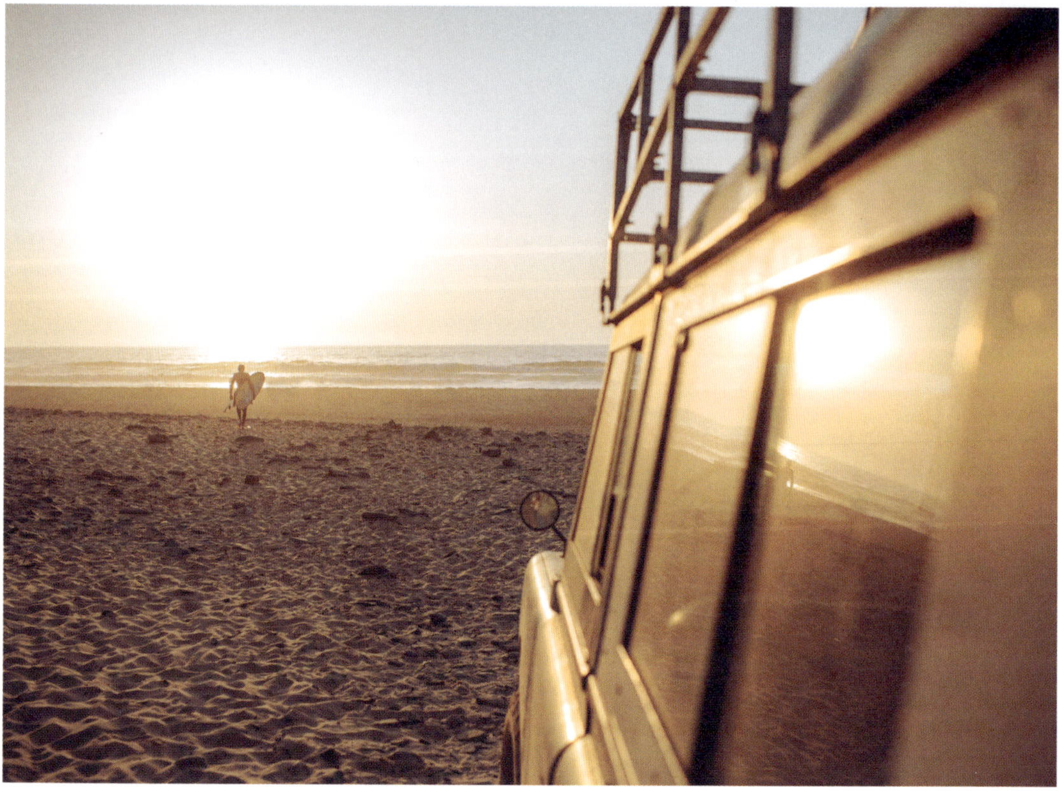

EVENT

So, what's going to happen in your story?

DRAMA

Once you've established your character's desires, the next step is to introduce obstacles that will raise the stakes. Interest is always increased if there is an apparent dilemma. We all love a bit of drama.

For my shoot I'm going to keep it pretty simple. What's the dream for every surfer? Finding the ultimate spot: a deserted beach with a perfect right-hander peeling flawlessly between two big rocks.

So, now we have a flag in the sand we can start to think about potential obstacles to reaching it. We could go off on all sorts of tangents here, but remember, I only have a day to shoot and a limited budget. We also need to keep in mind the client – the Land Rover. What tripwires can we introduce that keep the vehicle in the picture and ideally connected to the solutions for overcoming these obstacles?

Again, I'm going to keep it simple. Searching for the perfect spot is likely to take some time, so maybe we simply shoot him driving the car along a wind-blasted coast? We could shoot beautiful scenes, but ones that are only accessible using the vehicle. Dusty, axle-grinding clifftops, that sort of thing. The obstacle is the terrain and our Land Rover is our route to overcoming it.

SUSPENSE

Maybe we can add some uncertainty by incorporating a time constraint? Perhaps he's after a sunset surf, so has to reach the beach before the sun sinks below the horizon. Time is always an excellent element to play with – ultimately, it's our most precious resource.

SURPRISE

A good ending for a story is a satisfying surprise. Something unexpected, but when revealed is true to a story's purpose. Think of it like a joke – they always end with a punchline. Sometimes it's easier to decide on the punchline (or end image) first and work backwards from there, plotting all the scenarios that might lead to it. Think about how you can incorporate a situation at the beginning of your story that relates to the end.

ENVIRONMENTAL PORTRAITURE

When telling a story, whatever the medium, we need to set the scene. In a book, you can do this by describing a character's surroundings. For example:

The midday sun was unrelenting, and the shepherd sought solace under the shade of a nearby olive tree.

When working with pictures, the concept is no different, but we need to visually depict elements of our characters' surroundings to set the scene.

Environmental portraits show a person in their natural environment as opposed to a portrait in front of a neutral backdrop. I like making pictures of people this way because subjects tend to be more relaxed in their own setting, and, in turn, that atmosphere feeds into the captured image.

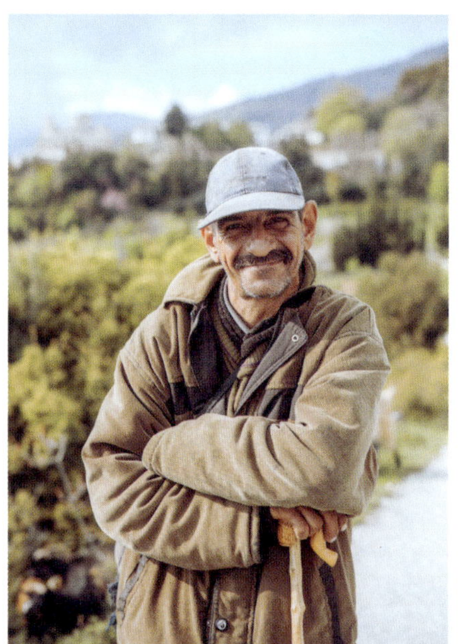

The 'environment' in this context is a place where a subject spends the majority of their time, so you can take this type of image anywhere – at home, in the local park, in the studio, at the gym, and so on.

I tend to shoot these images at a wide focal length (35mm or 24mm lens) to give the environment prominence in the shot, but there are no hard rules.

The trick with environmental portraiture is to balance your subject with their environment. The centre of attention should always be the person you are photographing, but you need to include enough environmental context to impart details about them and their life.

Ideally your location should:

- Illuminate the subject's life and surroundings.
- Provide interest without overwhelming the subject.
- Include small details that convey a message about the subject.

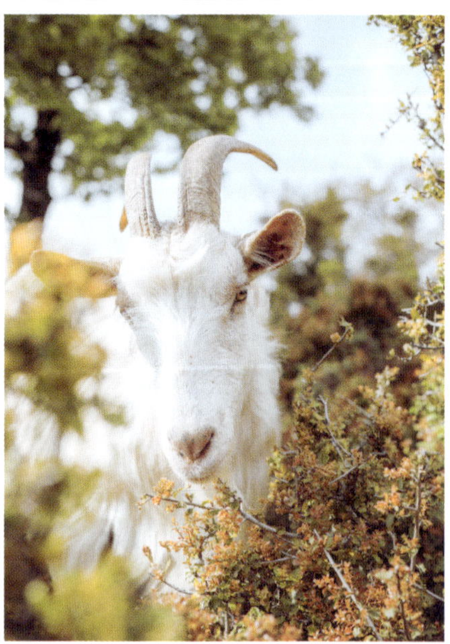

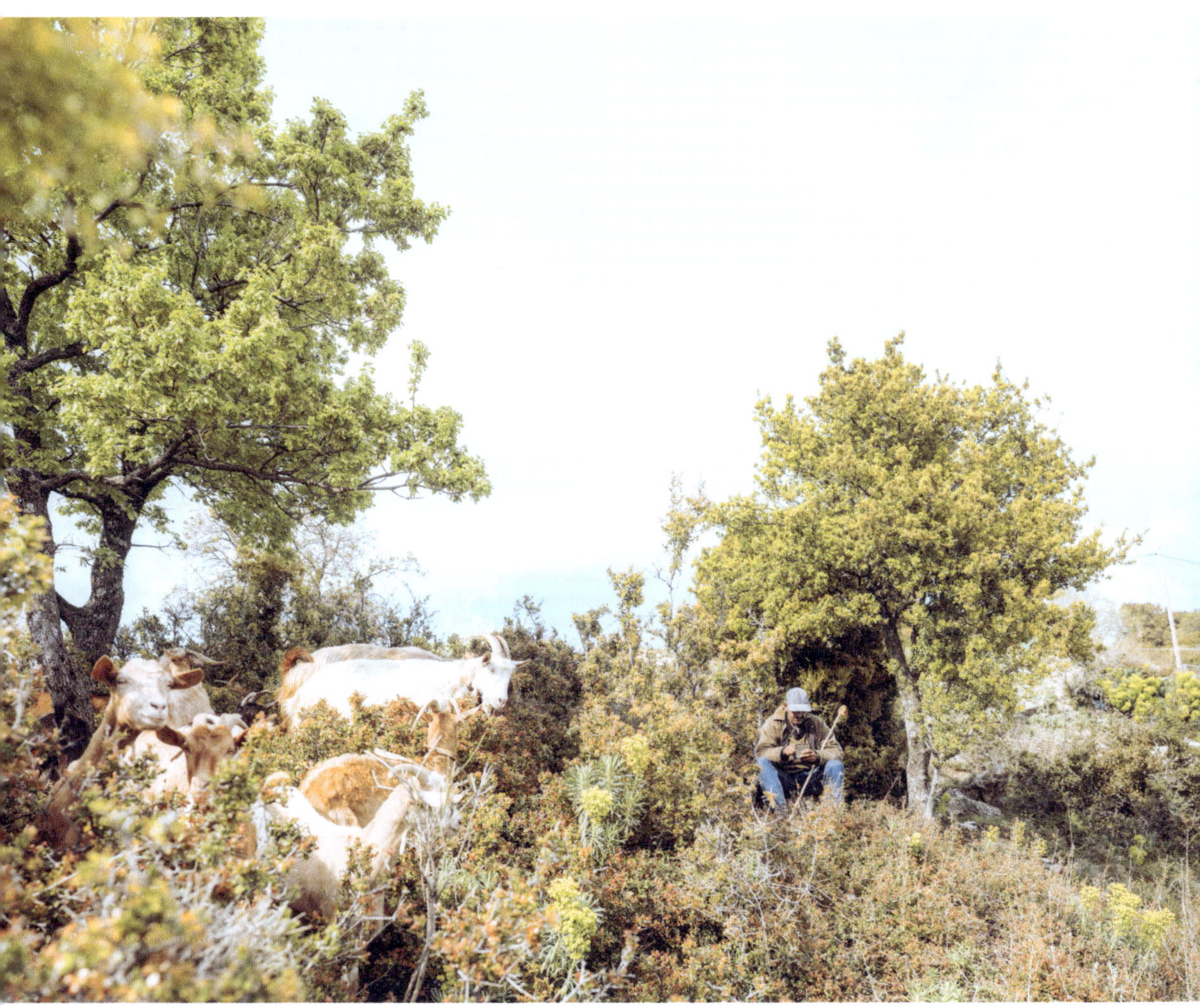

The image above depicts a shepherd I photographed in Greece. His herd of goats shows you the animals he works with: goats as opposed to sheep.

I positioned him in his natural environment – the hillside – and asked him to sit underneath a small tree as though he were taking some time to rest before moving on. The dominant form of the tree draws the eye, but the dark shadow that it casts helps to frame him in the scene.

By including his crook, the message that he is a shepherd (as opposed to a man sat next to a herd of goats) is reinforced.

TIP / The key to a good environmental portrait is the symbolism expressed by various elements in the image.

Project /
Capture an Environmental Portrait

+ Capture an intriguing environmental portrait of someone close to you.

+ Frame your subject so that the viewer can see something of their surrounding environment.

+ Use props to provide context.

+ Keep things natural. This is not a catwalk!

+ Tell a simple story about the character of your subject using the environment to provide context for your audience.

+ The viewer should be able to immediately comprehend the scene and understand the character depicted.

The aim of this project is to get you thinking about characters and the locations they inhabit. These elements are fundamental to visual storytelling, so it's important to practise making environmental portraits.

An understanding of your subject is key to making a compelling portrait, so planning ahead is essential. Obviously, this takes time and research, but you can begin immediately with family members. I'll warrant you know them reasonably well!

Try shooting a parent or sibling at their place of work, or maybe capture them doing a hobby they love. Just keep in mind the following three points:

• Decide on an aspect of their character you want to relay.

• Remember that location and props are vital to supporting the message.

• Keep it natural and pose your subject in a relaxed fashion.

The image of the goat farmer is an example of environmental details lending context to a portrait.

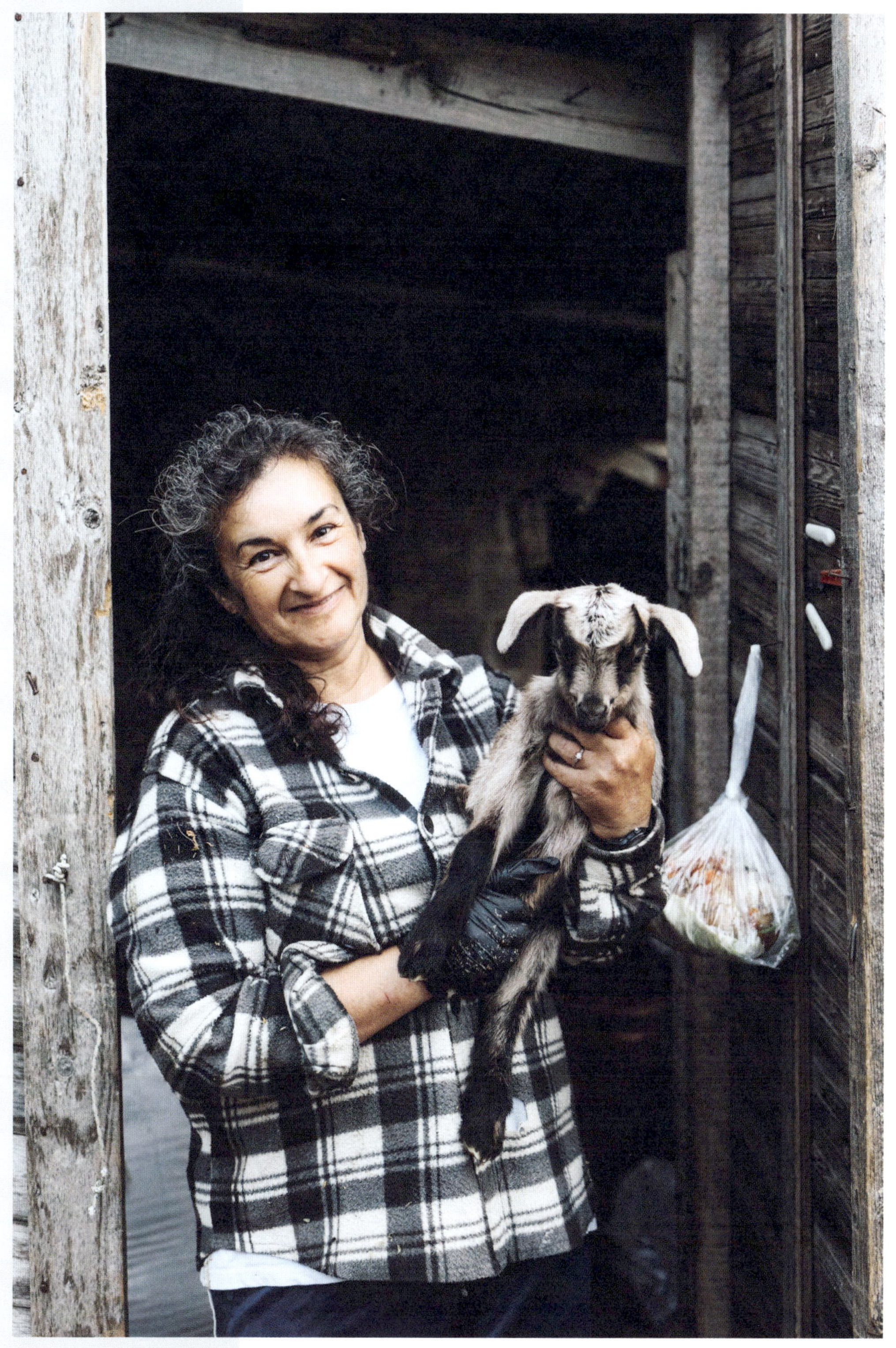

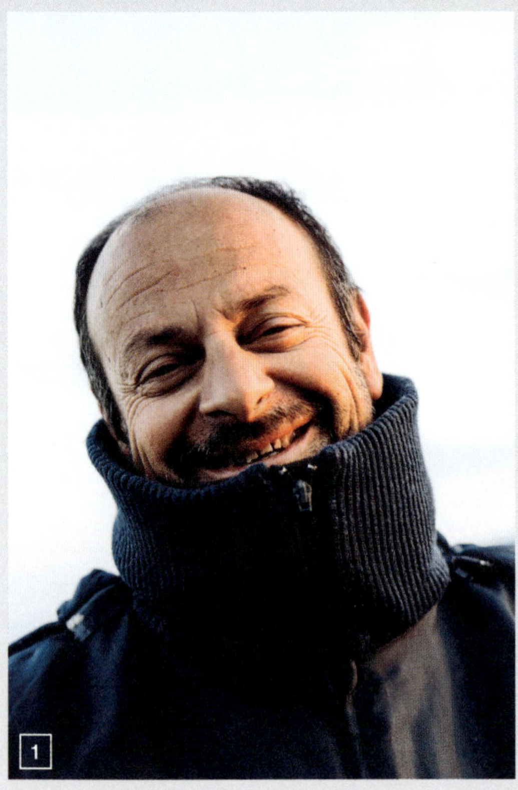

STEP 1 / **IDENTIFY YOUR CHARACTER**

Make a list of your subject's key character traits. Think about hobbies they love, their work or things they do to relax.

STEP 2 / **SELECT PROPS**

Select at least two or three things that represent the activity you have chosen to show your subject's character.

STEP 3 / **SELECT LOCATION AND LIGHTING STYLE**

Choose an appropriate location for the activity to be taking place. If outdoors, consider the time of day you'll hold the shoot and the strength of the sun. If indoors, consider your lighting setup.

STEP 4 / **POSE YOUR SUBJECT**

Allow your subject time to relax and engage with the props and their environment. The key is to get a natural portrait, so let them loosen up before providing helpful direction.

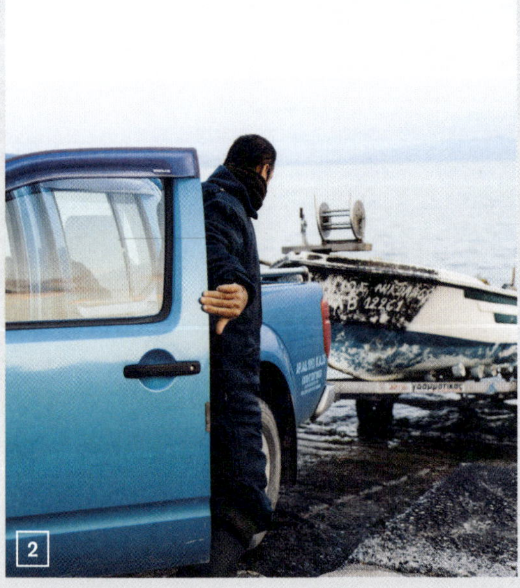

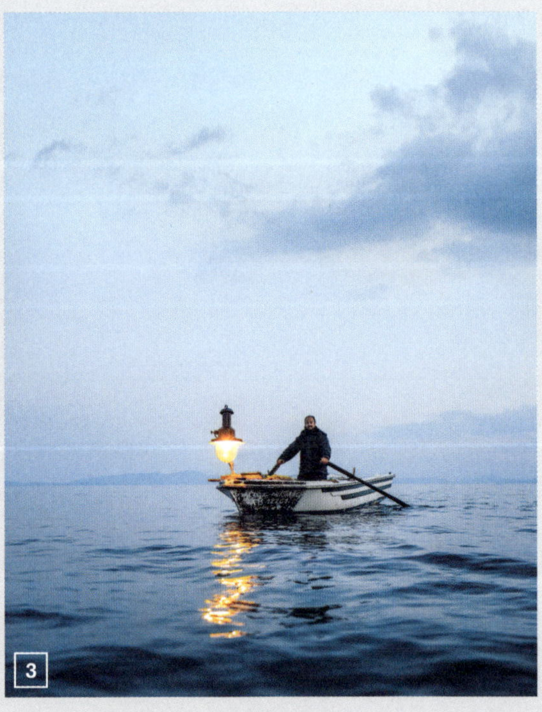

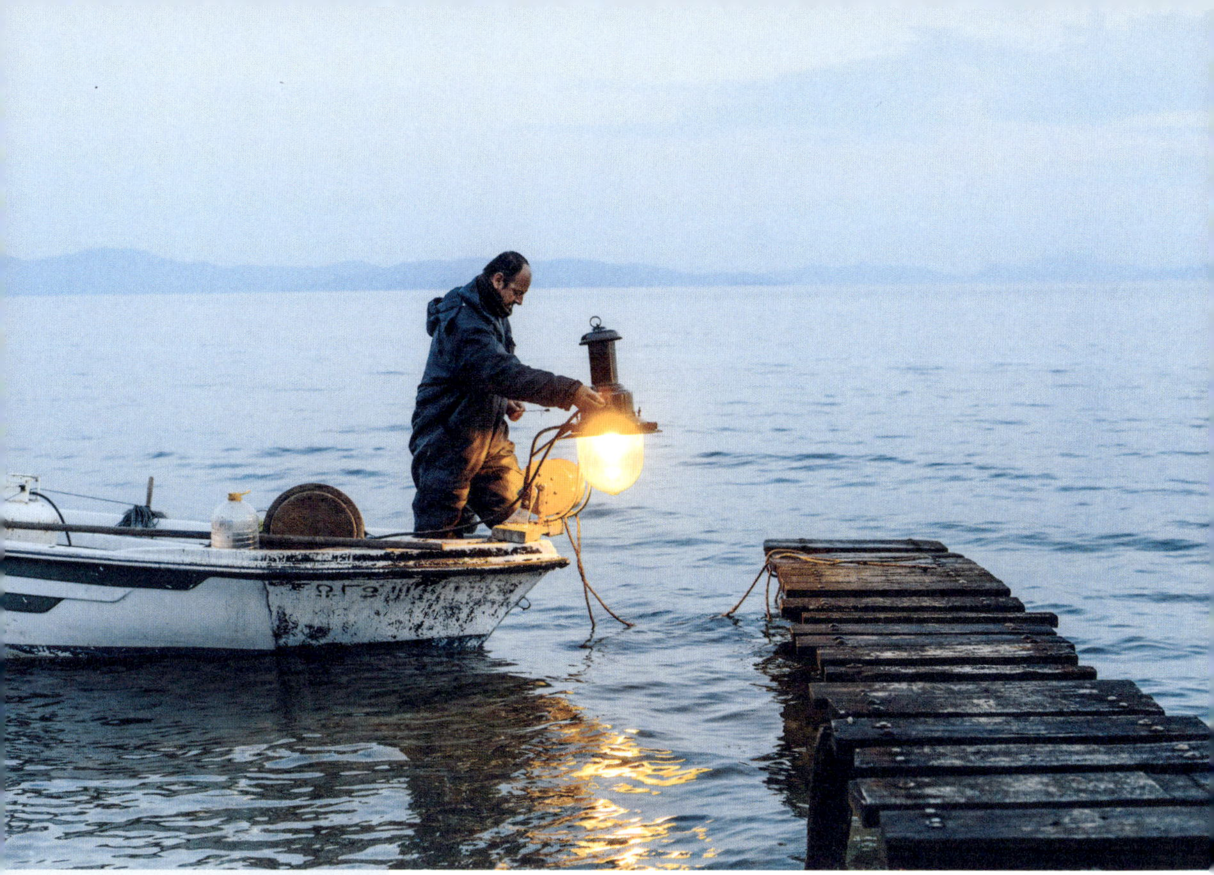

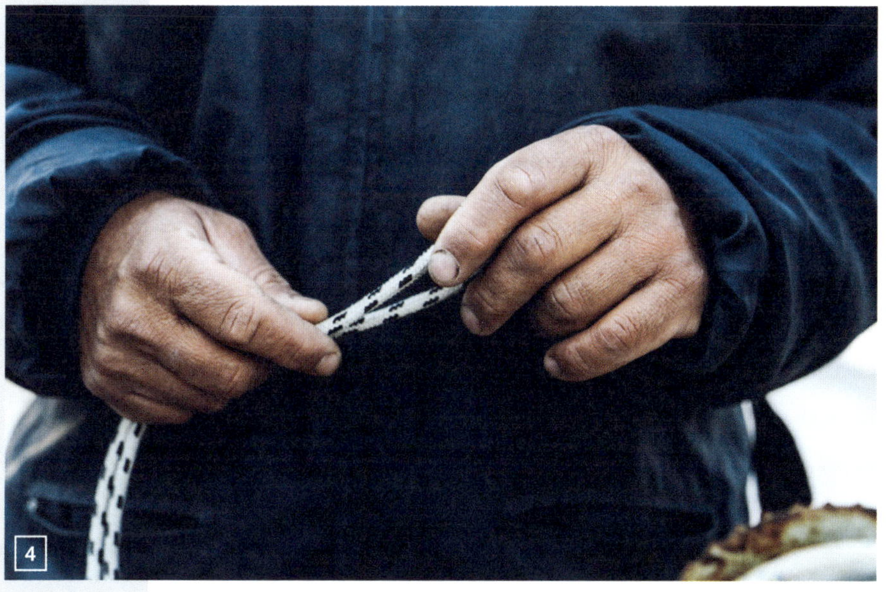

Vaios the night fisherman, photographed just after sunset. The large lantern at the bow serves to attract specific species to his boat and also allows him to select the catch according to size.

THE IMPORTANCE OF SHOT TYPE

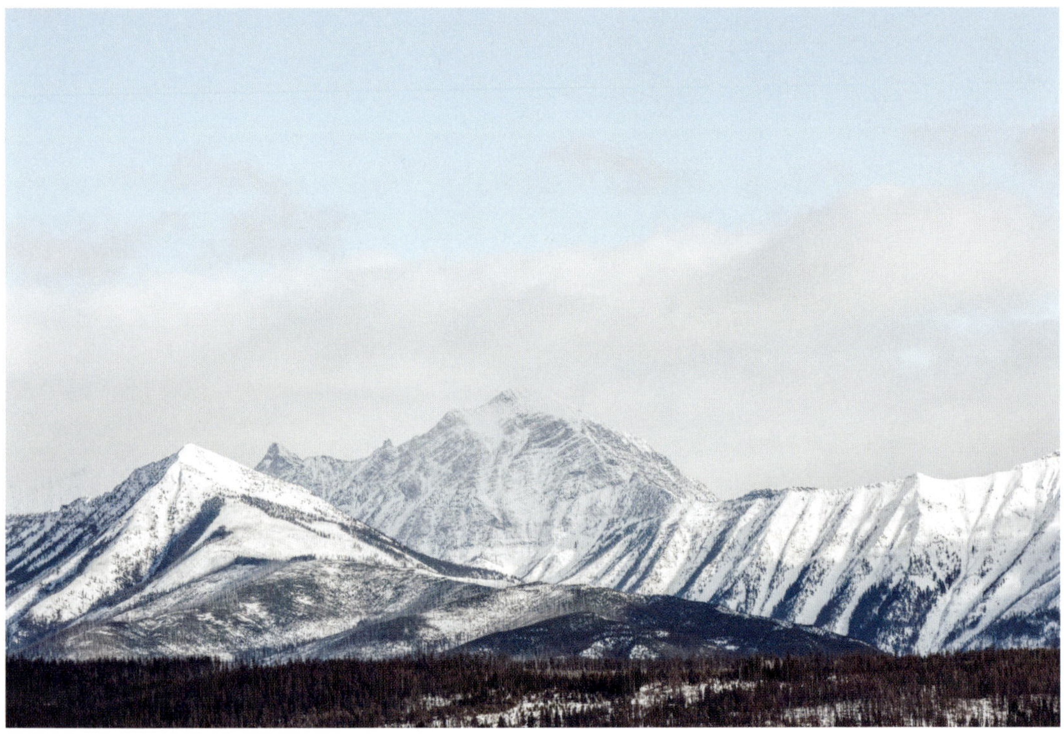

We've established that a good story can flow from a combination of character and location, but how do we use images as opposed to words to relay events?

Your choice of shot is absolutely key to visual storytelling. It's as important as the words used to tell a story in a book. They are your building blocks, and shot selection has a significant impact on the way a viewer interprets the action on screen.

The best stories take you on a journey, revealing information bit by bit. I like to construct this journey using four types of image:

1   Establishing shots
2   Transition shots
3   Cutaways/details
4   Reveals

In the same way that a book comprising of three words or a film shot from one camera angle might get pretty boring, a photo essay composed of the same type of shot will not have much visual interest. A variety of angles and compositions will help draw your viewers in and deliver a more engaging story.

Let's run through some of the key shot types and look at the qualities each one can bring to a story.

The fringes of Glacier National Park, Montana. This image could work as an establishing shot as well as a cutaway.

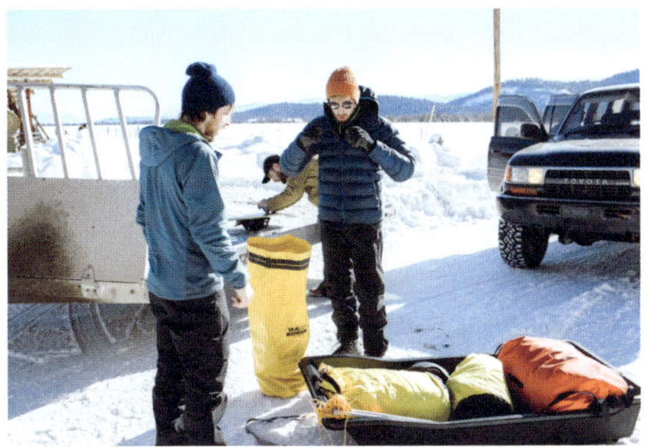

ESTABLISHING SHOTS

Introducing our character/scene and his/her desires.

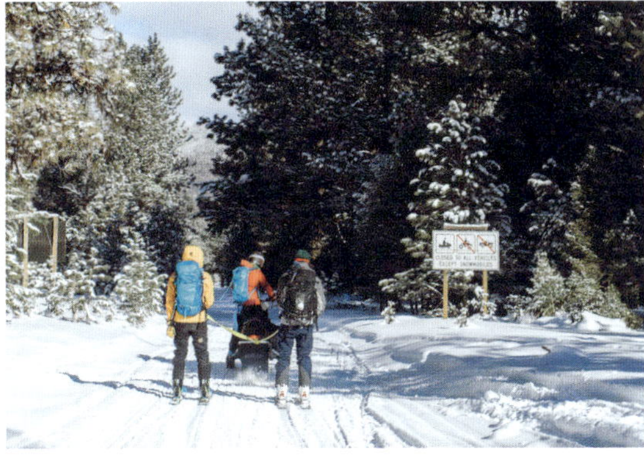

TRANSITION SHOTS

Images that relate to journey making: feet, walking, cars, roads and so on.

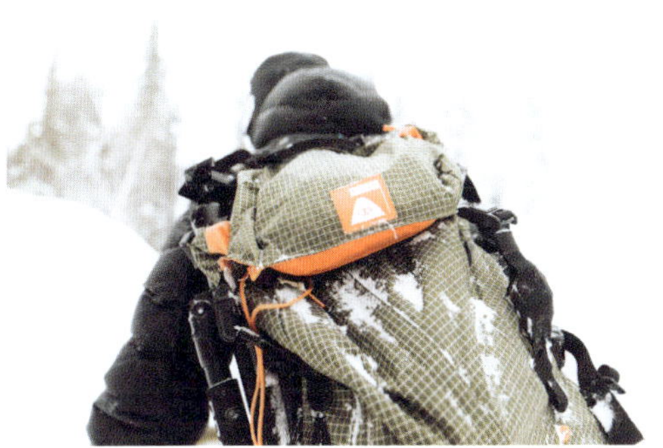

CUTAWAYS/DETAILS

Something related to, but outside, the main action of a scene. Useful for introducing peril/danger and adding suspense and building that all important sense of place.

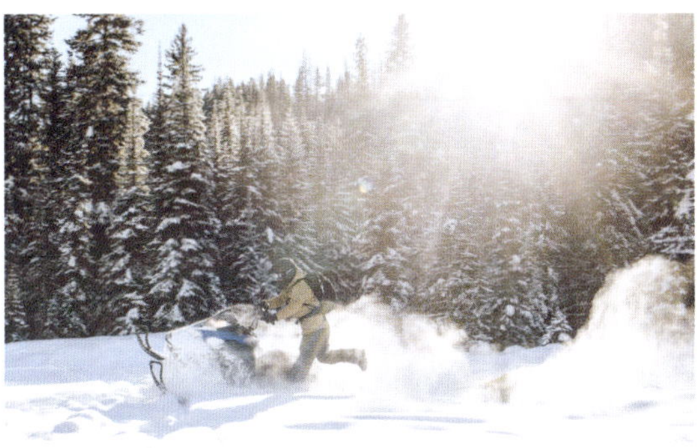

REVEAL

The end scene; the pay off.

SHOT TYPES: EXTREME LONG & LONG

EXTREME LONG SHOT

An extreme long shot is used to show a subject from a distance, or an area within which a scene is taking place. It's a study in scale and majesty. They're big, grand images – that lone climber isolated against a massive drift of snow, or a canoeist paddling across a huge lake. Often used as an establishing shot, an extreme long shot doesn't require any other contextual or supporting information.

Instagram is a one-shot platform so this sort of image works particularly well on there. You can immediately comprehend the scene and you don't actually need to read a caption to understand what's going on. I tend to use a telephoto lens to shoot these images. They help to compress distance and bring background elements closer to the foreground so there's more of a relationship between my subject and the environment they're operating in.

For storytelling purposes, I like to use this sort of image at the end of a set. It makes for a satisfying finish, like the end scene in a Western where the hero rides off into the distance. Such images provide an immediate sense of pleasure.

My lens choice for this is either an 85mm prime or a 70–200mm zoom. Both will appear to compress distance and relay the feeling you're after.

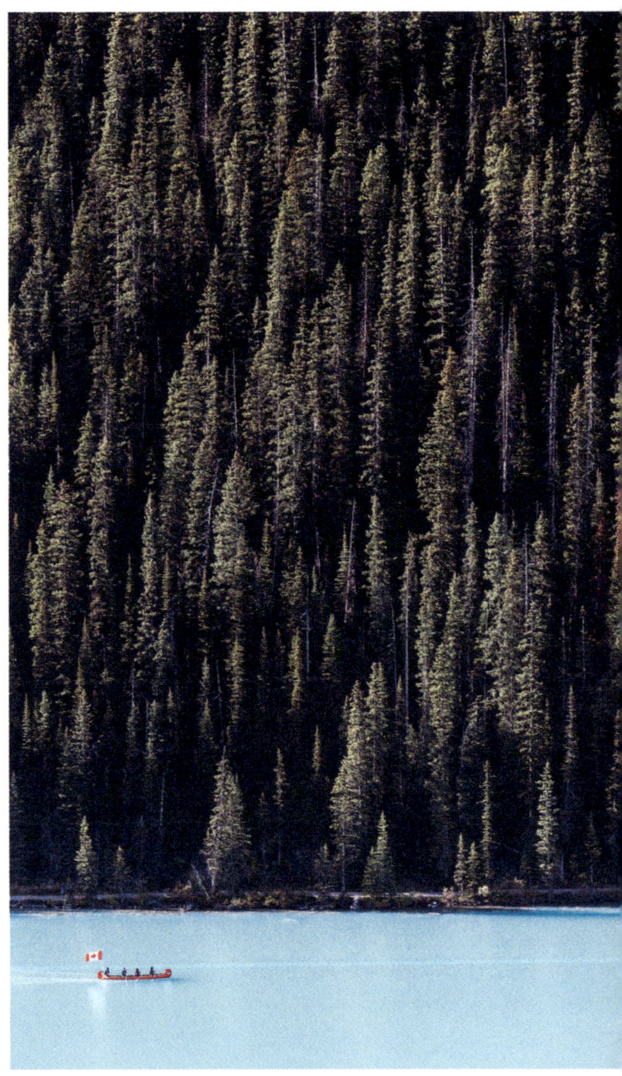

Lens choice: 85mm prime or a 70–200mm zoom.

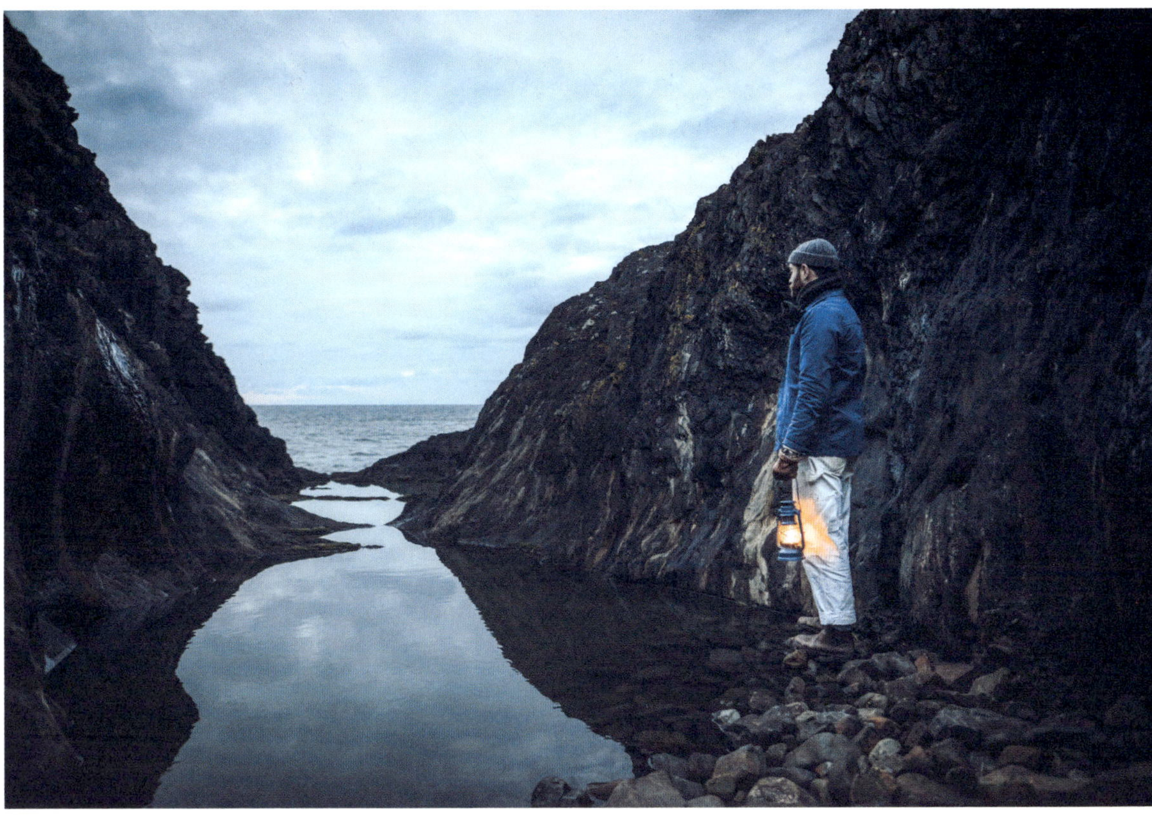

Lens choice: 24mm.

LONG SHOT

A long shot frames your subject from top to bottom. For a person, this would be head to toe, although not necessarily filling the frame. The character becomes more of a focus than in an extreme long shot, but the image still tends to be dominated by the scenery.

I used a 24mm lens for the shot here; anything wider would have introduced distortion and the scene would have felt unnatural. Depth perception is exaggerated when shooting this wide, and objects appear further apart than in reality. This front-to-back exaggeration means objects in the background become smaller, helping to create a feeling of space.

The distance of the camera from the subject can also create emotional distance; the audience doesn't get as involved in what's going on as they would if they were closer. I like to use this type of shot for creating intrigue – the audience is present, but observing. With their interest piqued I can then bring them deeper into a story.

SHOT TYPES: MEDIUM & MEDIUM CLOSE

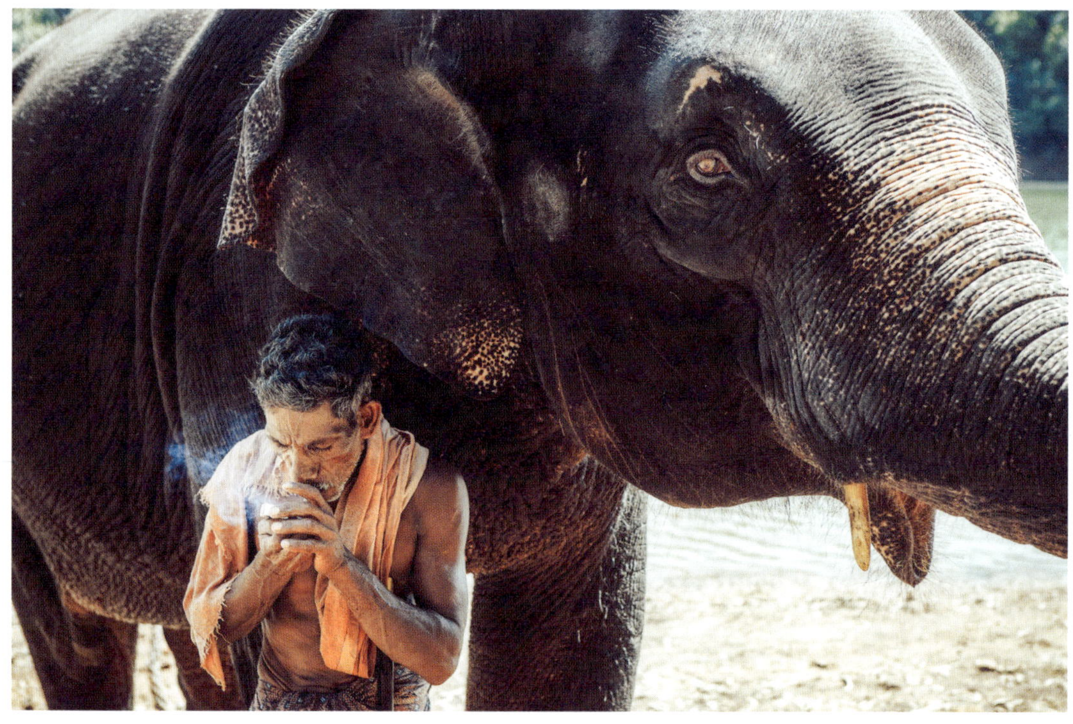

Lens choice: 35mm.

MEDIUM SHOT

A medium shot typically frames a person from the waist up. It focuses on a character (or characters) in a scene while still showing some of the surrounding environment. Try to frame your subjects without cutting through joints; framing a little higher or lower to avoid knees, the waist, elbows, etc.

Since we're now moving in closer to our subjects, avoid wide lenses and switch to a 35mm for this type of shot. This lens length is close to that of the human eye. It will give the viewer a realistic vantage point and lead to a more natural-looking image.

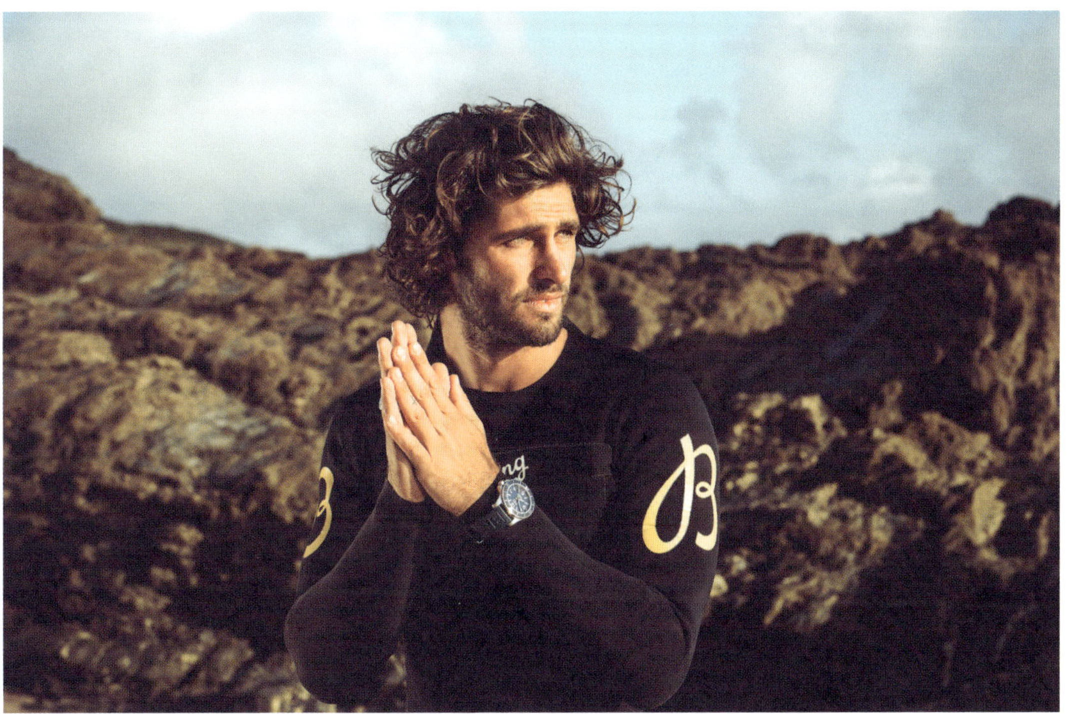

Lens choice: 50mm.

MEDIUM CLOSE SHOT

Whereas medium and long shots are more appropriate for delivering facts, orienting your audience or presenting stunning panoramic views, close-up shots reveal the emotion and/or details relating to the subject.

Such shots are rarely made with wide-angle lenses because this perspective causes objects in the center of the picture to look unnaturally enlarged. Go for a 50mm lens here. It makes beautiful portraits and the depth of field is awesome.

However, with this type of shot it is more difficult to tell the whole story. I think this is why you'll find less engagement on Instagram for medium close or close-up shots. It's hard for the audience to gain an understanding of what's going on without supporting imagery or, indeed, a caption.

SHOT TYPES:
CLOSE-UP & CUTAWAY

CLOSE-UP SHOT

A close-up shot tightly frames a person or object so the subject becomes the primary focus. Use it to keep your audience in-tune and 'connected'.

Concentrating solely on medium or long shots can quickly become boring if that's all an audience sees and you run the risk of them disconnecting from your characters. Using close-ups can keep your audience involved with a story.

We're moving into the realm of telephoto lenses here, but a 50mm will also do just fine if you're able to get up close to your subjects.

CUTAWAY SHOT

A cutaway is a shot of something related to, but outside, the main action of a scene. It's a shot that 'cuts away' to a separate or secondary action – hence the name.

Even if cutaways don't reveal anything new, they are useful when editing, because they help to transition the viewer from one image to another, into a new scene. They are also perfect for introducing suspense or a vague sense of danger to a series of images. In the example opposite, the cutaway reveals the wider rural landscape.

It's so easy to neglect to shoot these details, but they are invaluable for telling a more rounded story using a series of images. I can often be heard repeating to myself, *'details, details, details'* while on location. It's very easy to forget to shoot them, but I can't stress this enough: if you want to tell stories with images, you need cutaways.

My lens choice for this type of image is a 50mm: it's close to how the human eye sees, perfect for picking out details and delivers a natural-looking image.

RECAP

/ Think of different camera shots as a visual language.

/ Compile a shot list ahead of your shoot, and use different shot types to break down your story and structure the day.

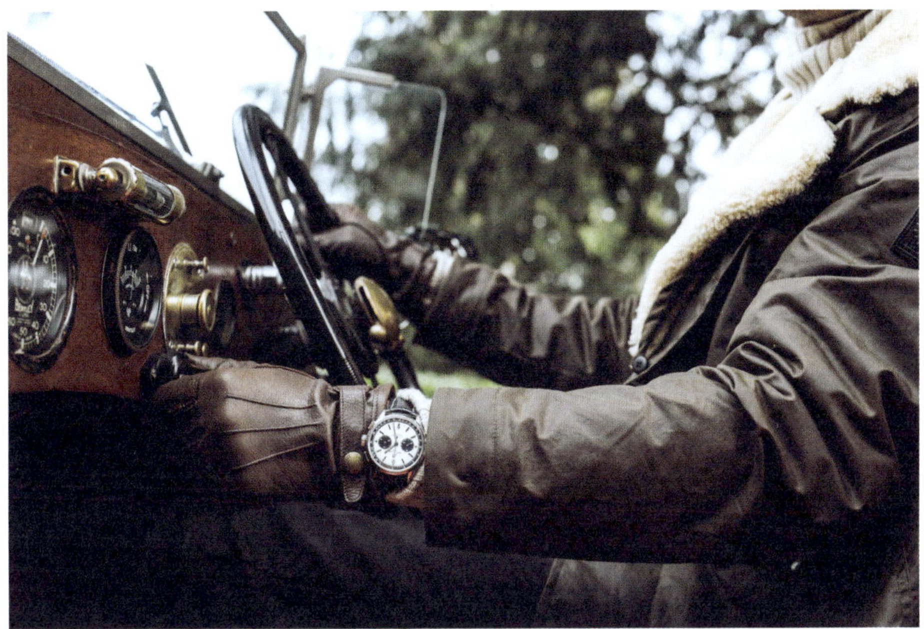

Lens choice: 50mm or 85mm.

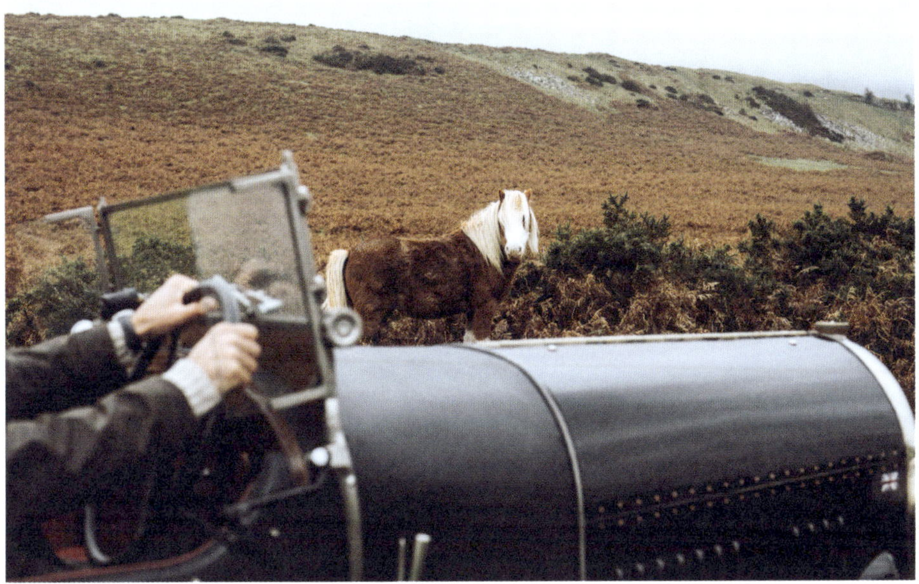

Lens choice: 50mm.

Project /
One Subject, Ten Ways

This is an age-old exercise often practiced by painters, but it translates well to photography, especially when it comes to visual storytelling. It's a simple exercise that you can do anywhere, but therein lies the challenge.

Think about composition, lighting, colour and even texture to create a variety of pictures of a single subject.

STEP 1 / **CHOOSE AN OBJECT**
Choose a simple object to photograph. The classic choice is an egg, because you can change the state of it fairly easily, but any simple, everyday object will suffice. I've chosen a pile of books for this example.

STEP 2 / **TAKE TEN PHOTOS**
Try to make ten completely different images of your subject. You are allowed to change the state of your subject (like breaking your egg) but also consider using light, composition, reflections, texture, depth of field or refer back to 'Shot Types' on pages 40–45 for some additional ideas.

STEP 3 / **ADD OTHER ELEMENTS**
There are no rules (aside from the restriction of shooting just one subject). You are allowed to add other elements to the scene – such as the bookcase opposite – or change the background or location. The aim is to get you thinking creatively about presenting the same subject in as many different ways as possible.

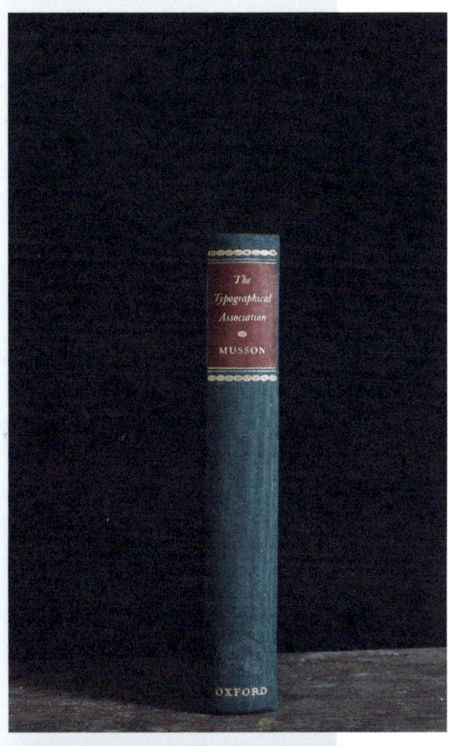

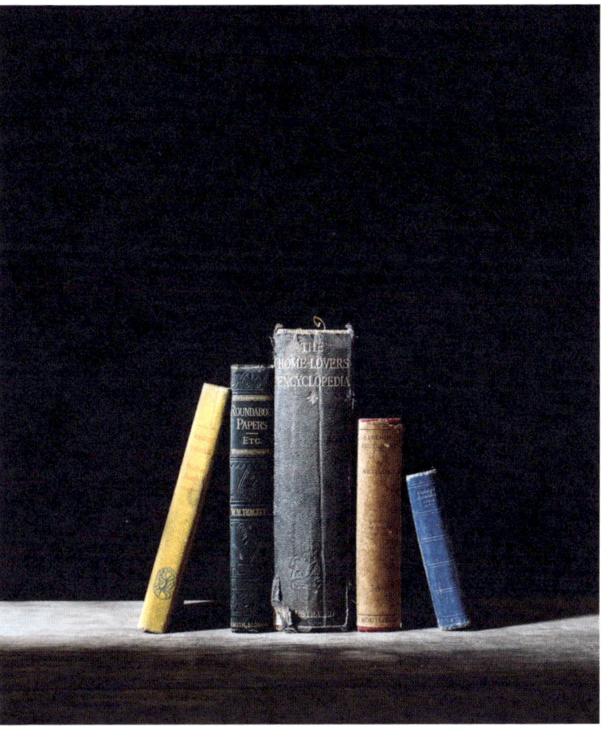

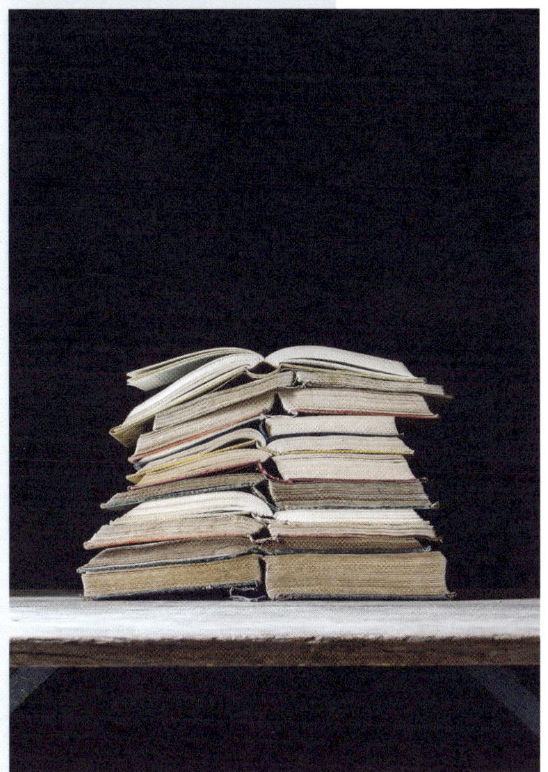

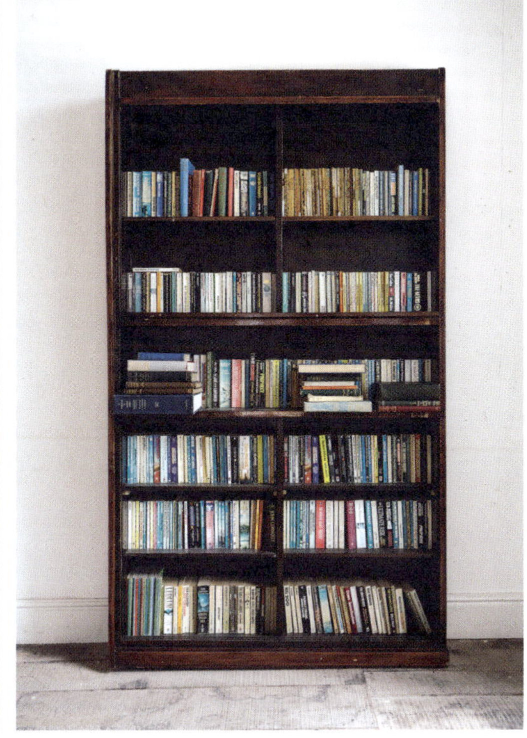

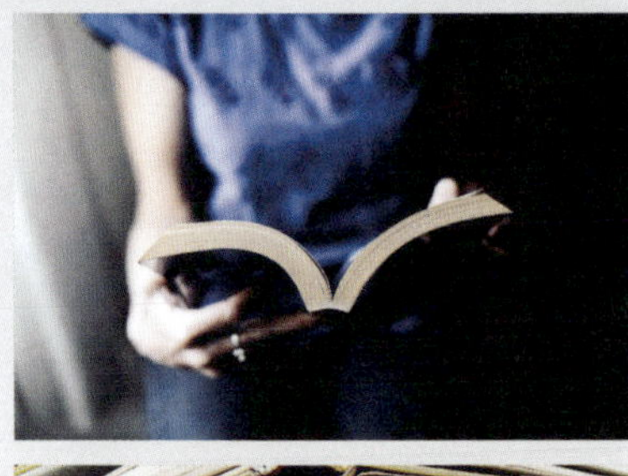

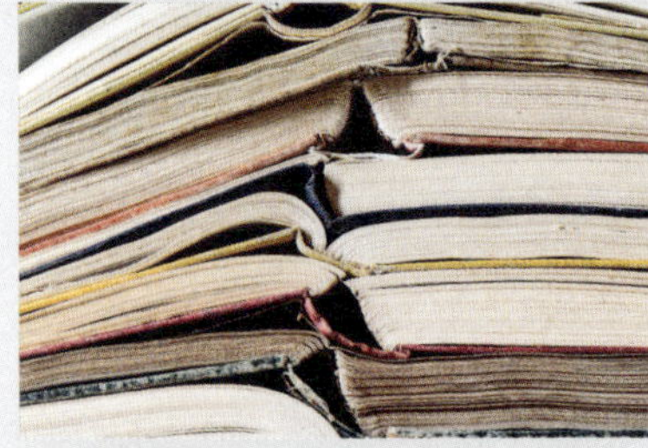

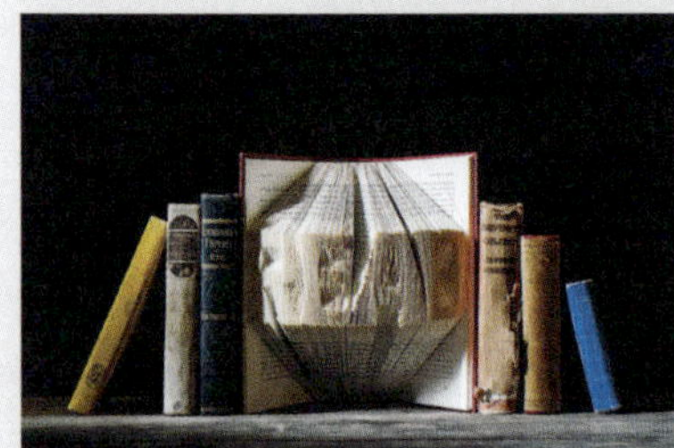

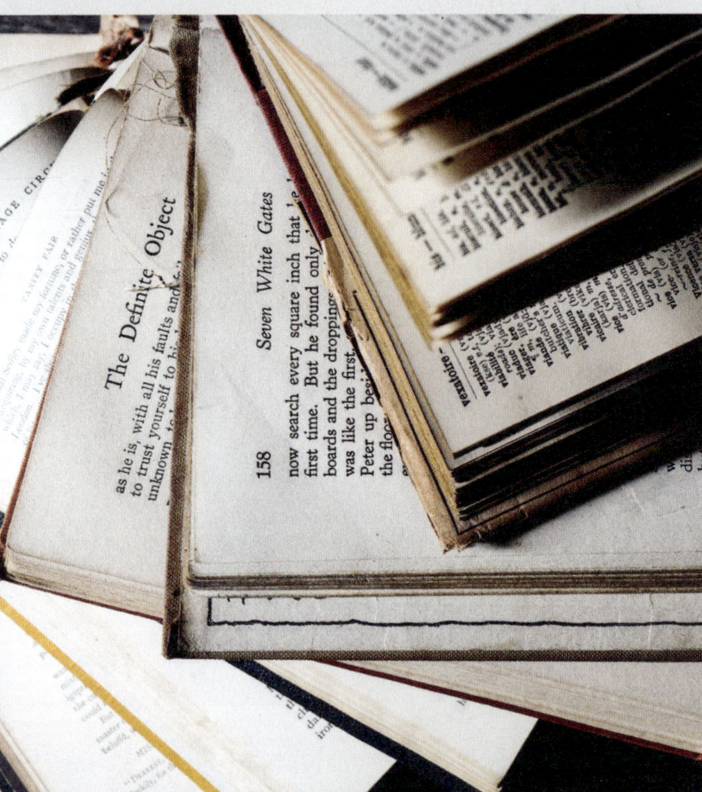

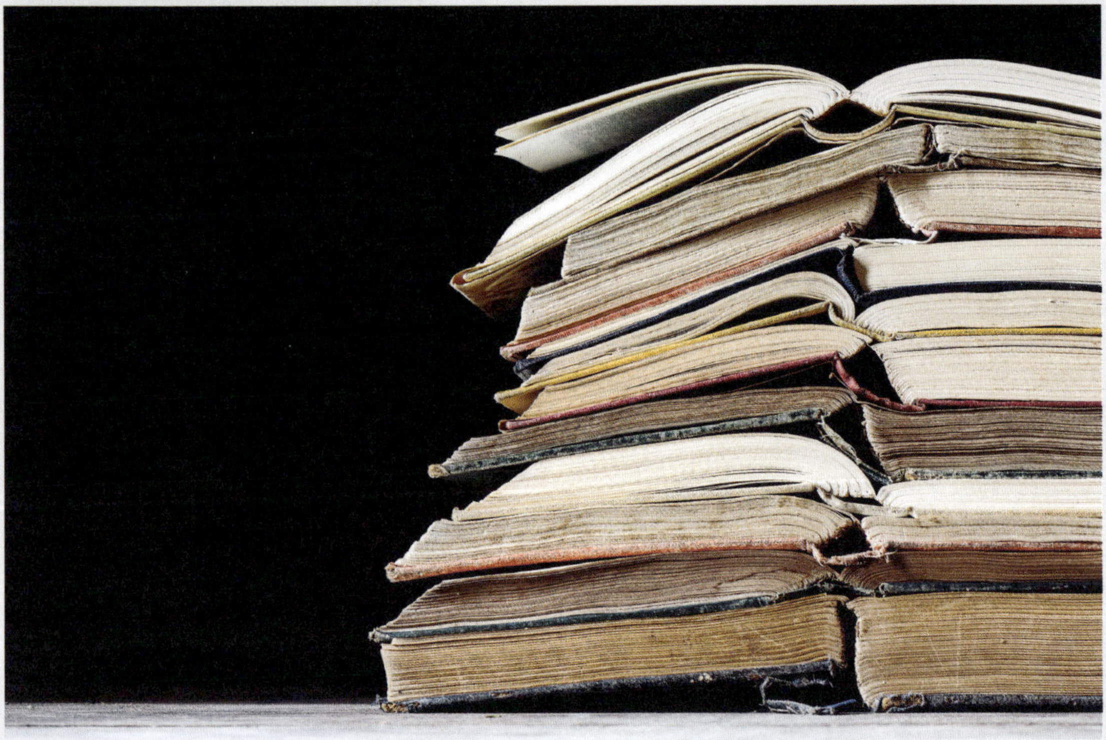

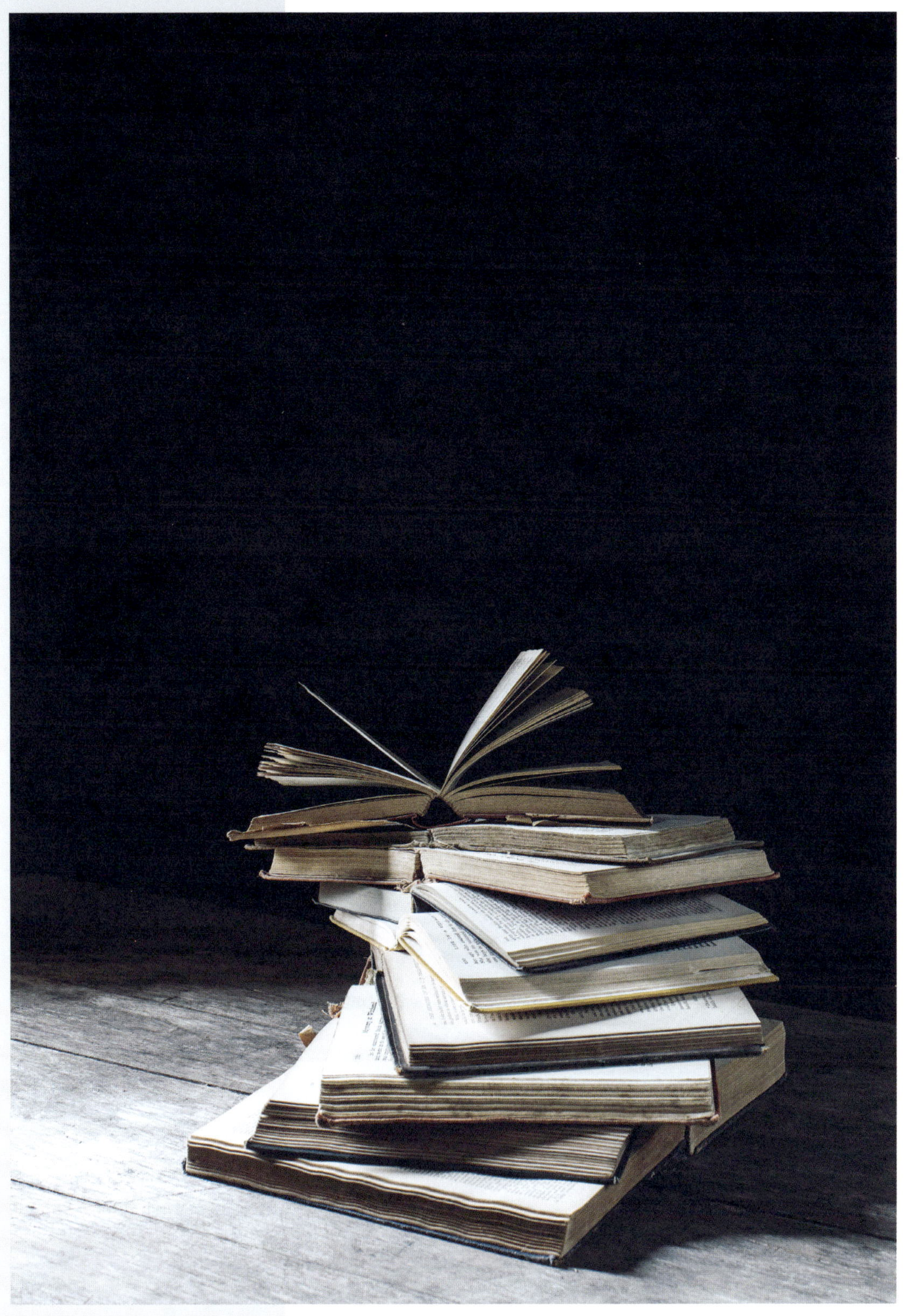

CREATING A BODY OF WORK

Editing is every bit as hard as making photographs, and you can easily corrupt a body of excellent images with a bad edit. However, the 'right' order cannot be determined by rule, and it's often difficult to decide whether a picture should be included at all.

FIRST IMPRESSIONS

First impressions are crucial; they bring your audience deeper into the story. We are moving beyond your role as a photographer here and into the editing world, a separate profession entirely in the film industry. Just as a good photographer knows when not to take a picture, a good editor knows when not to use an image, even if (individually) it's the best image from a shoot. If it doesn't add to the story, if it doesn't work with the other photos in the set, it should be left out. You can always repurpose it elsewhere – sell it as a print or post it to Instagram, for example.

OBJECTIVITY

Part of the problem is that you need to free yourself from the memory of standing in situ and taking the photograph. Look at the image objectively with a stranger's eye. Every single image you include should reinforce the narrative you are trying to relay.

ORDER

I often lead a body of work with an establishing shot to set the scene. However, this isn't a hard and fast rule. Sometimes it's better to start with something that creates more intrigue, such as a tightly cropped close-up shot revealing a detail of your main character. Remember, such shots can pique your audience's interest, creating intrigue and encouraging them to dig deeper. Work with that.

Over the years, you will inevitably build an archive of photographs from which to draw stories, and sequencing images from different shoots can lead to some fun results and give pictures a whole new meaning. The effect of pairing unrelated imagery is really quite magical – the two images opposite sit together on a spread in my printed portfolio.

TIPS

/ Spend time on your edit.

/ Try to free yourself from the memories you made while making the photographs and view your work with a stranger's eye.

/ Use colour instead of subject matter to pair work – it can lead to unexpected results!

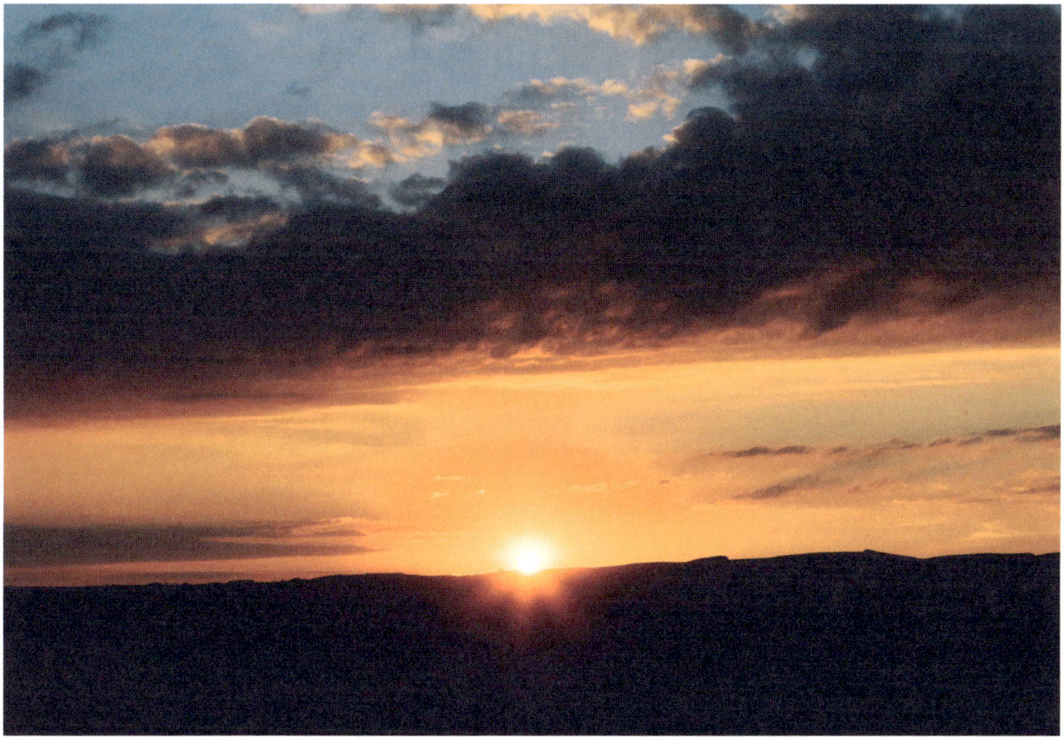

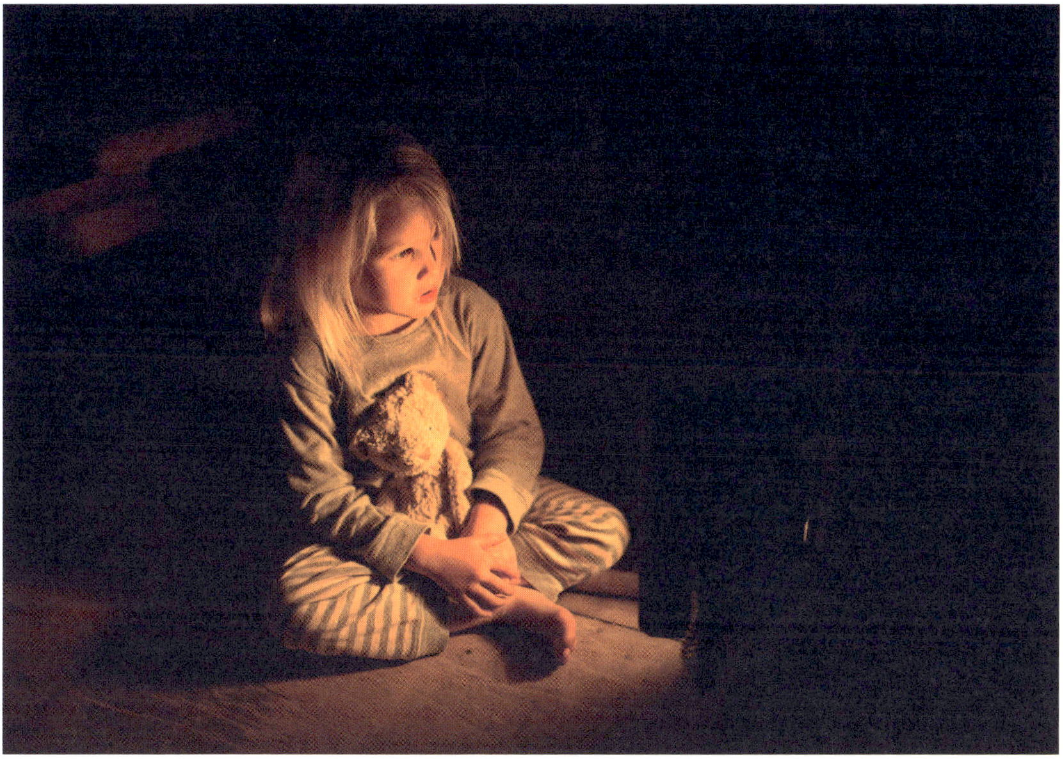

Project /

Everyday Cinematic

BRIEF

+ Make an everyday situation cinematic.

REQUIREMENTS

+ Establish your location.

+ Intrigue your viewer by slowly revealing the event.

+ Involve your viewer and maintain their interest by using a variety of shot types.

+ Finish the story using something introduced at or related to the beginning.

OBJECTIVE

+ Create an engaging photo story from an everyday occurance using at least four different shot types.

Choose an everyday situation to document with your camera. For example: preparing a meal, a birthday party, planting a flower... it can be anything. Your job here is to make an engaging photo set out of an everyday occurence using the variety of shot types detailed on pages 40–45.

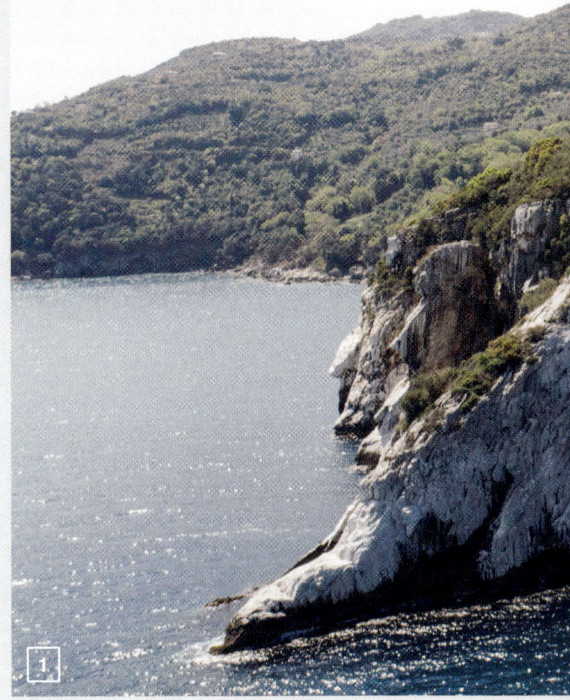

STEP 1 / ESTABLISH

Establish the scene by showing the location. This is a drone shot of the beach where my event is taking place. An extreme long shot like this is great for setting the scene.

STEP 2 / INTRIGUE

Close crops begin to reveal a character and introduce an event associated with the location.

STEP 3 / REVEAL

The full event is revealed and more characters show that we're witnessing a family picnic.

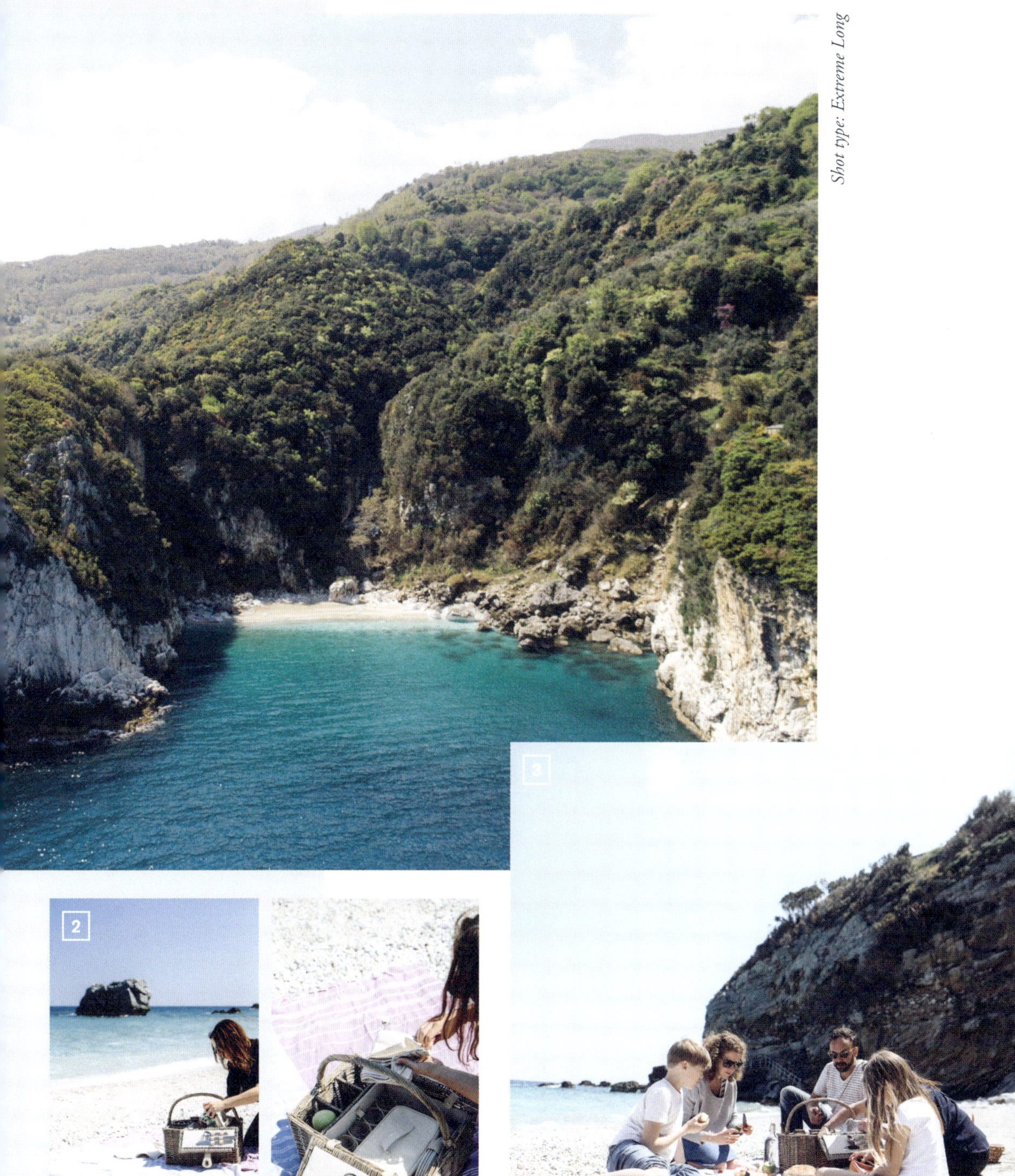

Shot type: close-up.

Shot type: medium.

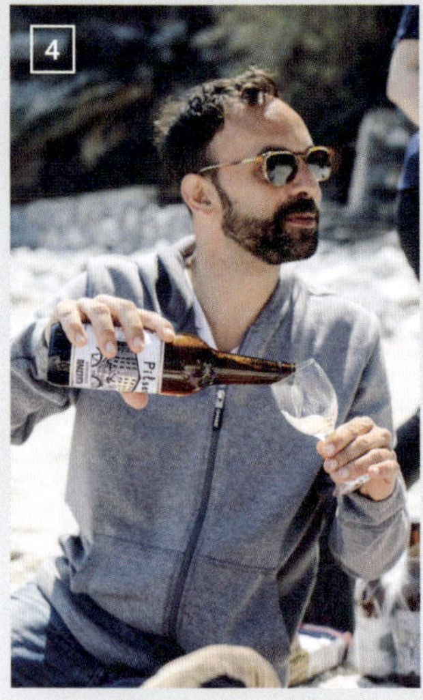

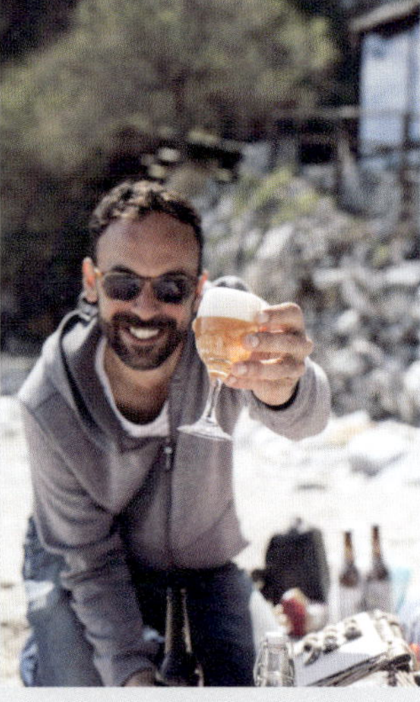

STEP 4 / **INVOLVE**

Image sequence shot from the point of view of one of the characters. Up until this point, viewers have been a fly on the wall, watching the scene evolve. This is a clever way of putting them directly into the scene.

STEP 5 / **ENGAGE**

Cutaway to a bird's-eye view of the scene. The change of angle gives a different perspective and keeps the viewer engaged.

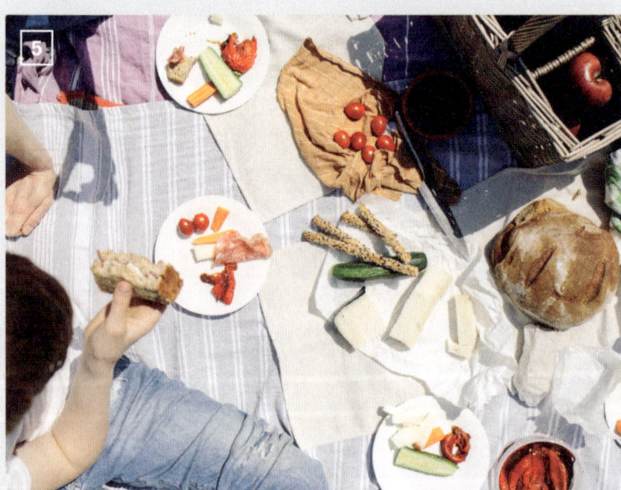

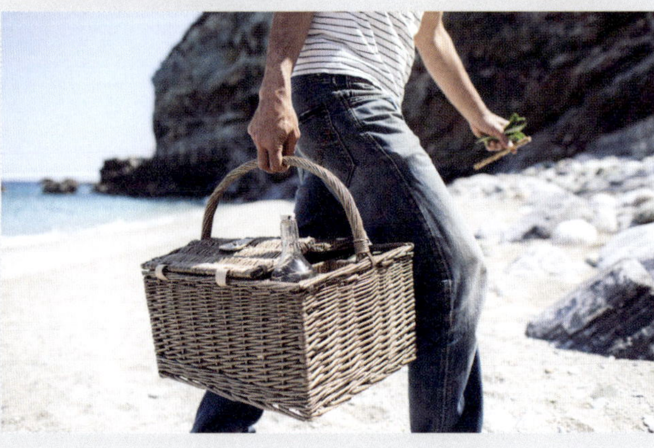

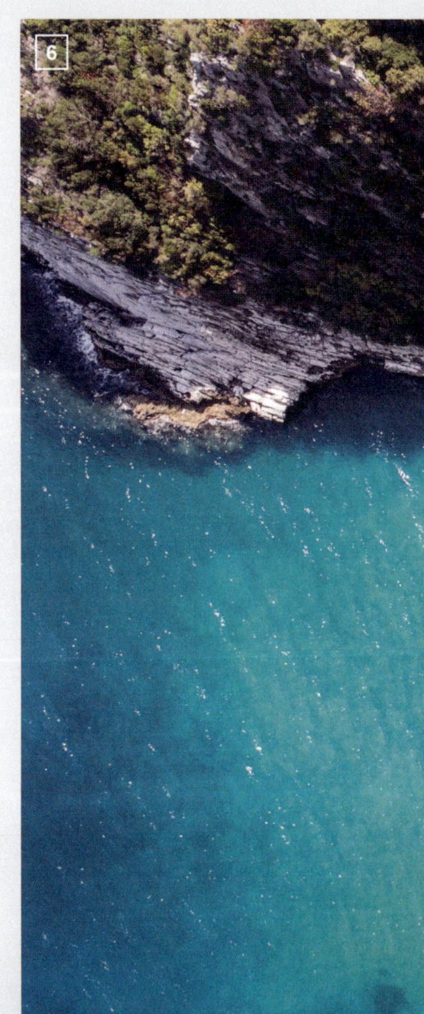

Another bird's-eye view of the same scene signals the beginning of the end of the story by pulling the viewer away from the scene. A closed hamper – introduced in the initial scenes – ends the sequence.

Shot type: extreme long.

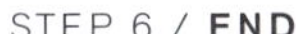

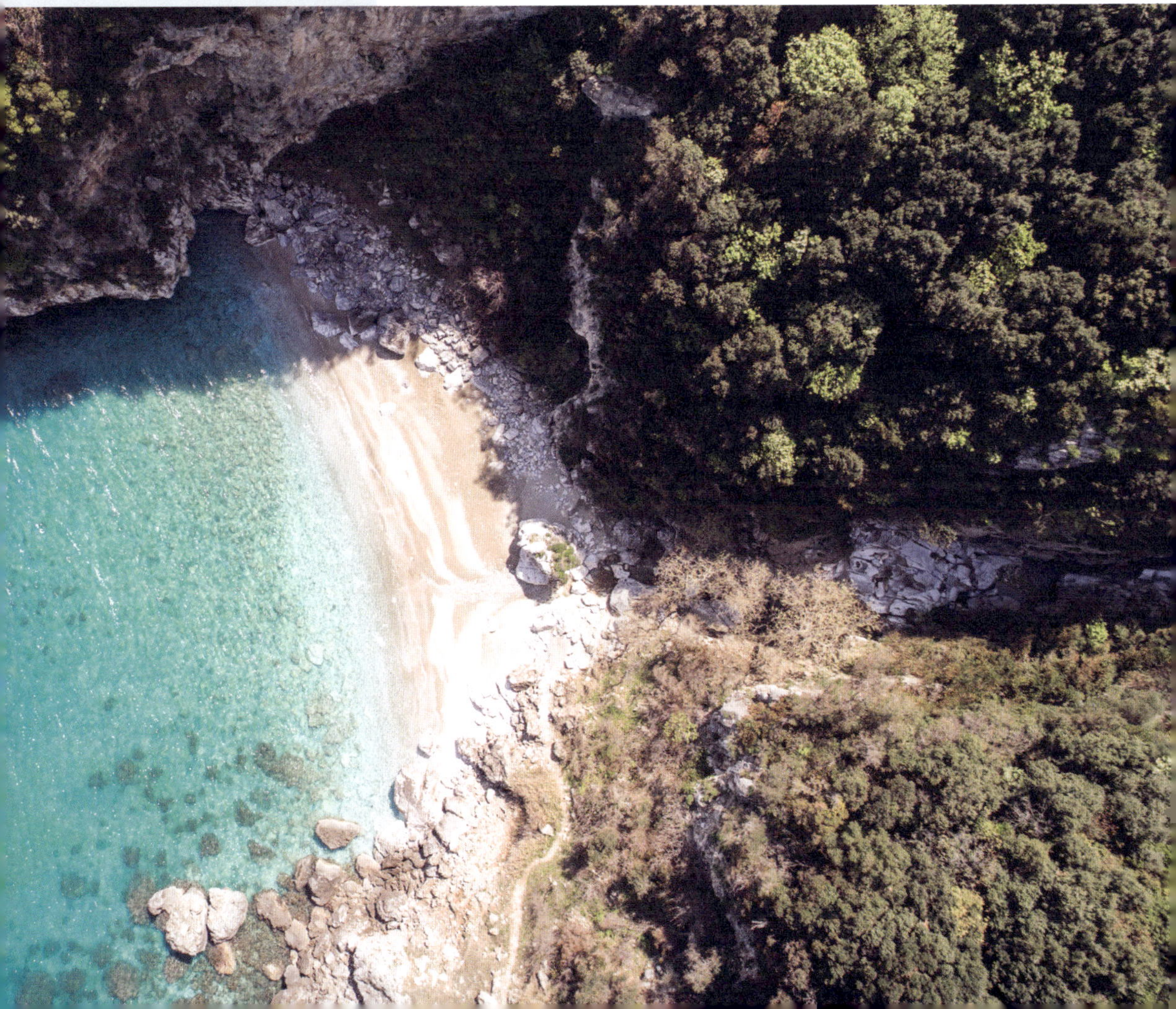

Step 1: Pitch

A strong online presence is an essential part of any photographer's business and it's necessary to present a polished and professional shop front. However, it's just as important to deliver a sense of your own personality to prospective clients. Let's face it, *everyone* wants to be a photographer these days! You can't rely on your image-making capabilities alone to win contracts; you've got to show you're cool to work with too!

In this chapter, we'll run through building websites, curating an Instagram feed, the art of negotiation and how to handle yourself on client calls – essentially, everything you need to start landing work and getting paid for the images you make.

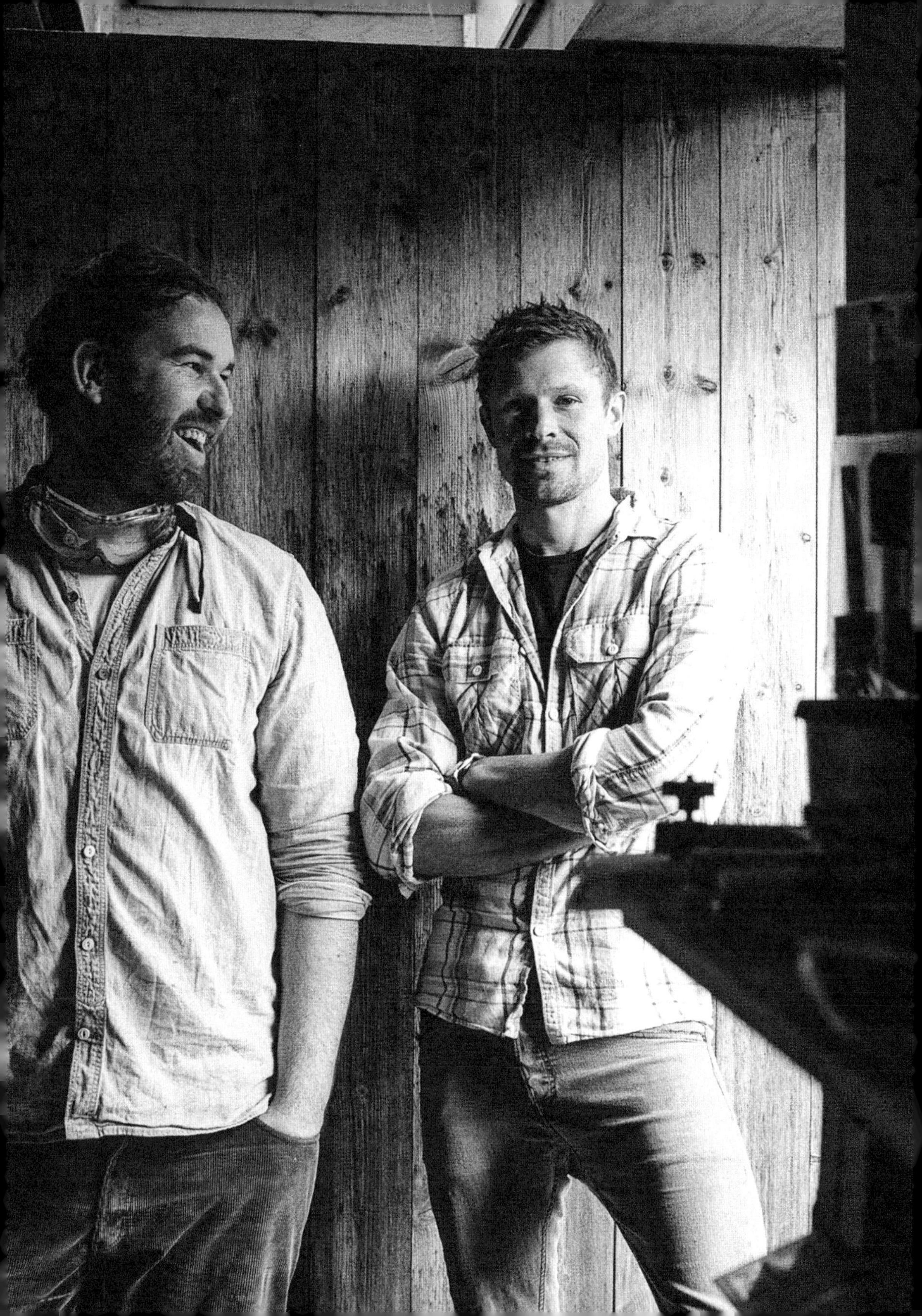

WEBSITE

You might think Instagram has removed the need for a photographer to bother with a website, but a solid portfolio site is still a vital marketing tool. Instagram is hard to beat when it comes to maintaining a personal connection with audiences, but the lifespan of an image on that platform is short and a website gives you a platform to curate and display a collection of your best work, as well as legacy personal projects.

Maybe you're starting from scratch or perhaps you have a website already and you're thinking of reworking it. Either way, ask yourself the following questions before you begin:

WHO ARE YOU?

What type of work do you want to make? When starting out, photographers experiment and shoot all sorts of subject matter. In fact, I highly recommend it in order to find your niche and style, but a mish-mash of subjects can lead to a jumbled body of work when viewed together. Hone your website so that you're only displaying the type of work you want to be employed to shoot.

Perhaps you are shooting weddings at the weekend to pay bills, but really you have a hankering to shoot automotive work. It's a common scenario, as we don't all land dream assignments from the get-go. In this case, consider creating two sites – one for your bread-and-butter wedding clients and a second to showcase the very best of your auto work to potential editors. The way you present your work demonstrates where your focus lies, and a confused portfolio gives the impression that you don't know who you are.

WHO IS YOUR AUDIENCE?

This is not your mum, dad, friend or colleague... I'm talking potential clients looking to commission you as a photographer: art buyers, magazine editors, social media managers and so on. These people are busy and review a ton of pictures each day! It's imperative to capture and maintain their attention from the outset.

As before, a tightly edited selection of images is the only way to go. A website showcasing 20 killer pics in a consistent and coherent style will always win more work than a wide-ranging jumbled body of work.

IS IT EASY TO USE?

Remember, you are advertising your skills as a photographer not a web designer. Keep it simple and let your pictures do the talking. Look at template platforms like Squarespace, Format and Cargo Collective. They offer well-designed, hosted portfolios that work on multiple devices and are easy to navigate. Make life easy for your audience: no one has an abundance of time today and the longer it takes for a potential client to access what they're looking for, the more likely they are to hit close and move on to the next name on their list.

IS YOUR BRANDING COHESIVE?

Does your domain name match your email address or does it read *yourname@gmail.com*

I see this a lot and still don't understand why. Gmail email addresses work just fine for emailing your friends and family, but when dealing with clients it pays to look professional. Hosted platforms like Squarespace and Gmail itself make it super easy to create an email that matches your domain name, so there's no excuse.

FINN BEALES

DIRECTOR / PHOTOGRAPHER

HOME   COMMISSIONS   72 HRS IN...   PERSONAL   WORKSHOP   MOTION   ABOUT

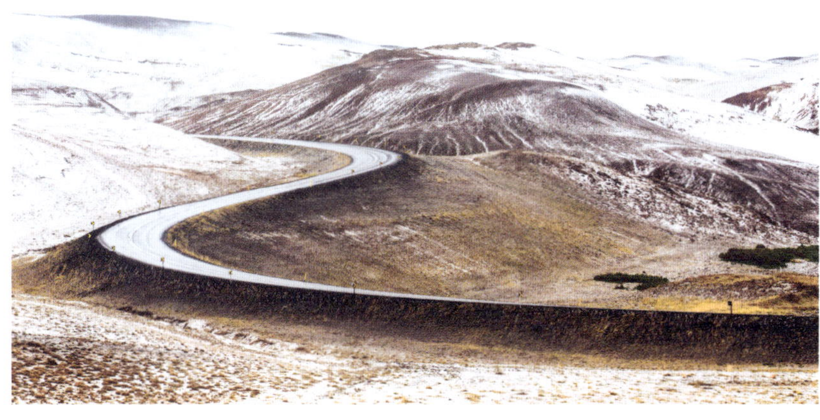

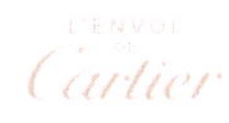

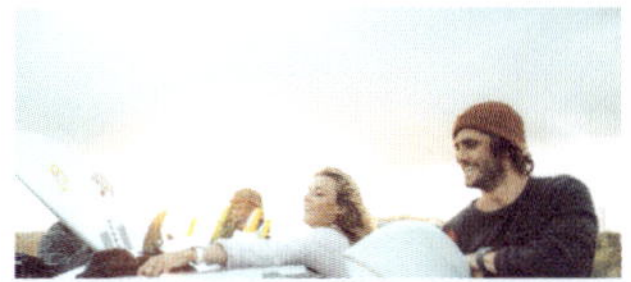

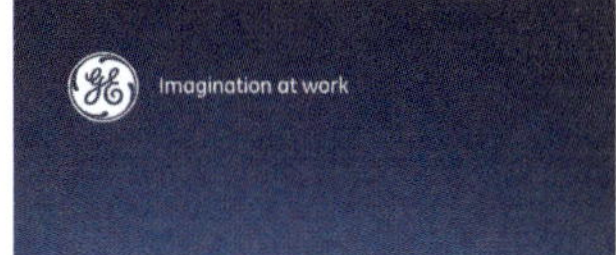

FINN BEALES

DIRECTOR / PHOTOGRAPHER

HOME   COMMISSIONS   72 HRS IN...   PERSONAL   WORKSHOP   MOTION   ABOUT

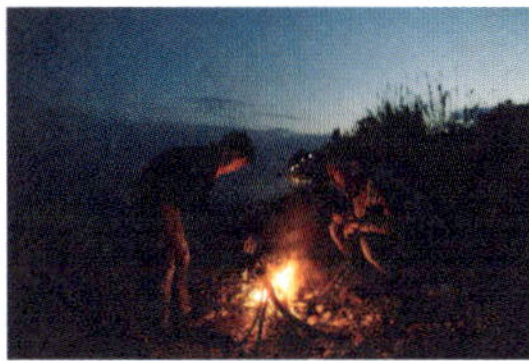

72hrs in Poilon, Greece

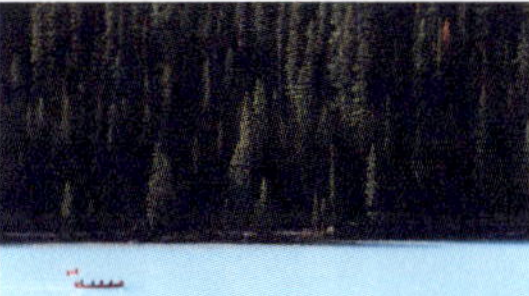

72hrs in Alberta, Canada

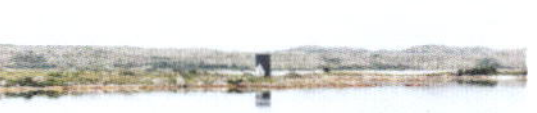

72hrs on Fogo Island

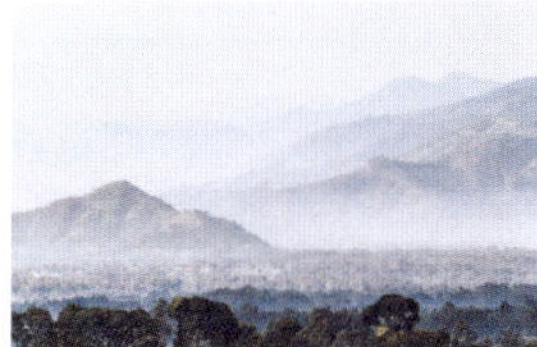

72hrs in Rwanda

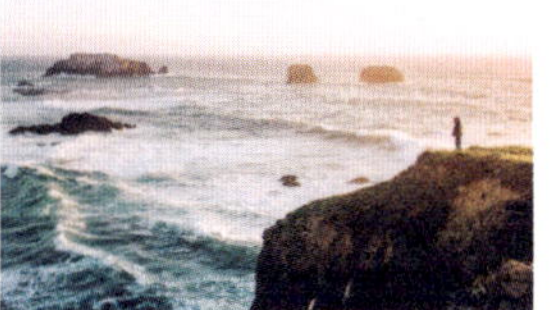

72hrs in Northen California

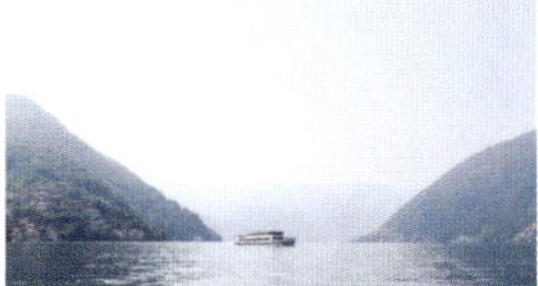

72hrs in Lake Como

Instagram

Search

finn
Edit Profile
6   2
1,801 posts   591k followers   944 following
Finn Beales
Stories of course
Photographer / Director
Online photo classes
www.madebyfinn.com/workshop

2019   BTS   JAPAN   TIMEOUT   BREITLING   LA/SING...   MARSHALL

POSTS   IGTV   SAVED   TAGGED

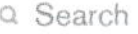

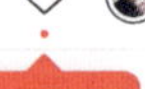

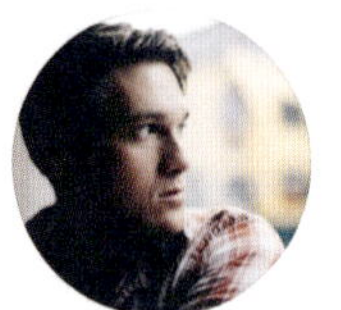

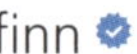

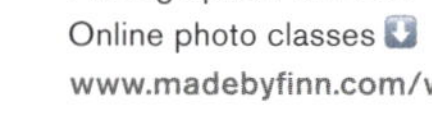

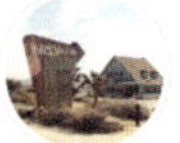

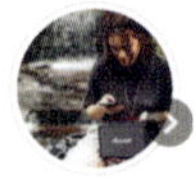

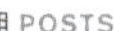

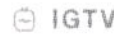

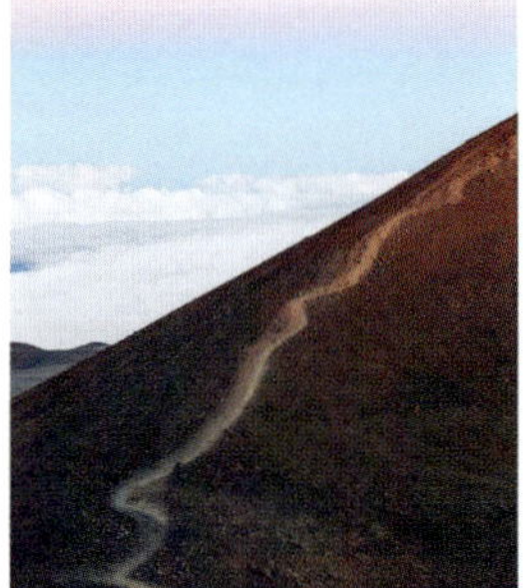

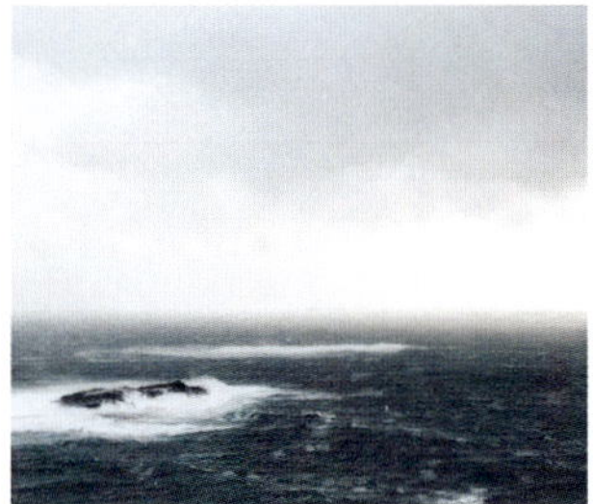

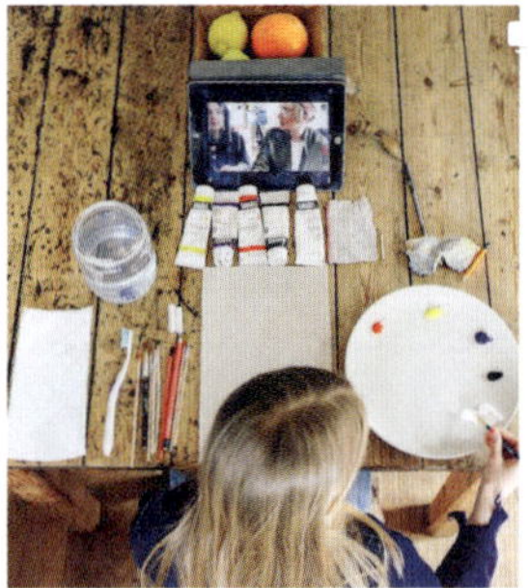

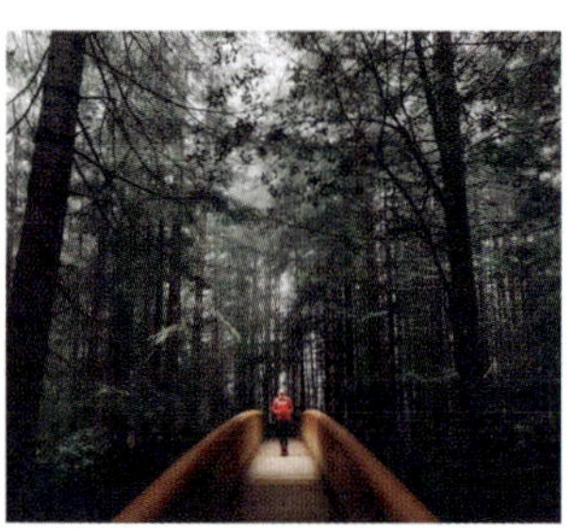

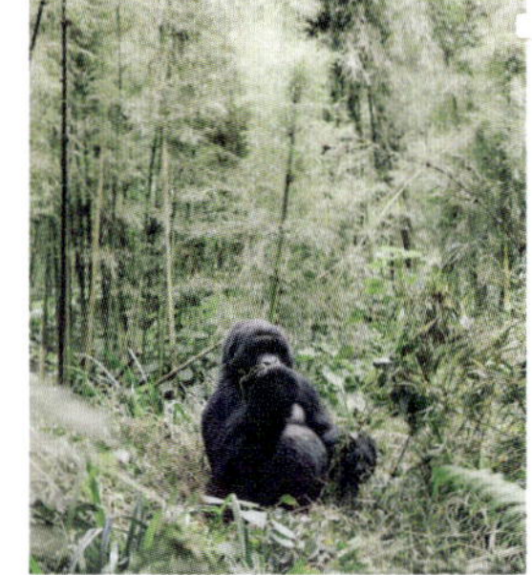

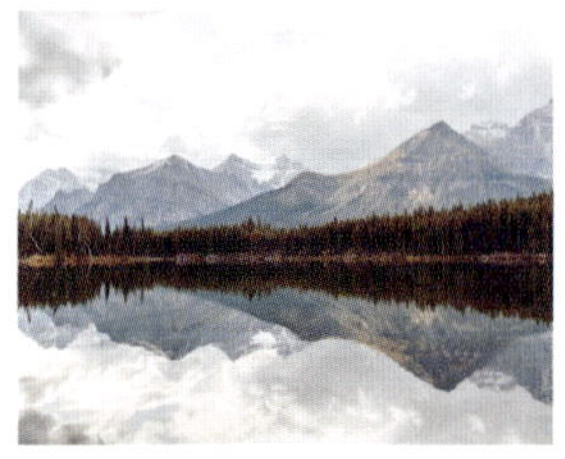

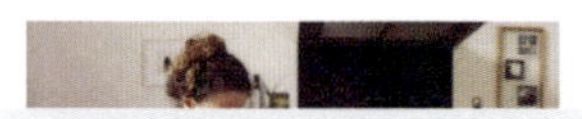

INSTAGRAM

Instagram now has over one billion active users. Although that might seem like an overwhelming level of competition, there are still plenty of opportunities for photographers on the platform. In this section, we'll look at some of the tips, tricks and methods you can use to grow your presence on the platform.

POST REGULARLY

Instagram only works if people keep posting content to the platform, so it makes sense for them to 'reward' accounts that are more active, rather than those that have been left to gather dust – and that reward comes in the form of exposure.

Unfortunately, the visibility of your account is determined algorithmically. The more you post, the more you engage, the more visible your account will become. I aim to post once a day, Monday to Friday, and take the weekend off, unless I'm travelling, in which case I post pretty much every day.

ENGAGE WITH FOLLOWERS

Engaging with people is one of the best ways to grow your profile, remain inspired and get the most out of the platform. Liken it to the real world – say you spend an evening in the corner of a bar not speaking to anyone, you will leave at the end of the night with no new friends or connections. Spend the evening chatting and getting to know people and you'll leave with new friends and all the opportunities that arise from such encounters.

Engaging on Instagram is no different. Chat with other photographers, art buyers, editors or even your dream clients. Engaging with such accounts will lead to an increase in their awareness of your work and in followers who can potentially lead to new work.

Identify accounts you'd like to build a relationship with and commit. Engage regularly, liking and commenting. Leave thoughtful comments. I don't just mean '*awesome*' or '*great shot*' – these comments are unlikely to catch attention. Post interesting responses and ask questions. Consistently interacting along these lines will eventually get you noticed and hopefully lead to opportunities further down the line.

CONSISTENCY

Just as with your website, you need to keep your posts consistent, and by that I mean consistent in terms of the brand image you are looking to project. If you are using Instagram as a professional you are going to want to post your best work in the hope of attracting clients.

However, instead of posting the same images found on your website, you can afford to be a little looser. Try to find a balance between images that demonstrate your ability as a photographer and photographs that deliver a sense of personality to your followers. The latter can be more personal, such as images from home, pets, kids… anything that gives prospective clients an understanding of what you are like as a person.

CAPTIONS

I'm actually a man of few words when it comes to my Instagram captions, but this isn't best practice if you want to build followers on the platform. When I spend time 'crafting' a caption related to the image, perhaps expanding on the story the picture is telling, I always notice a spike in engagement. Keep your captions to around three lines in length and ensure they are genuine and in your own voice. Again, it's important to deliver a sense of your own personality and show clients what you're like to work with.

HASHTAGS

Although not quite as relevant today as they were in the early days of Instagram, hashtags can still play a part in revealing your content to users outside your following provided you are using the right tags.

Every hashtag has its own 'gallery' and photo editors sometimes browse these galleries in search of new talent. Each gallery has a 'Top' and a 'Recent' section. The posts in 'Top' are determined by a combination of how recent the post is, and how many likes/comments it is receiving.

Use a site such as Display Purposes to generate relevant hashtags from the specific genre of image you are posting, whether it's landscape, travel, portrait or something else.

You can apply tags by writing them in the caption, but I prefer to drop them into the first comment just after I have posted the image. I'd also recommend starting that comment with five dots, each on their own line, as this forces Instagram to collapse the comment, which hides it, creating a cleaner look and feel.

GEOTAGS

While hashtags can present your work to new users according to genre, geotags make it easier for people searching for a particular place to find your pictures. Turn on GPS tracking in your phone or camera or alternatively search for the location when you come to post your picture, it's more than likely someone has posted an image from nearby so the coordinates will already be logged on the platform.

COLLABORATE

Everything I have mentioned so far will help you develop 'virtual' relationships via Instagram, but don't forget that there are real people on the end of those likes and comments. I have made some great 'real world' friends via the platform. Relationships that began with a simple comment posted on their account have flourished over the years as I made the effort to meet them.

Over time you will find like-minded folk and start building relationships. Collaborating with fellow photographers or creatives is one of the most rewarding aspects of the platform, on a personal as well as professional basis.

The following collaborations were all the result of connections I made through Instagram.

1 *Collaborating with Jared Chambers and Rishad Daroowala for Explore Canada.*

2 *Myself, Julian Pircher and Alex Strohl filming the video workshop that inspired this book (madebyfinn.com/workshop).*

3 *Me shooting on location in Portugal for the workshop.*

4 *Andrea Dabene in Montana – personal work.*

5 *A behind-the-scenes shot of Alex and myself shooting the workshop in Portugal.*

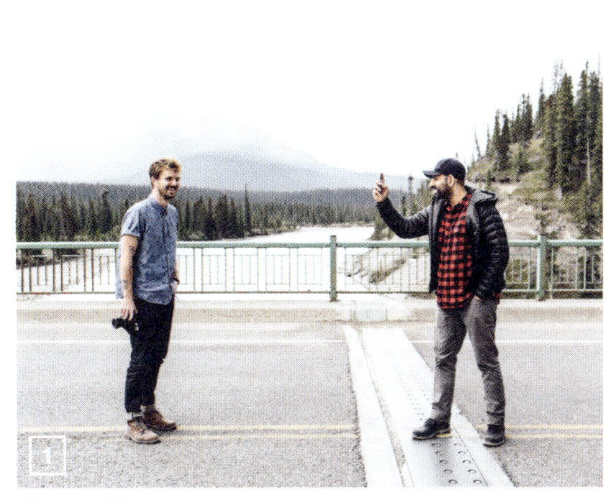

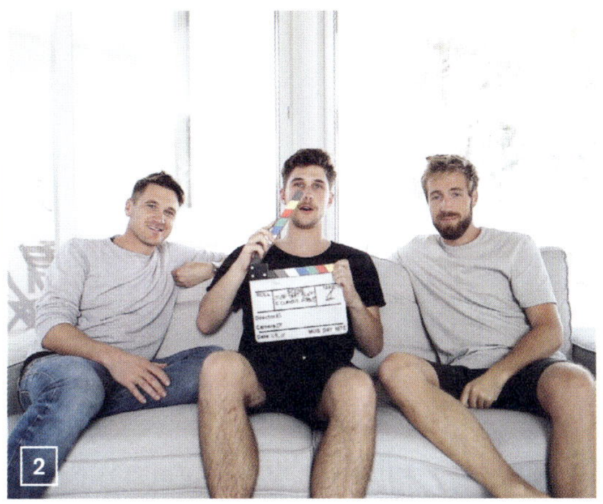

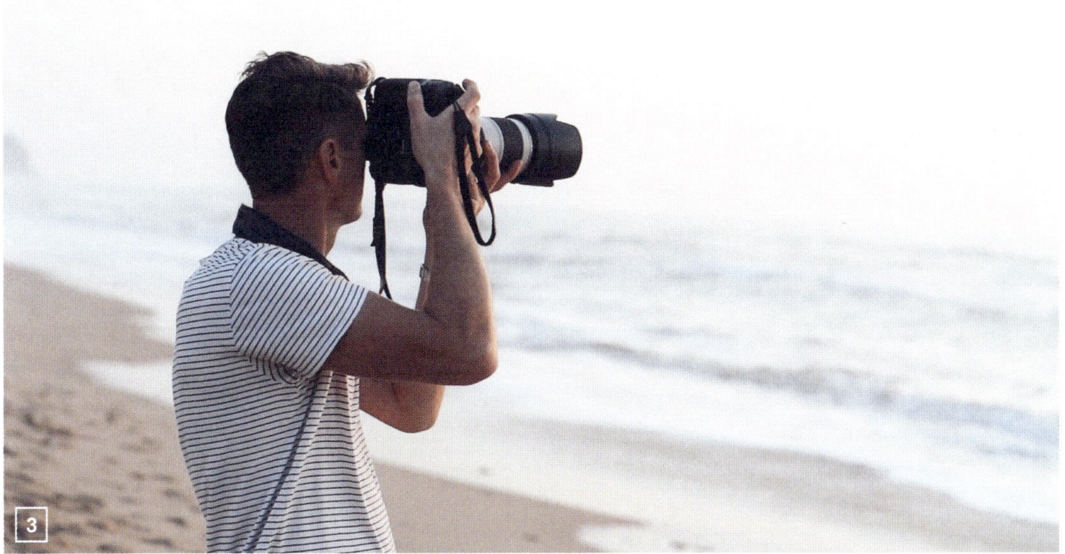

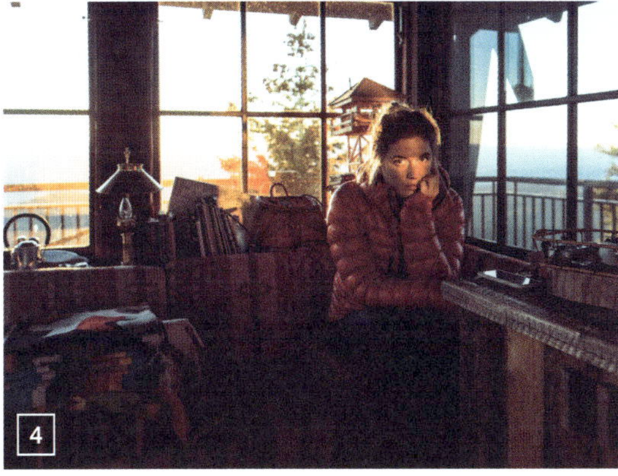

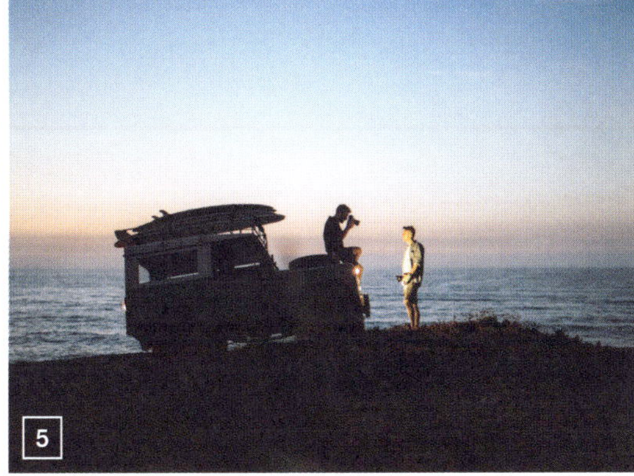

ASK THE RIGHT QUESTIONS

So you have a killer looking website and you're posting regularly to Instagram. Then one day, lo and behold, you receive an email from a prospective client asking if you would be interested in shooting for them. How do you move that email into a paid shoot?

To start with, always respond positively:

Hey there! Thanks for your email. I'm really excited about the prospect of working with you and would love to hear more.

Then you need to drill down on their expectations:

Do you have a project brief you can share?

Sometimes, prospective clients already have a brief sorted, so you can cut out a lot of work by asking for that. If not, I ask them to fill out several bullet points as best they can, so I can get more of an idea of their project and their requirements.

⊕ **CREATIVE SPECIFICATIONS**
This might be mood boards, or any example imagery. I'm a visual person and work better with pictures than words. Example imagery helps me get into their groove and deliver on their expectations. Ask about particular subjects: What am I shooting? Is it a product? Is it a location? I may have addressed this in the opening line, but I still like to put it here so we have it in writing.

⊕ **SHOOT DATES AND THE TIMELINE FOR DELIVERABLES**
Really, really crucial, because if it's a summer campaign that needs to be shot in December,

I can't shoot that in my backyard in Wales; it's very grey in Wales in the middle of winter, so I'm going to have to fly to a different location to get those sunny scenes. Knowing the answer to this question will help determine the location, which will have a knock-on effect on the costs.

⊕ **DESIRED REGIONS AND LOCATIONS**
They may already have some thoughts in mind. If not, it's good to get them thinking about it and manage expectations from the outset.

⊕ **SHOT LIST OR AT LEAST A NUMBER OF DELIVERABLES**
I need to know what they want from me from the outset.

⊕ **ANY SOCIAL MEDIA ASKS**
This will have ramifications on cost, but it will also have implications on how I approach the job. If I'm putting images on my Instagram account, I need to create imagery that's going to sit well with the rest of my content. I'm not going to put just anything on my Instagram account, because I'm aware people follow me for a reason. The images need to sit right in this context.

⊕ **FULL USAGE TERMS AND ALSO USAGE PERIOD**
This is how the image(s) will be used and for how long. Are they going to be used on a billboard campaign? Are they going to be used on a client's social media account? Are they going to be used for TV ads? All of these questions will help me start to price the job. A billboard campaign will be highly lucrative, whereas a magazine article will be lower down the pay scale. This information is needed for me to start to produce

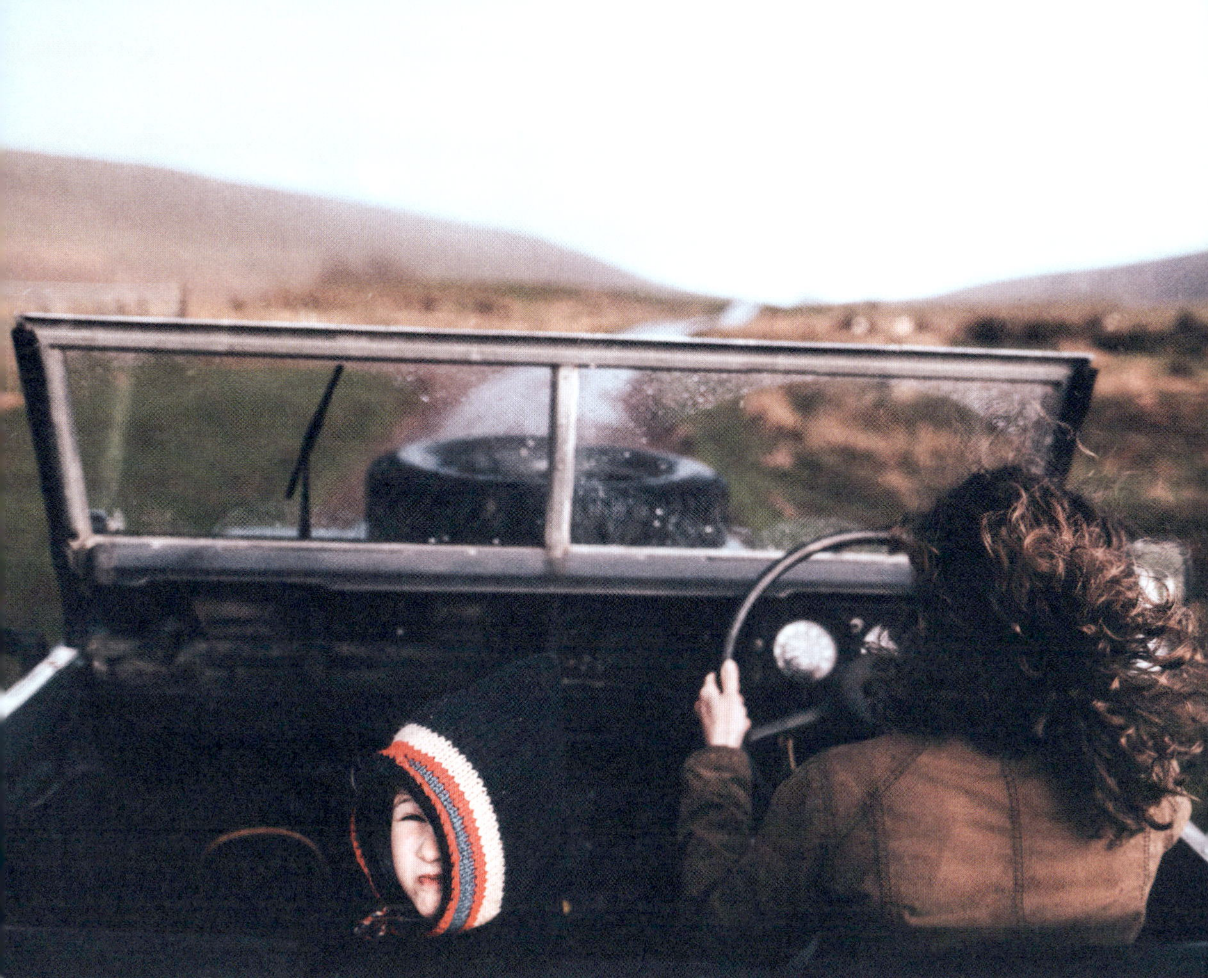

the shoot and work out how much everything's going to cost. You should also ask about the 'use of your likeness' in this section. Increasingly I'm being asked to feature in 'behind the scenes' videos. This is where a brand uses your profile to advertise their product. That has a value. Don't let that slide.

COMPETITOR BRANDS AND EXCLUSIVITY TERMS

If a car company approaches you to shoot a campaign, they may have a line in their contract that says you can't work for any other car brand for a set period of time after you deliver the shots. This is really key, because it signs you into an exclusivity deal. If the campaign isn't worth much money, and you agree to it for portfolio-

boosting reasons, you won't be able to take on a competitor's campaign that may turn out to be worth more money. Check the small print.

BUDGET PARAMETERS

It's unlikely you'll get a straight answer to this, but try to tease out a ballpark figure from the get-go.

Once you have answers to all these questions, you can start building a project brief for your client. You can start doing the legwork for them. They'll take you more seriously, and, hopefully, this is going to transition into a commissioned job.

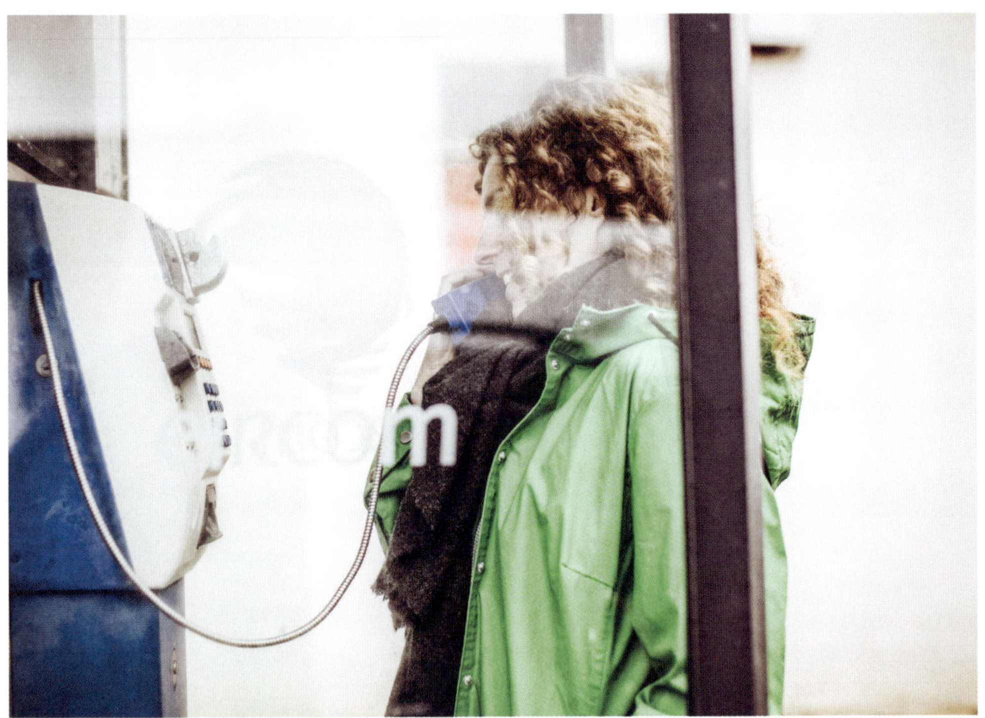

The creative call is a make or break moment. Take them seriously. Don't conduct them in a phone box!

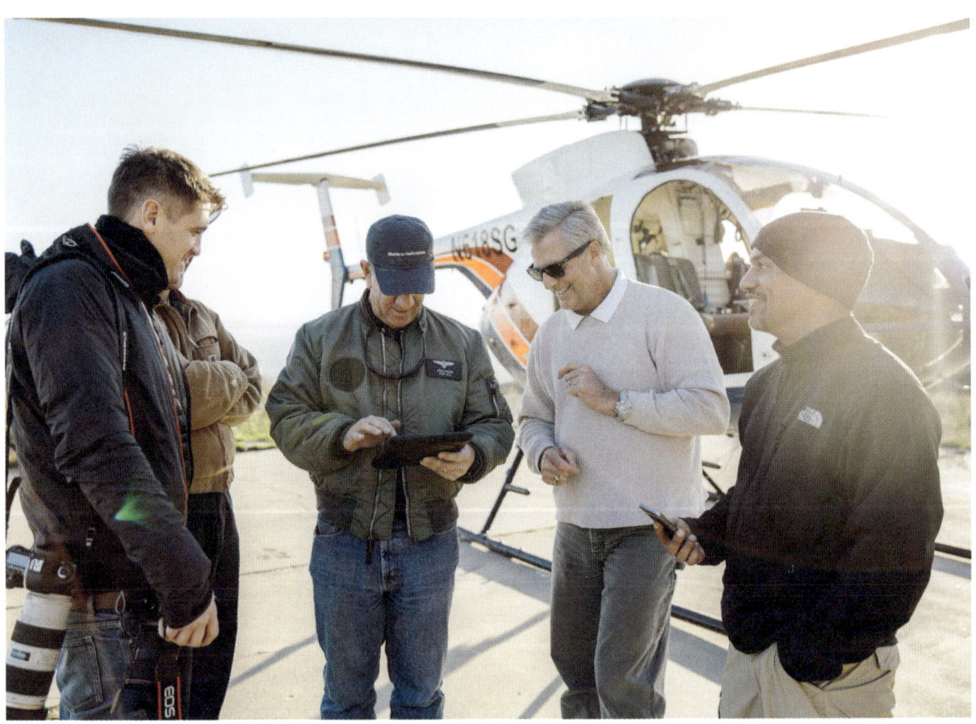

Shooting on location with a production team in Los Angeles. Photo: Seth Carnill.

THE CREATIVE CALL

While your portfolio (website, book, Instagram) can get you to the point of consideration by a client, it's how you articulate your experience and ability in a way that will add value to a production that will determine whether you win the contract or not.

Sometimes a client (typically the art buyer at an ad agency or a photo editor at a magazine) will send across some notes in an email and will ask to have a quick call to enquire about how you might approach their brief.

For more significant assignments, these calls get scheduled in advance. They involve not only the art buyer/producer, but also their creative director, art director and/or account executives that are involved with the project. These phone calls can be a little intimidating, but they are vital. No matter how suited your portfolio might be, if your impression as a person isn't on point, you are unlikely to get the job.

What do you need to project? The three C's as my dad would say:

CONFIDENCE

The creative call is your chance to shine, and enthusiasm is your friend. Meeting over the phone is different to meeting face to face. It's your voice and energy that matter, so make it count.

CAPABILITY

Do your homework. Look at the brief and read around it. Have questions prepared and show that you have the ability and experience to add value to the project.

CHARACTER

The client is more than likely to be talking to several other photographers about the job, so don't assume you have it in the bag just because you are on the phone with them. You need to prove you are the one they want for the job; someone who is easy to travel with and calm in high-pressure situations. They want to ensure that you are like-minded and enjoyable to work with.

TIP / Don't talk about the budget on a creative call. That is a conversation that happens when you have convinced them there is no one else on earth who can do the job as well as you can!

Project /
Develop a Treatment

BRIEF

+ Develop a treatment for a job tailored to your client.

+ Show, rather than tell, how you will approach their brief.

REQUIREMENTS

+ Include information about you as a photographer.

+ Feature a mood board of imagery including photos you have taken yourself and reference images from other sources.

+ Keep your design and branding consistent to present a polished and professional image.

OBJECTIVE

+ Secure a job by demonstrating to the client you have thought carefully about their brief and have the best approach to achieving their goals.

So you nailed the call and everything's going well. The next step is to create a treatment. This is not always requested by a client, but I like to go the extra mile to ensure I win the job, so in this project we'll walk through the process of putting one together.

The aim of a treatment is to shift from email language to images. I'm a visual artist after all, and much better at talking with pictures than with words. Developing a treatment is a slick method of delivering additional information and conveying a sense of professionalism to your client.

The treatment document goes to the client before they've actually booked you. It will show them how you approach your photography and how you would tackle their brief.

STEP 1 / **TITLE SLIDE**
Begin with your logo, so it's clear who you are and what you do. You should also tailor this slide to your client by including their logo and the campaign title.

Ensure your treatment looks professional and ties in with the rest of your marketing collateral. The regular use of your logo, colour palette and font across multiple touchpoints is vital in the treatment presentation.

**SOLID BLACK
BACKGROUND**

Choose a font and stick to the
same one for all the text in your
treatment for consistency.

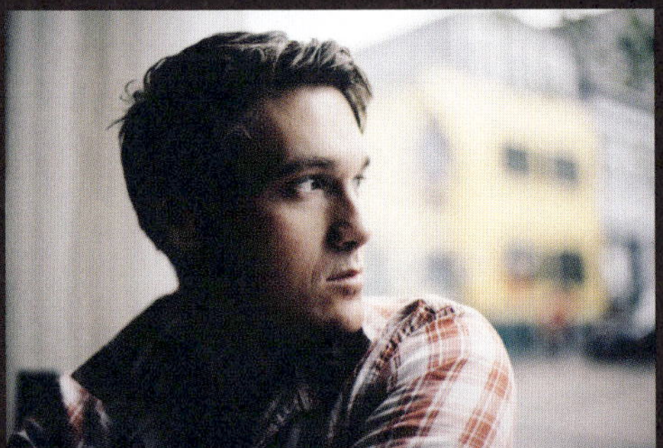

INTRODUCTION

Thanks so much for considering me to shoot the campaign. It's an engaging concept with which I sympathise. The following line, taken from a letter Hunter S. Thompson wrote to a friend on the topic of finding one's purpose in life, eloquently summarises my own approach:

"A man must choose a path which will let his abilities function at maximum efficiency toward the gratification of his desires… In short, he must not dedicate his life to reaching a pre-defined goal, but rather choose a way of life he knows he will enjoy. The goal is absolutely secondary: it is the functioning toward the goal which is important."

Photography is a way of life for me and I fundamentally believe the enjoyment I receive from my work will feed through to the pictures I make with you.

Thanks again for your consideration.

FINN BEALES

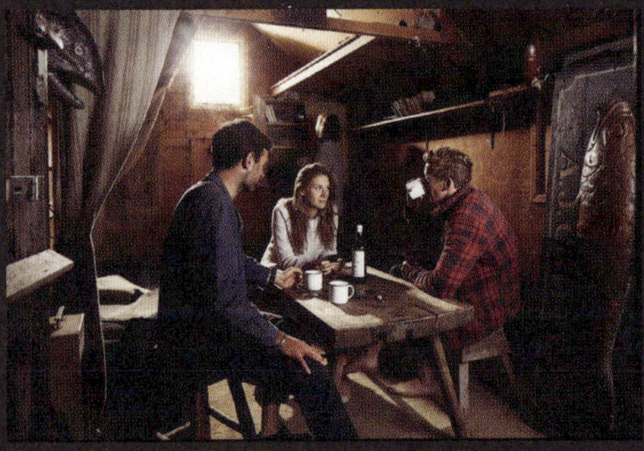

APPROACH: ON LOCATION

Any decent production should make the most out of people's time, but this is especially true when it comes to travelling to multiple locations. To ensure a smooth production, I propose the following:

1) Investigate all of our subjects and define a shot list in pre-production that allows for a degree of flexibility. Often things happen on location that cannot be planned for and staying 'open' to capturing these 'moments' can lead to the best results.

2) Scout and decide together the best places to shoot within our desired location. Observe what times of day are best for natural light, and what gear needs to be considered to enhance the environment.

3) Begin photography and bring our concept to life. Once everyone is confident we have the shot, we can move on to the next variation or setup.

STEP 2 / **PERSONAL NOTE**

The second page is a brief introduction to
me and why I'm interested in this campaign. You
don't have to include this, but anything you can do
to personalise the treatment will pay dividends.

STEP 3 / **MOOD BOARD**

We know the client is interested and believes you
are appropriate for the project, but it's always good
to remind them of this. Include a handful of images
related to the project and show you have the
experience they are looking for.

STEP 4 / **APPROACH**

This page details how you approach the job. Things
like how you scout locations ahead of a shoot and
how you work with models (especially if they're
not professional). You might also want to touch on
colour grading (see pages 144–149) and retouching
within these pages. Basically, detail your method
to your work.

STEP 5 / **BIOGRAPHY & CONTACT**

The final page is a biography. This is just a quick
rundown of who you are, who you've worked with.
I also list my agent, my website and my Instagram
account.

STEP 6 / **SUPPLY A PDF**

Supply the treatment to your client in a reduced size
PDF (below 20MB) to ensure universal readability.
All being well, your client will deem you a professional
enough photographer to handle their brief and you
can move onto estimating the job in hand.

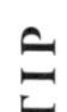

TIP / Set up a template that can be adapted to
suit each campaign. I use Photoshop to
create my treatments. As these tend to
be viewed on a screen, I use a landscape
layout. Don't go crazy on the design –
keep it clean and easy to understand.

PRICING

Time is money   – **Benjamin Franklin**

Many photographers fail to factor in the cost of all the time and labour they invest in an assignment: pre-production, travelling, meeting with the client, the cost of equipment, the actual shoot time, post-production, and so on. For these reasons, you should steer clear of a straight day rate method of pricing and break down the job into line items that your client can understand.

As photographers, we all know how much time and effort goes into making an image, but you can't expect your client to. The estimate is your chance to educate them by detailing the work involved in bringing their vision to life.

There are many variables at play for each shoot so it pays to estimate each job separately. Essential costs that you should build into your estimate include:

FEES

CREATIVE FEES
This is your shooting day rate.

USAGE OR LICENSING FEES
Photographs are in essence intellectual property, and licensing their use is how you generate income. Much like software or a book, you can purchase the use, but the creator still owns the material. The fees for a specific project are based on your time as well as the use of the photographs, because the more the images are used, the greater value they have. Since they're worth more, they cost more.

PRE-PRODUCTION DAY(S)
If you are self-producing, you'll be booking travel, taking phone calls, meetings to discuss the shoot and countless other things. This is all chargeable time.

TRAVEL DAY(S)
Every day you take to travel to do a job is a day you can't work for someone else. This is chargeable time.

EXPENSES

ASSISTANTS
Will you need help on the day? Don't forget to charge for their travel days too.

HAIR/MAKEUP STYLIST
Not always essential (especially for lower budget shoots) but keep it in for your client's information.

TALENT FEES
Will you need to pay your models?

LOCATION FEES OR PERMITS
Something to consider if you are shooting in some cities or parks.

EQUIPMENT
Even if you're shooting with your own gear you should always include a line for equipment hire.

AIRFARES/CAR RENTAL
Think about all travel related to the job and pass this onto your client.

ACCOMMODATION
Hotel rooms for yourself and your assistant.

PARKING, TOLLS, MISC.
Include a line for smaller items and unexpected events.

PER DIEMS
This for the cost of food/meals while on the job.

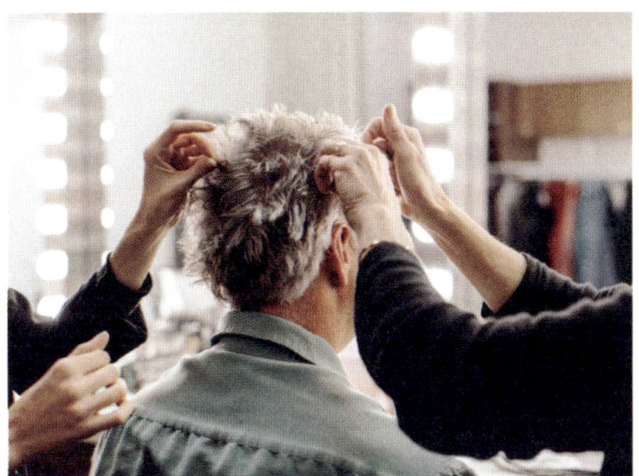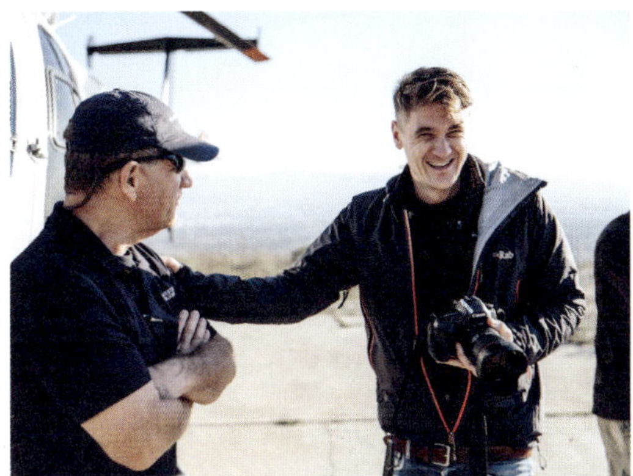

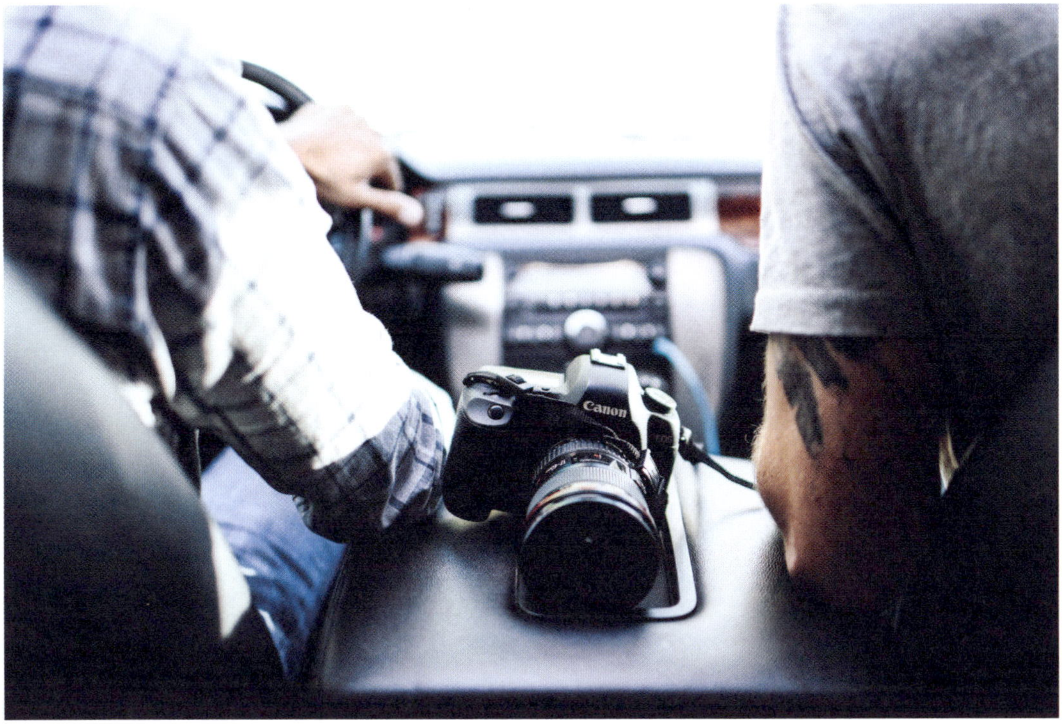

IMAGE PROCESSING

You will spend a good chunk of time running through your images and making a first edit for your client to make their selects from an online gallery.

RETOUCHING

Charge for this on a per image basis.

Breaking down the job into line items gives you room to negotiate should your client push back. For example, you could agree to waive your equipment fees, or reduce your travel day rate. Remember, the art of negotiation is to allow the other party to feel they are a winner too, so expect to give some ground.

SELLING THE ESTIMATE

Once you have prepared an estimate for a job you need to sell it to your client. Don't assume your client will understand all of the line items discussed on the previous page.

EXAMPLE ONE

Sell your estimate in polite, explicit language and elaborate on some of the included line items in your covering email.

EXAMPLE TWO

More often than not, the licensing line causes trouble as clients tend to find it difficult to understand why they don't own the images you are making for them.

Here is some example email copy you can bounce back to a client who is querying fees in language that may help bring them around.

EXAMPLE THREE

You can always trim some line items from the estimate, giving some ground to your client if you think it might help you win the job. Remember, negotiation is all about give and take. Perhaps you can concede the equipment line item (especially if shooting with your own gear), or maybe lose the assistant? However, always try to keep your creative/licensing fees intact.

It's also sometimes worth referencing Getty's Usage Calculator to convince prospective clients that you haven't just plucked your figures from thin air. Run the usage they specify through Getty's Calculator and you'll receive a rate you can quote to them with a screenshot of the calculation.

Here is some more example email copy explaining your reasoning behind the figures quoted.

---

1 *Dear [Client Name],*

Please see an estimate attached. Deliverables for this type of job average around 10–15 images per day. As you list 12 key visuals, I have based the estimate on 1 shoot day. You can multiply this out should you foresee the need to book another day. Some notes regarding the estimate below:

Creative/Licensing Fee: *I have tried to keep this as low as possible and am basing it on a typical collateral library rate negotiated with other clients of a similar size.*

Travel Day: *I understand that the location is overseas and fairly remote so I have included two travel days to account for the return trip.*

Assistant Days: *I have included an assistant as I foresee the need for lighting equipment on location and an extra set of hands will be useful.*

Equipment: *This covers the one-day rental costs for a DSLR, a backup DSLR, grip equipment and a portable lighting kit.*

Shoot Processing for Client Review: *This covers the time, equipment and costs to handle the initial edit, batch colour correction and upload of the images to Dropbox for your selection.*

Selects Processed for Reproduction: *This covers colour correction and basic touch-up of the 12 selects. Any further retouching would be estimated and billed separately.*

Mileage, Parking, Tolls, Meals, Misc: *This covers the basic expenses accrued during travel, meals for myself and my assistant on travel days, and miscellaneous expenses that may arise.*

Best wishes,
[Name]

2 *Dear* [Client Name],

I understand your question regarding licensing, and I appreciate this area of the estimate can seem a little confusing.

Photographs are, in essence, intellectual property, and licensing their use is how I generate income. Much like software or a book, you can purchase their application, but the creator still owns the material. The fees for a specific project are based on the use of the photographs because the more the images are used, the higher value they have. Since they're worth more, they cost more.

Compare photography with software: When you buy one copy of a piece of software, you get it for one computer, not for all computers in the office, even though it's no more extra work for them to give you 100 copies of Microsoft Word. If you use a picture 10 ways, then there is a fee for 10 ways. If you're using a photo 50 ways, it's not going to be 50 times that, but it's going to be more.

I am more than happy to license a full package of rights for the photographs, but you may end up paying for uses you do not need. Standard use is generally one year from shoot date in a specific medium unless otherwise negotiated. I have started at three years for publications that you produce, such as a magazine, annual report, brochure or website, and whose audience are employees, customers, shareholders or the public.

My goal here is, of course, to build a long-term business relationship, so if you tell me what your plans are, I'm sure we can work out an equitable license.

Best wishes,
[Name]

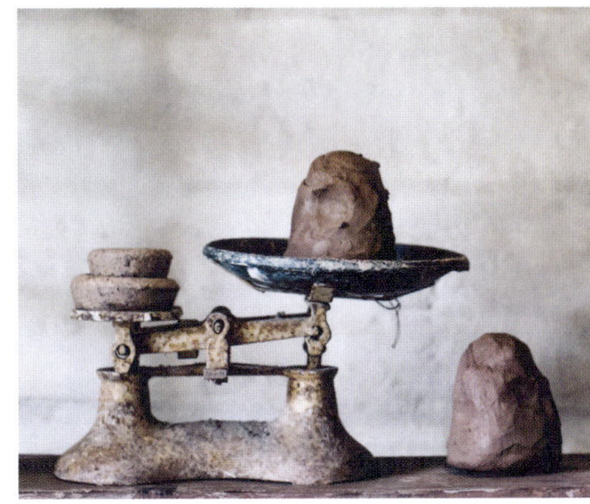

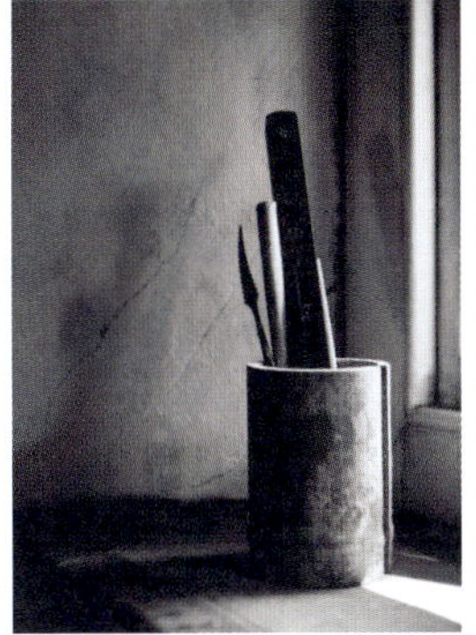

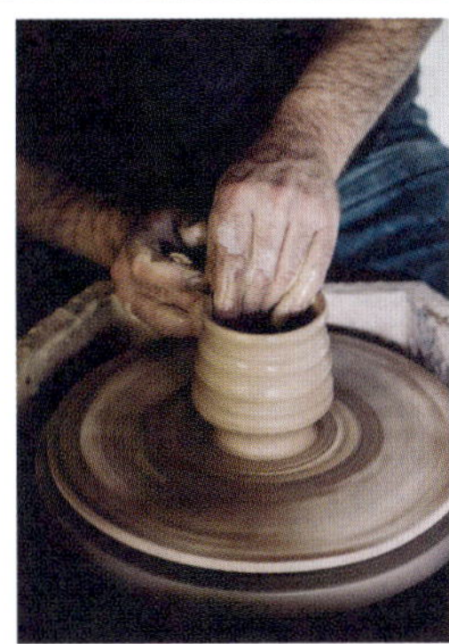

3 *Dear* [Client Name],

Please see the revised estimate attached in which I have detailed a range of licensing options for you.

I suggest we stick with the three-year usage period and you can always extend after three years have passed should you still want to use the images. This way, you aren't paying for unnecessary usage.

I used Getty's pricing calculator to establish a fair market rate for the usage you specified (magazine circulation figures are around 60k) and have attached a screen grab for your information. I have also reduced the equipment fees for the job, as I am keen to make this happen!

Best wishes,
[Name]

Step 2: Prepare

By failing to prepare, you prepare to fail   – **Benjamin Franklin**

I live by the above quote, and I am meticulous when it comes to
shooting preparation, from building mood boards and shot lists right
through to considering the psychological properties of colour.

A vast amount of planning and prep work is needed ahead of the
shoot day. In this chapter, we'll dig into these different tasks and
techniques, which will help you work more efficiently and produce
more impactful images.

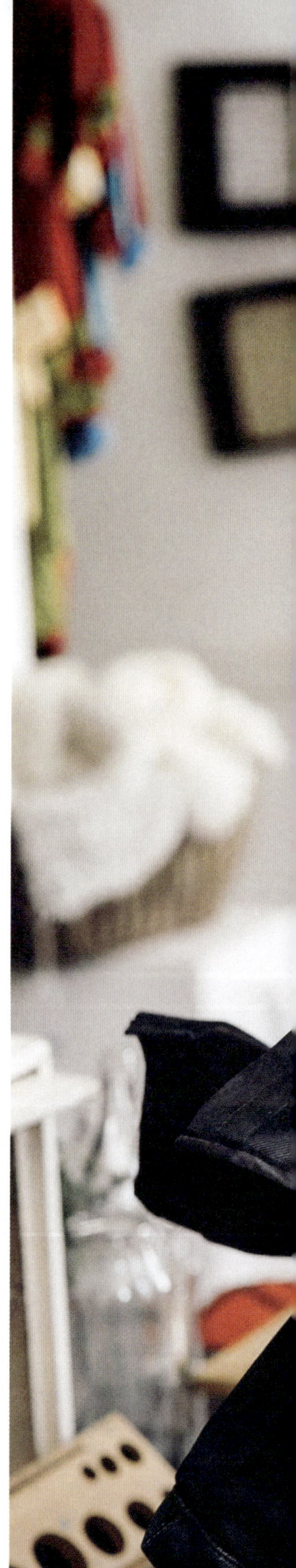

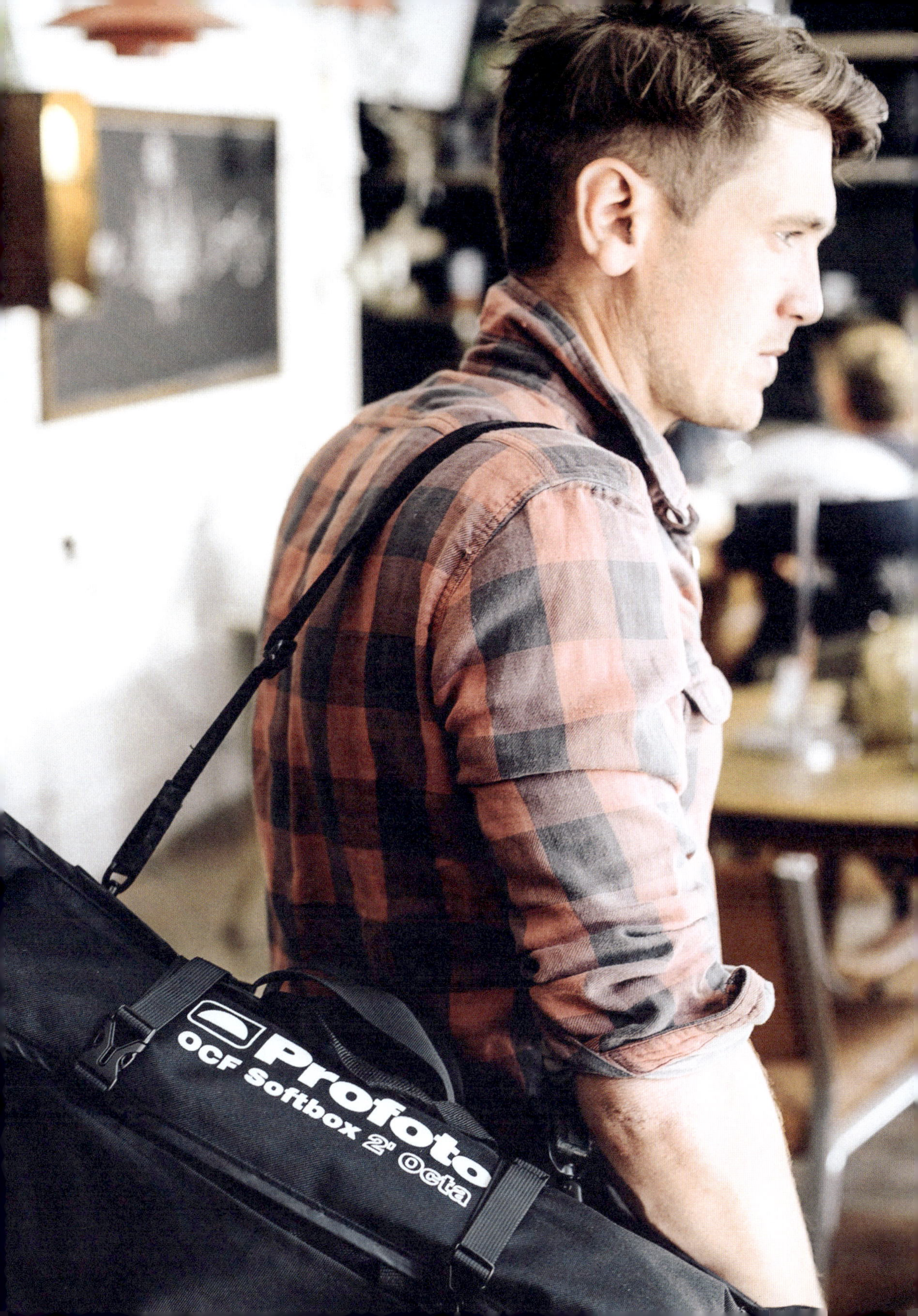
Profoto
OCF Softbox 2' Octa

DEVELOPING A MOOD BOARD

Congratulations! You've won the job. Now you can focus on the fun bit. I like to use mood boards to direct my approach, as well as manage client expectations. They can also be a useful method of kick-starting a project.

SOURCES

I use lots of different sources for developing mood boards. Obviously, I draw on my own photo archive, but I also look into the backstories of the brands I'm working for.

The first port of call is usually an online resource called Designspiration. It's been around for a long time and has an active user base that makes it super valuable for visual art. Taking the Cool & Vintage shoot as an example, I used search terms such as 'vintage Land Rover' which returned a whole host of inspirational material. I'm not looking to copy these images but they will give me ideas for compositions and potentially a direction to follow when it comes to colour grading and lighting design.

For example, here is an image of a 1950s surfer that I found on Designspiration. I love the light leak running through the image and used that as a retouching reference for my own shoot. Remember, my client is called Cool & Vintage, so I am looking to deliver a retro vibe. Polaroid-inspired grading and light leak effects (see page 150) help reinforce the 'feeling' for my story.

COMMERCIAL AND PERSONAL

This method of finding inspiration shouldn't be limited to commercial projects either – it is just as effective for personal projects. It's way harder to start when staring at a blank piece of paper, and a simple image search can lead you down some pretty inspiring paths for your own work.

OFFLINE

So far I have only talked about online methods of image research because search engines are easy to use and fast. However, the internet relies on your use of keywords. Although you can get at the information you are looking for very quickly, it narrows your chances of stumbling on something completely unrelated, which is a shame, as such encounters can be just as inspiring. Don't overlook the offline world, especially secondhand bookshops, which can be a fantastic resource. There is great value in random chance. By leafing through topics in an old bookstore that bear no relation to what you think you need, you'll be surprised at the thought processes triggered.

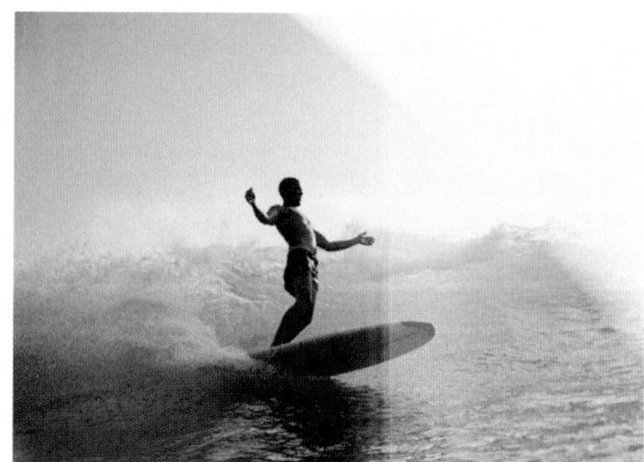

Photo © Ron Church Estate

<table>
<tr><td rowspan="4">**TIPS**</td><td>/</td><td>Search around a topic using keywords.</td></tr>
<tr><td>/</td><td>Look into the backstory of the brand and product.</td></tr>
<tr><td>/</td><td>Don't forget offine sources of inspiration.</td></tr>
<tr><td>/</td><td>Embrace unrelated subjects as avenues of inspiration.</td></tr>
</table>

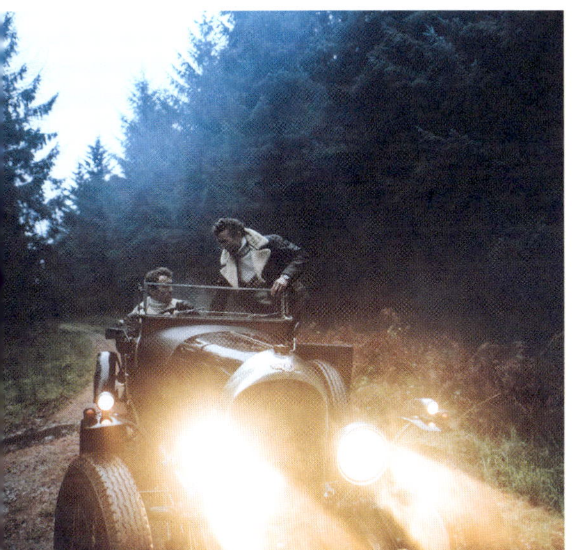

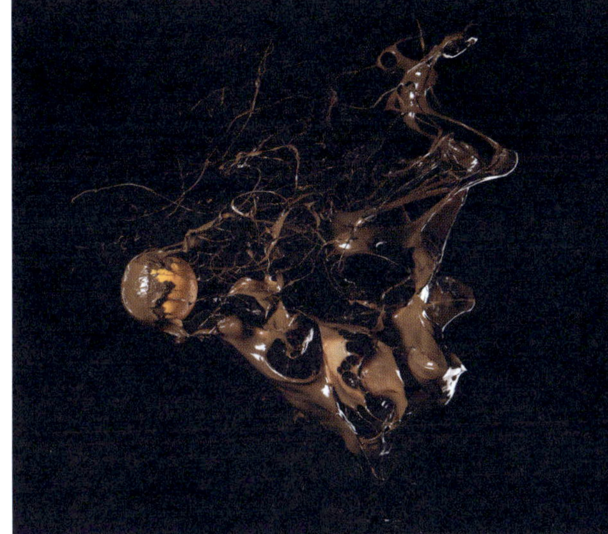

BREITLING PREMIER CHRONOGRAPH

This is a campaign shot for Breitling to showcase their Premier B01 Chronograph; a watch inspired by their first collection of elegant timepieces introduced in the 1940s.

I wanted the creative for the shoot to reference that era and the quality of the timeless designs. I spent a day researching images on the internet using terms like '1940s advertising', '1950s Britain Photography', '1940s fashion'. This research delivered a lot of material that helped me design the wardrobe for my characters and a find in a secondhand bookstore gave me the inspiration to feature an old Bentley. It transpired that Bentley and Breitling had a long-running business partnership, making it a solid match.

View the full story at:

www.madebyfinn.com/breitling-b01

WILLY WONKA NOMNOM CHOCOLATE CANNON

The owner of a chocolate company called NomNom is a young entrepreneur who gladly compares himself to Willy Wonka. His brief to me was very clear:

'Put the magic back into chocolate and try to visualise the impact our flavour combinations deliver when you eat a bar of NomNom.'

After the brief came in, I reread *Charlie and the Chocolate Factory* to put myself in Wonka's shoes. Story first remember. How would he combine flavours with chocolate? He'd build a chocolate cannon of course! I also figured capturing the impact and freezing the ingredients colliding at high speed would result in some great-looking imagery.

View the full story at:

www.madebyfinn.com/chocolate-cannon

MOOD-BOARDING FOR COLOUR

I don't think enough consideration is given to the topic of colour theory today. Platforms like Instagram make it all too easy to hit a colour filter button and post an image, all without actually understanding how the colour change is affecting a viewer's response to your image on a psychological level. When it comes to persuasion, emotion is the driver, and nothing – not even words – appeals more to a viewer's emotions than colour.

The choices you make when colour grading your work can actually affect the mental state of your viewer. Let's have a look at the psychological properties of the visible colour spectrum (the rainbow of colours we can see with the human eye). After that we'll explore how you can evoke distinct emotional responses from the viewer by combining different colour tones.

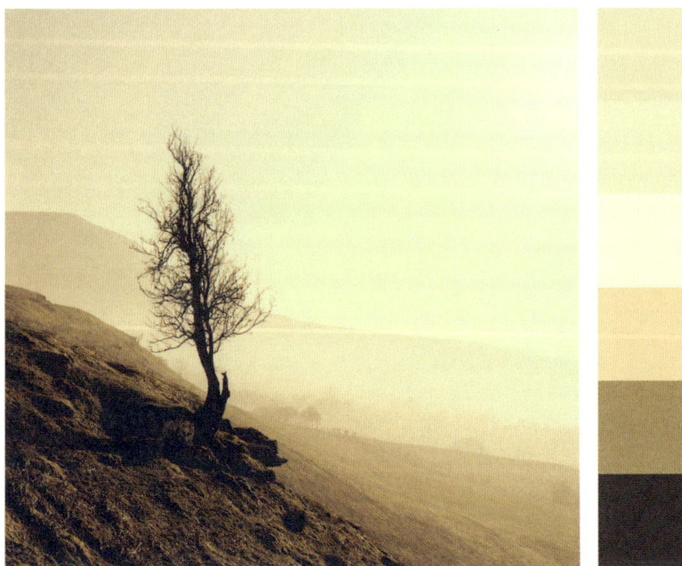

Optimism / Confidence
Self-esteem / Friendliness
Creativity

Think of yellow as a colour of confidence, hope and power. Psychologically strong, it is the most luminous and noticeable to the human eye. In the natural world, yellow is the colour of the sun and of light and heat. Think of it as a colour of strength.

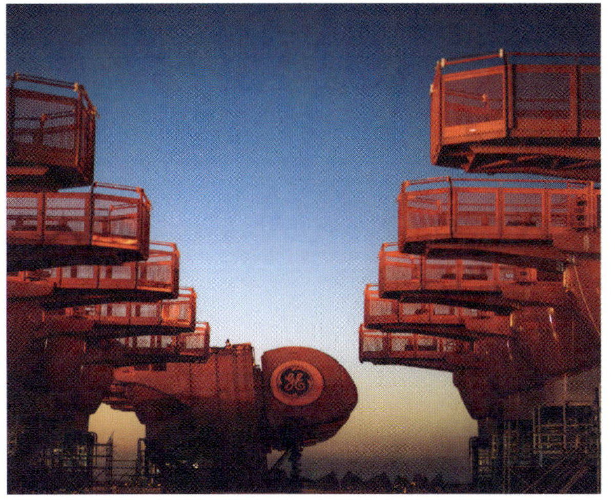

Physical / Strength / Warmth
Energy / Excitement

Red is a powerful colour. Its effect is physical and raises the pulse rate. Red is strong, basic and lively. It evokes passion, energy and desire, but it can also convey power and danger.

Intellectual / Intelligence / Trust
Efficiency / Reflection / Calm

The world's favourite colour blue, affects us mentally, as opposed to the physical reaction we have with red. Blue is serene and soothing. Strong blues allow for clear thought and lighter hues aid concentration and calm the mind. Look at the multitude of mindfulness apps on the market today… all use blue in their branding for these reasons.

Spiritual awareness / Vision / Luxury
Authenticity / Truth / Quality

Violet is the last visible wavelength in the colour spectrum before ultraviolet rays, so naturally, or should I say 'supernaturally', it has associations with time and space. It brings a higher level of thought to an image, and even drifts into the realms of spiritual enlightenment. It promotes a range of contemplative emotions.

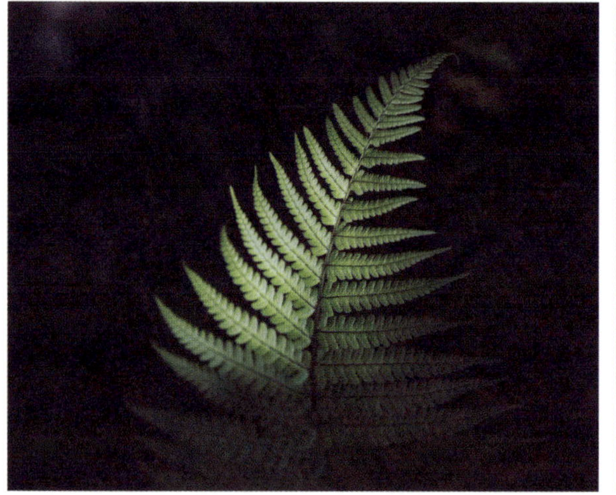

Harmony / Balance / Refreshment
Rest / Restoration / Reassurance
Environmental awareness
Equilibrium / Peace

So closely related to the natural world, green can deliver feelings of reassurance on a very primitive level. A mix of blue and yellow, it is the colour of growth, rest and balance and is useful for promoting a feeling of well being.

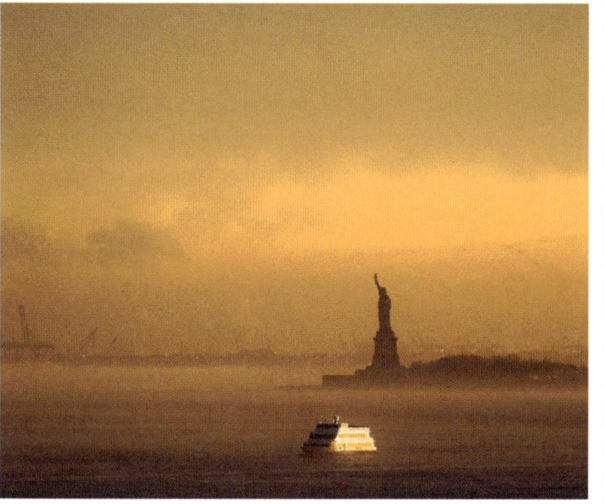

Physical comfort / Food / Warmth
Security / Sensuality / Passion
Abundance / Fun

Orange delivers feelings of comfort and warmth. It's a fun colour and being a combination of red and yellow, it is stimulating physically as well as emotionally. It helps to focus our mind and provides a feeling of safety and security.

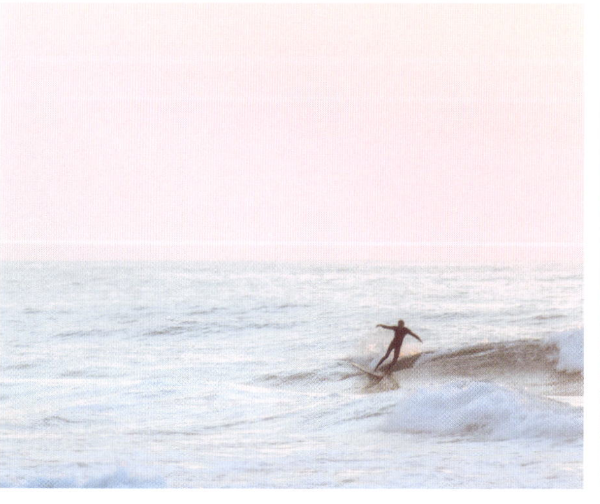

Physical tranquillity / Nurture
Warmth / Femininity / Love
Sexuality

Like the colour blue, pink soothes rather than stimulates. However, since pink is a tint of red, the effect is more of a physical reaction. Think of pink as refreshing, joyful and kind.

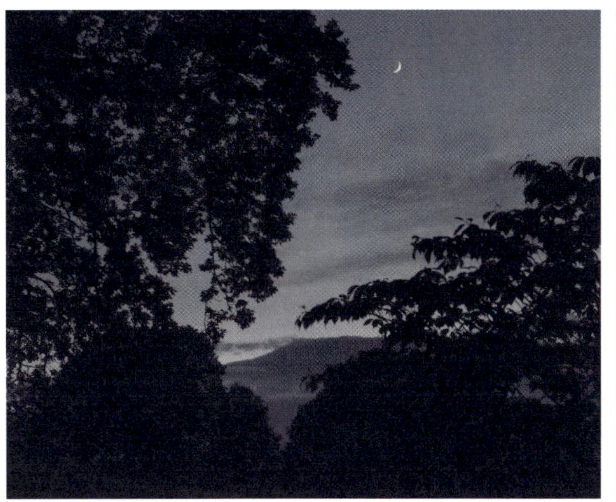

BLACK

Sophistication / Glamour
Security / Emotional safety
Efficiency / Substance

Black is essentially the absence of light and it can be menacing – have you ever been afraid of the dark? On the other hand, it communicates feelings of sophistication, and an unsurpassed level of excellence, particularly when combined with white.

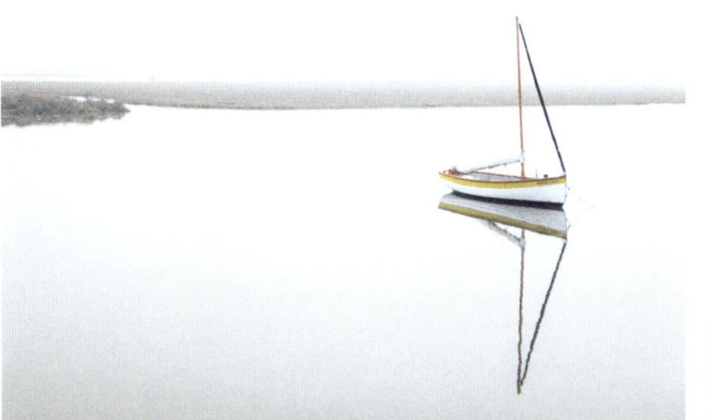

WHITE

Hygiene / Sterility / Clarity
Purity / Cleanliness / Simplicity
Sophistication / Efficiency

White reflects the full spectrum of colours and where black is total absorption, white is total reflection. White is pure and, like black, uncompromising. Think of white as clean, hygienic and sterile. It can also deliver an increased perception of space.

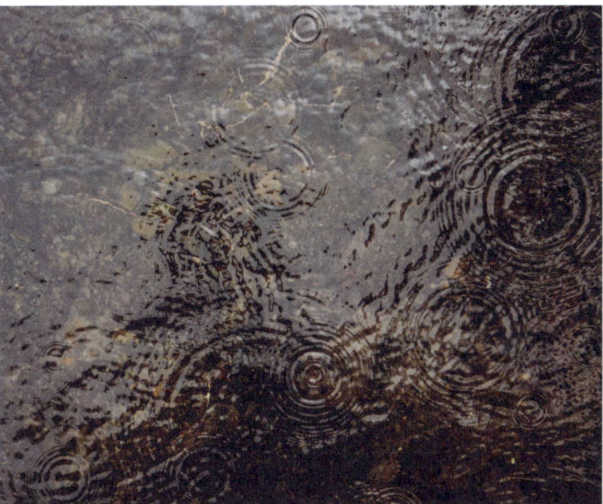

BROWN

Seriousness / Warmth / Nature
Reliability / Support

Brown is a combination of red, yellow and black, but it's warmer and less threatening than pure black. Like green, it's closely connected to the natural world and many people find it safe, secure and supportive.

COMBINING COLOUR PALETTES

Now that you know colours possess certain meanings you can begin to combine them to evoke those feelings in the viewer. This is especially important when working for a client. Researching the traits and expectations of a target audience is vital for fine-tuning positive emotional responses to your chosen colour scheme.

Have a look at some example palettes I developed for client projects below. I've detailed the emotional response I was looking to evoke and how these relate to the brand values of each client.

/ Colour theory is a vast topic and I have only touched the surface here. For more information, there is a huge resource on colour psychology at the following link: *www.about-colors.com/*

/ Based on the distinct emotional responses different colours draw from viewers, I have added a series of Lightroom Presets for you to download from my website. These won't just make your photos look pretty, they will help your images connect with a viewer: *madebyfinn.com/workshop*

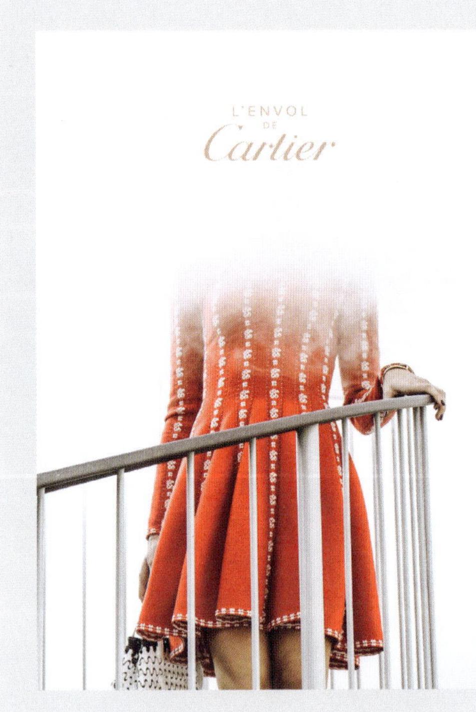

CLIENT Cartier

A stable thermal stratification system was created so that a 'cloud' of Cartier's new fragrance could be held in position. A spiral staircase led through a 'cloud of scent'. The red dress delivers a physical feeling of energy and excitement and when paired against the white cloud of scent we get a feeling of clarity, purity and sophistication, befitting of the Cartier brand.

RED

*Physical strength /
Energy / Excitement*

WHITE

*Clarity / Purity /
Sophistication / Efficiency*

This campfire scene was photographed during the 'blue hour' – just after sunset. I wanted to contrast the orange from the campfire against the blues in the sky to evoke the attributes listed on the right, all positive associations for a company providing holiday accommodation.

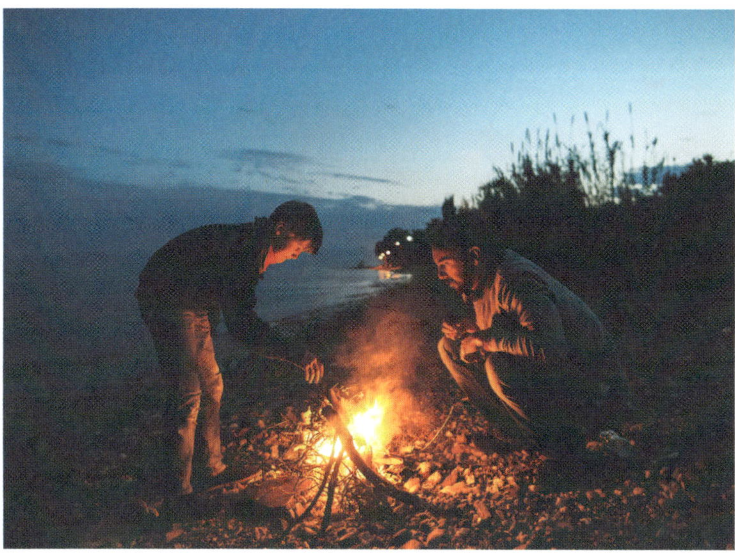

BLUE

Intelligence
Reflection
Calm

ORANGE

Physical comfort
Warmth
Security

CLIENT **Visit California**

Reflecting on the view high above the Mendoccino Coastline. By pairing the blue sky against the brown-green landscape we evoke positive attributes and align them with the brand.

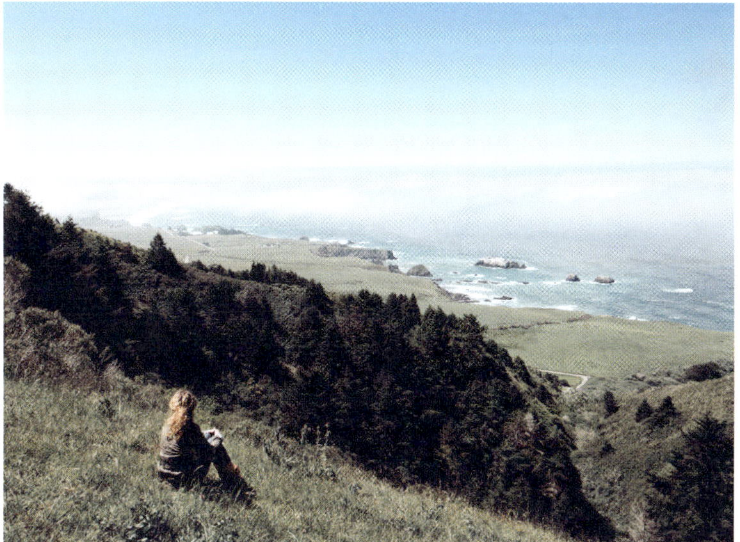

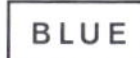

BLUE

Trust
Reflection
Calm

BROWN

Warmth
Nature
Reliability

DEVELOPING YOUR OWN COLOUR PALETTE FOR IMAGE GRADING

Since colour can convey feeling just as effectively as subject matter, it's vital to consider it before a job. But where should you start?

Let's return to the mood board I mentioned previously. As well as kick-starting the creative direction for a job, we can also use mood boards to develop a colour grade. Hours of research and a lot of money will have already been spent by advertising agencies profiling their audiences, so existing campaigns are an excellent place to start.

For the Cool & Vintage shoot, I looked at old Land Rover adverts and vintage surfing posters on Designspiration. I discovered they both used a similar colour palette, so it made perfect sense to use these tones to inform my own work.

After creating a collage of related imagery in Photoshop, I use a nifty little trick to average out the colour tones as outlined below.

Exercise /
Making the Grade

Follow these steps to reduce the number of colours in your mood board and average them out. You can use Photoshop's Dropper tool to sample the colours and build them into your own grade.

If you don't have Photoshop, try using an alternative, Pinetools, which can be found here: pinetools.com/pixelate-effect-image.

1 Flatten your collage so that all of your images are on one single layer.

2 Hit: Filter > Pixelate > Mosaic.

3 Make the cell size around 150 to average out the colours.

4 You can then use the colour dropper to sample these values and drop them into the Split Toning panel of your editing programme.

5 Here I used earthy tones from my mood board in the shadows and blues in the highlights.

6 Once you're happy with the look you can create a preset and apply it across all of the images in the set.

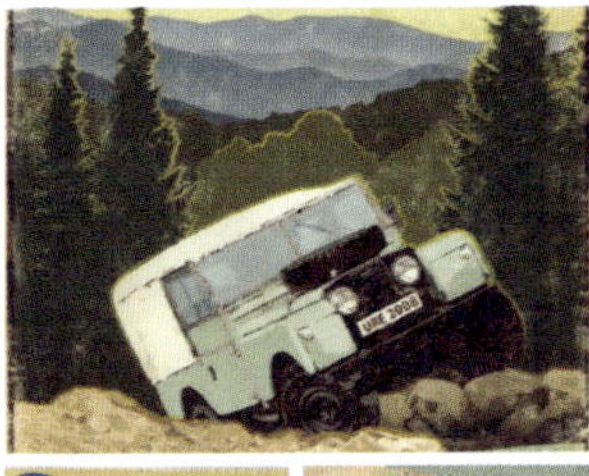
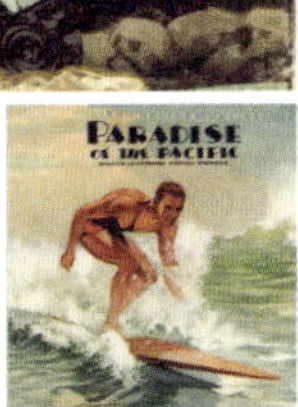
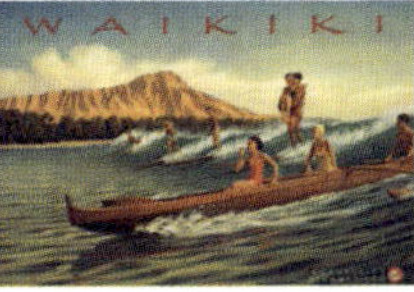
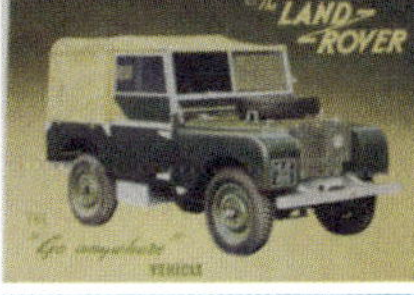
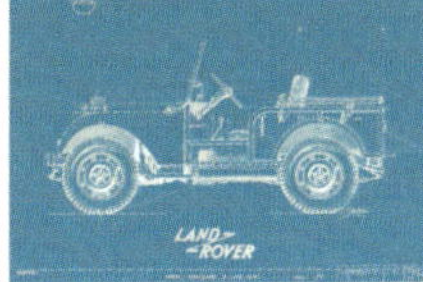
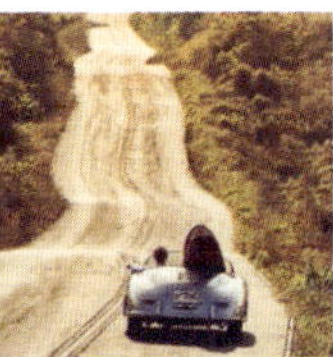
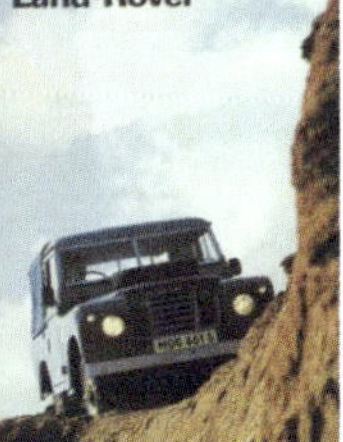
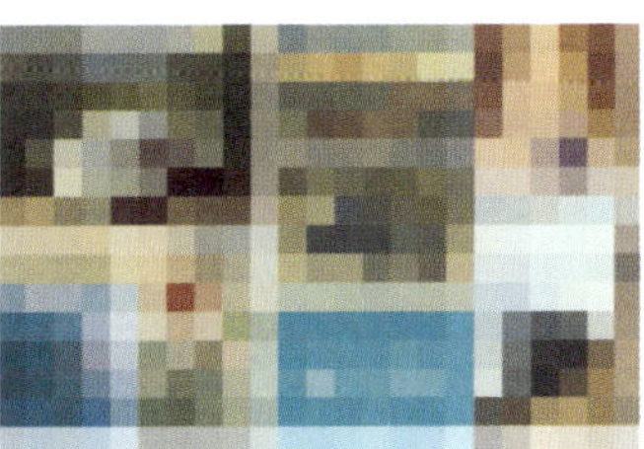

Land Rover brochure and promotional imagery copyright of Jaguar Land Rover Limited, reproduced with permission. Waikiki postcard © Kerne Erickson.

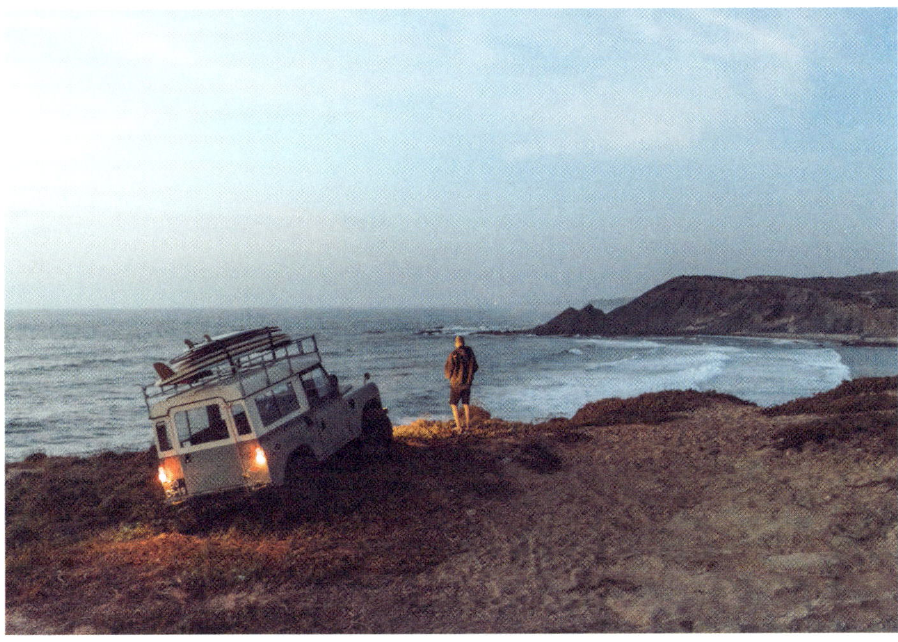
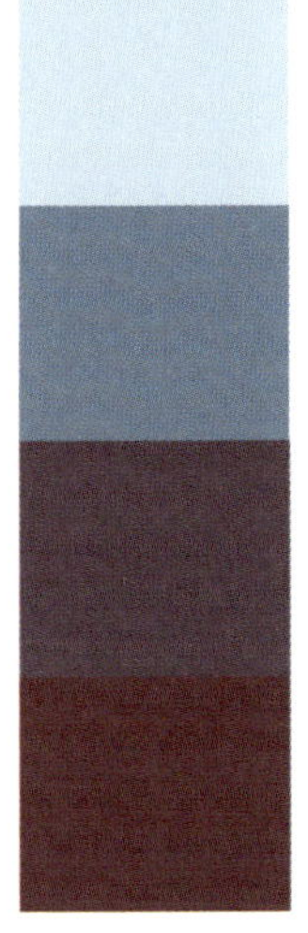

TIP

/ Colour can convey feelings just as effectively as subject matter. Instead of randomly applying presets to your images, decide on the feelings you want to convey and choose your props, wardrobe and colour grade accordingly. Creating a colour grade based on the heritage of the brand will help you develop a cohesive set of images that will resonate with the target audience.

Project /
Edit Like a Painter

BRIEF

+ Select three different images and develop two colour grades for each image.

REQUIREMENTS

+ The two colour grades for each image should project a different feeling.

+ Use the Split Toning panel within your editing programme to change the colour of your images and the emotion you want to convey to your audience.

+ Show your graded images to friends and family and ask them what they feel when viewing.

OBJECTIVE

+ Study the emotions different colours stir in a viewer on pages 80–83. The objective is to elicit alternative emotional responses to the same picture by changing the colour tone of the image alone. This is what happens when you choose a 'filter' on Instagram. By changing the colours, you change the mood. This exercise will give you a better understanding of how and why this works.

The aim of this project is to change the feeling or emotion associated with a photograph using colour. It's important to decide on the emotions you want to evoke before you begin this exercise.

Select an image and develop your colours according to your chosen emotions. For example:

RED   *Excitement / Energy / Strong*

YELLOW   *Optimism / Friendly / Creative*

BLUE   *Intelligent / Reflective / Calm*

On completion, ask friends or family to identify what emotions the images provoke.

EXAMPLE

In the example opposite, a subtle change in colour tone makes a noticable difference.

1 *A cool blue tone runs across the entire grade, delivering a sense of relaxation and calm. Where the colour runs into shadows, the darker tone, suggests reliability. Too much blue can make an image feel a little sad, so a hint of red in the shadows brings some warmth and energy to the picture.*

2 *This is a bold and uncompromising tone, the photo uses the colour yellow through shadows and highlights. Psychologically strong, it harks back to sun-faded photos of yesteryear and provides a pleasing nostalgic feeling.*

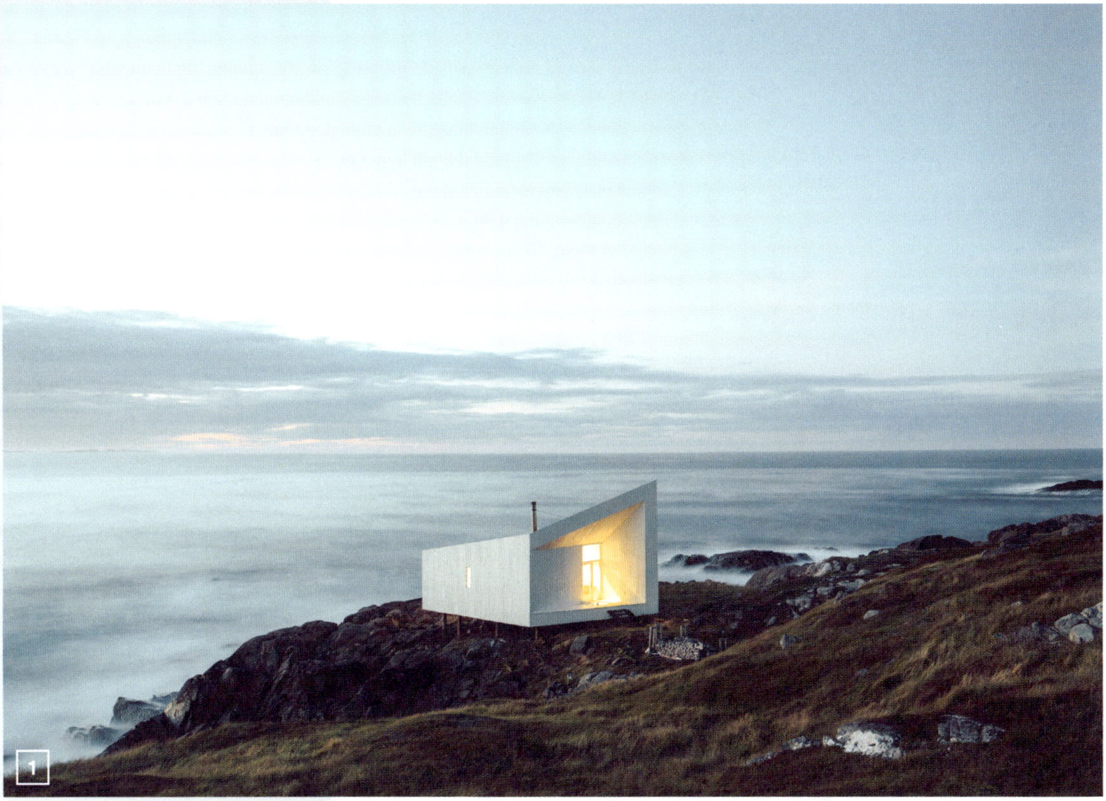

1

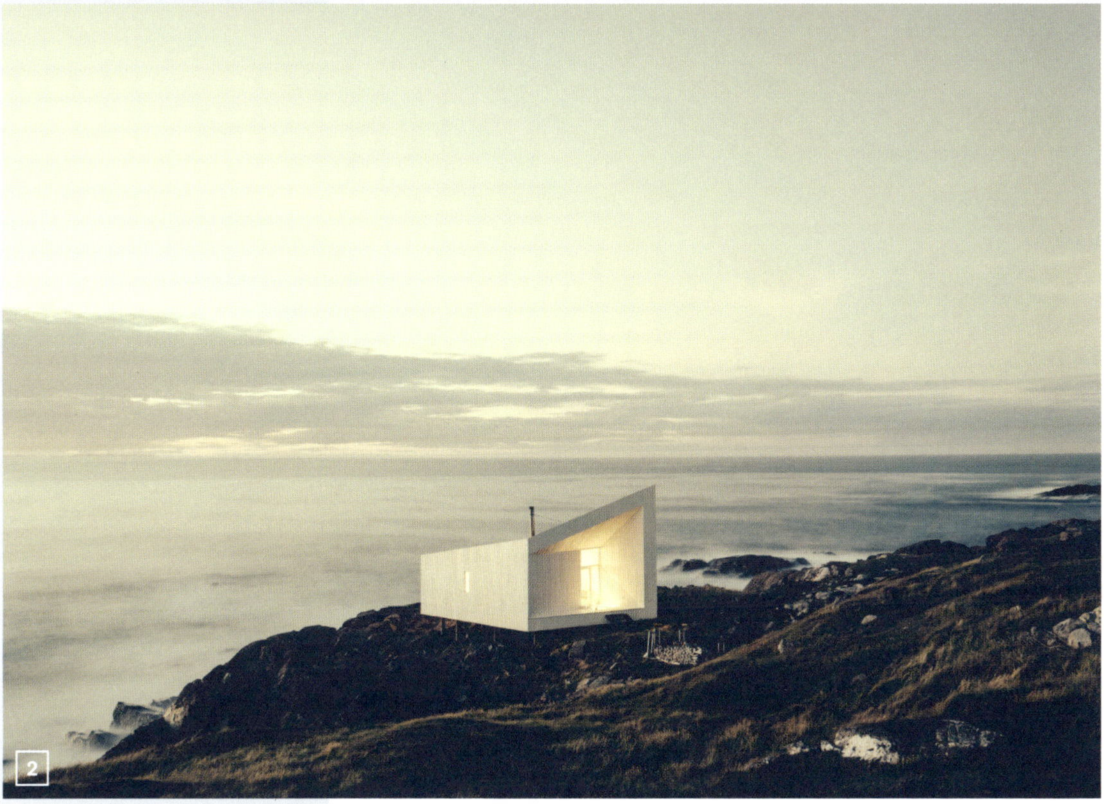

2

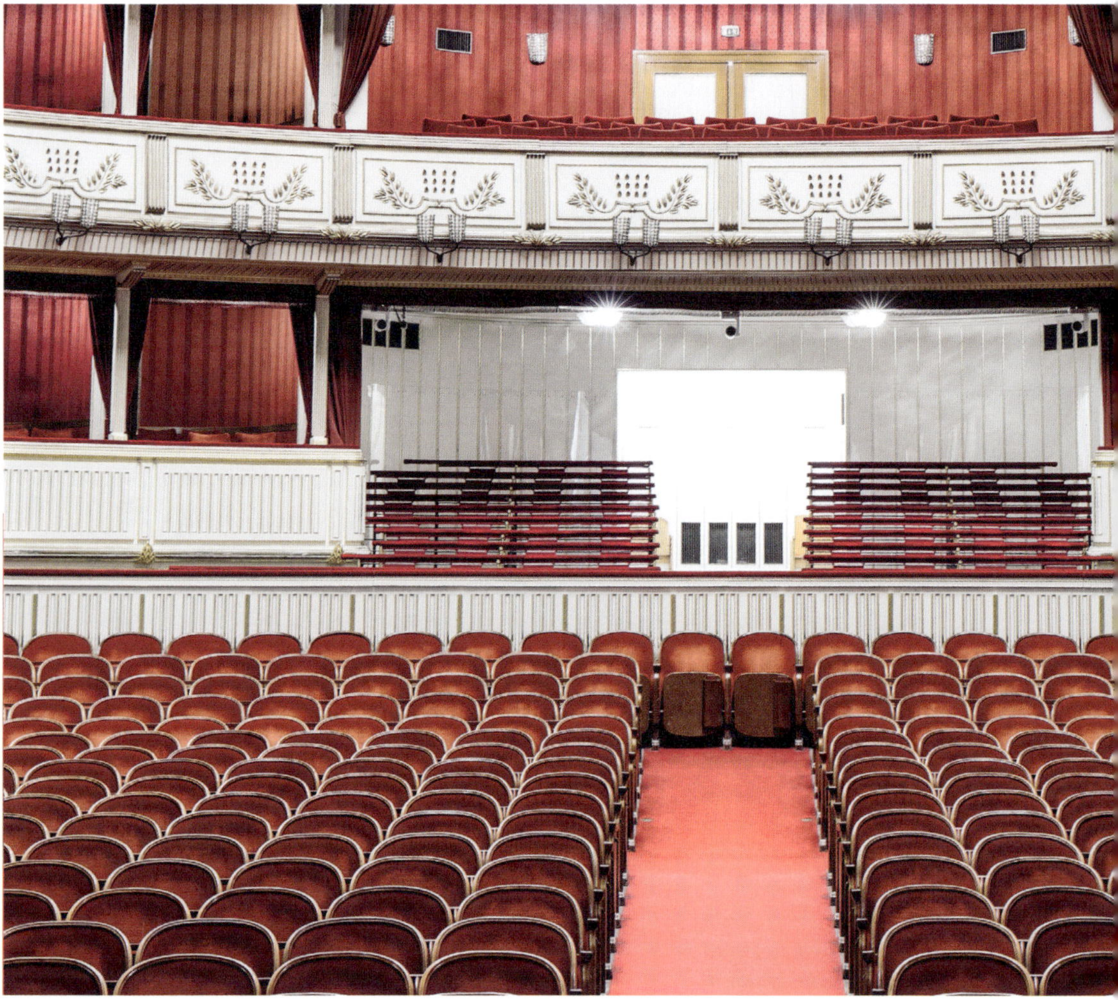

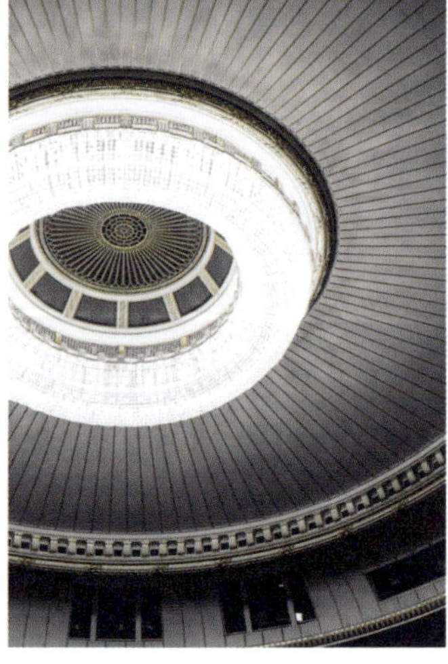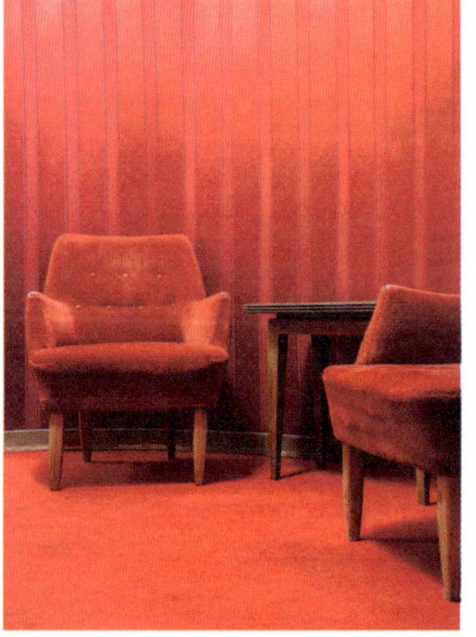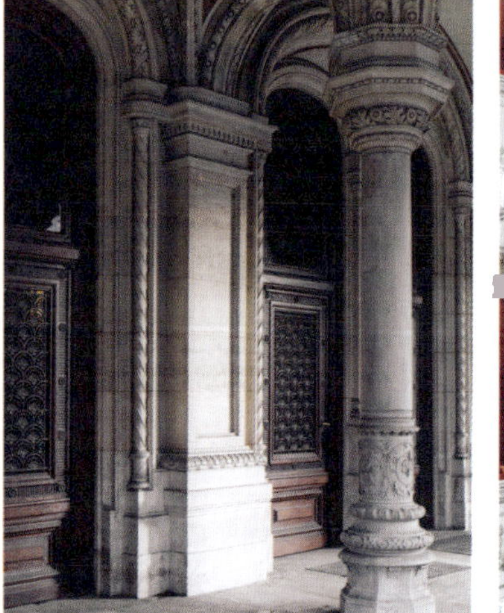

THE LOCATION RECCE

Finding the right location for your story is a vital part of your role as a photographer. You can never prepare for everything, but knowing where and when you want to photograph can alleviate a considerable amount of stress when it comes to the shoot day.

WHY RECCE?

Having hired you for a project, a client will often expect you to source the ideal location to bring their vision to life. Essentially, a recce is a low-stress test run ahead of a shoot day. It's your chance to visit several different locations and weigh up the pros and cons of each, before presenting a shortlist to the client so they can make the final decision.

WHAT HAPPENS?

Your job on a recce is to gather as much information as you can about the shooting environment. Lighting conditions can change dramatically throughout the day, so it's important to know how the sun will track across the sky. Smartphone apps like Sunseeker (see page 20 for others) can show you the path of the sun, making it an invaluable tool.

If you're shooting outside, knowing where the sun will be and when will play a big part in your decision-making. For example, you may have identified the perfect street corner from picture research online, but it's unlikely to be 'lit' appropriately throughout the day. By physically scouting the location, you can determine the optimum time of day to shoot. You can also assess appropriate shooting angles, which will have a knock-on effect in terms of what equipment you need to use and the call time (see page 95). The same is the case if you are shooting indoors: is there enough natural light coming from windows or will you need to artificially light a scene?

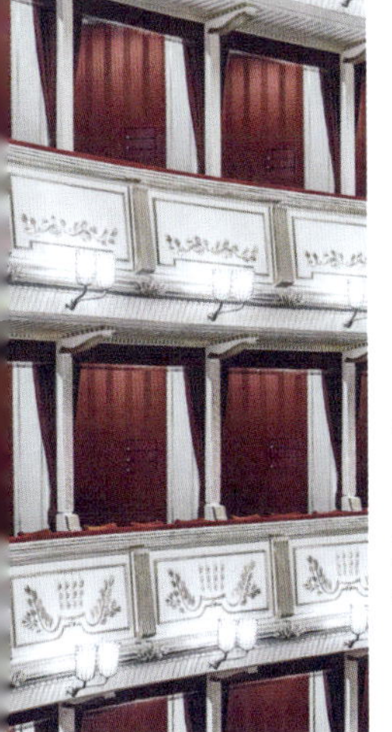

Photographed for Cereal magazine.

/ Sunseeker is an invaluable tool for tracking the sun across the sky. It helps you plan your shoot according to the golden hour or blue hour, optimal sunlight conditions and the sunrise and sunset time and directions.

/ Cadrage allows you to simulate different camera and lens setups using just your smartphone. Use it to frame shots on a recce so you don't need to lug heavy equipment around.

MISSION CONTROL

Shot-listing is a technique I have borrowed from the film industry to keep a production organised. Think of it as a visual script. By studying my lines (pictures) ahead of the shoot day, I know what I need to say (capture).

I like to combine this list with other information more usually found in a call sheet, so I end up with a hybridised master document that I refer to as 'Mission Control'.

WHAT'S INCLUDED?
Mission Control keeps everyone involved in a production on track. It details the types of shot required for each scene, camera equipment, props, locations and call times for talent. It even lists the expected weather conditions on the day of the shoot – it helps if everyone is dressed appropriately!

CREATING A SHOT LIST
Writing a call sheet and a shot list will challenge you to consider all aspects of a production and will help flag up any issues or problems before they arise. Think of it as part of the creative process. It's a lot of work, but it will pay dividends in the long run.

The idea is to anticipate everyone's needs before you even get to set.

Opposite: Photographed for Audi at Fforest.

> **TIP**
>
> / You can never predict everything and often serendipitous moments will arise on set that you could never have forseen. Think of Mission Control as your guide, but always remain open to the unexpected.

SHOT NUMBER
A reference number assigned to each shot.

SCENARIO
Description of the scene including simple directions. Keep this short, so it's easy to scan.

EXAMPLE IMAGERY
Include example imagery taken from your mood board to help direct talent.

SHOT TYPE
Long shot, medium shot and so on. I also like to describe how the camera will frame subjects.

CAMERA AND LENS
The camera/lens required to capture each shot. This helps assistants prepare equipment ahead of time.

SCENE LOCATIONS
Include a postcode and Google Maps link.

CALL TIME
Specify the time you want crew/talent on set for each scene.

WEATHER
Include a brief weather forecast, so that everyone is aware of any inclement conditions and is dressed appropriately.

SUNRISE AND SUNSET
Include times for sunrise and sunset as well as the 'first available' light and 'last available' light (usually an hour before/after sunrise/sunset).

CONTACT DETAILS
Mobile phone numbers and email addresses for everyone involved (with permission).

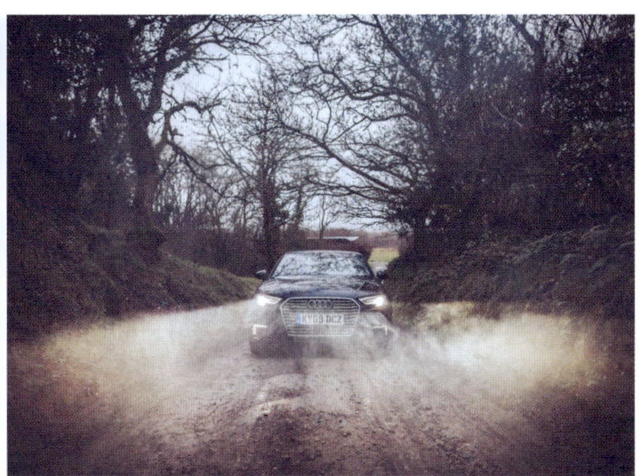
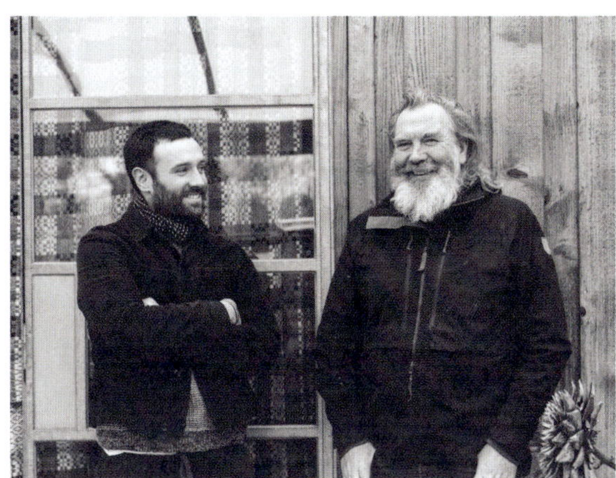
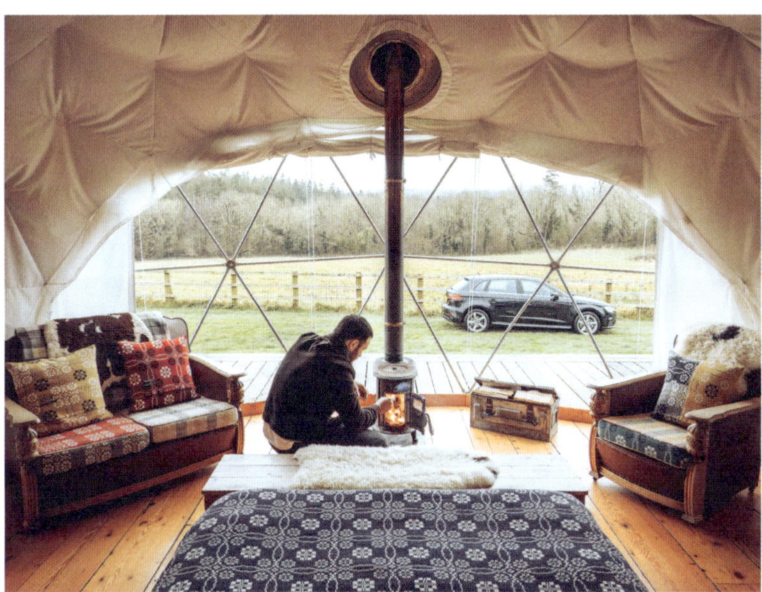
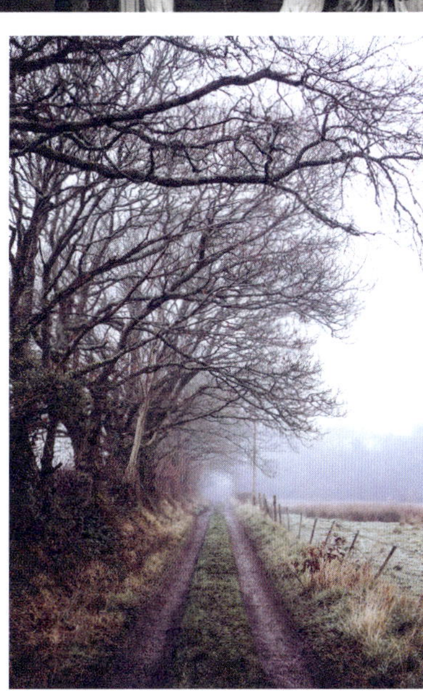
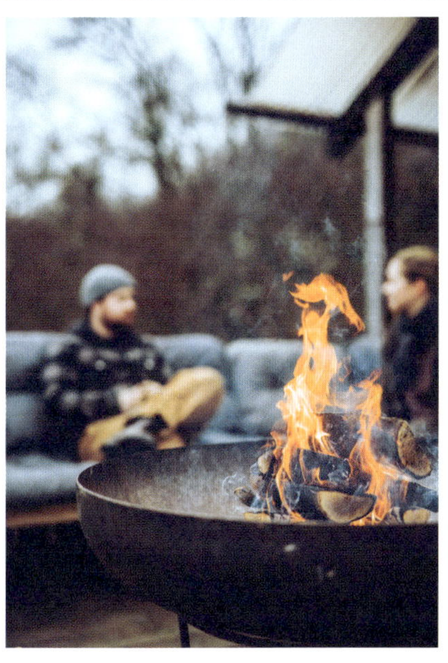
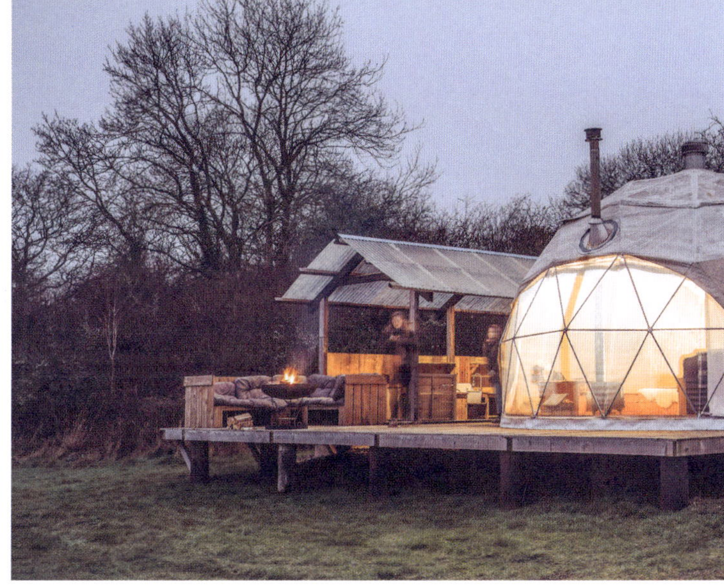

This is a page from one of my Mission Control documents.
As you can see, it lists a lot of the information you find in a
typical call sheet (see opposite), as well as creative direction
for myself and the talent, as well as production information
for others involved in the shoot, such as styling, wardrobe
and lighting details.

Location
Moylegrove Beach

Parking
Location, no charge

Dawn	07:35
Sunrise	08:15
Sunset	16:07
Dusk	16:47

CREW CALL   **15:30**
SHOOTING CALL   **16.00**

Weather
Saturday will remain cold and
sunny with isolated snow showers
and winds easing. Temperature
between 0 and 5 degrees Celcius.

WRAP UP WARM!

SCENARIO
Jackson guiding a friend to shore with a lantern.
Blue hour scene – It's important to ensure the lamplight
is visible along with the surrounding environment.

CREATIVE DIRECTION
Jackson holding up lamp with right hand.
Finn to shoot over shoulder.

Someone else in canoe on water in the
background – out of focus.

Canoeist ideally wearing yellow (oilskins?) for
a pop of colour off the ocean.

Watch visible on wrist – Note: may need a reflector
to bounce light back from lantern onto watch.

Hands of watch at 10:10 and date window set to 8.

PROPS
Storm lantern
Canoe

WARDROBE
Fisherman's jumper or Norwegian sweater
Yellow oilskins?
Fisherman's hat

Here's a page from a typical call sheet. Used more for production purposes, it allows a producer to run the day. Note the call times for the photographer, wardrobe, hair and makeup are well before the arrival of the agency, client and talent on set.

CALL SHEET
Wednesday, February 23rd

8:00 AM	Call time photo, wardrobe, production
8:30 AM	Call time hair/makeup
9:00 AM	Call time agency. Review wardrobe.
9:30 AM	Call time LARRY, clients,
--	grooming & wardrobe.
10:00 AM	Call time MARGERY & MELINDA
10:30 AM	SHOOT LARRY
11:00 AM	
11:30 AM	SHOOT MARGERY. Call time PAUL
12:00 PM	SHOOT MELINDA
12:30 PM	Call time SID, TOMMY, FRANKIE, JOY
1:00 PM	Working lunch
1:30 PM	SHOOT GROUP SHOT
2:00 PM	SHOOT PAUL
2:30 PM	
3:00 PM	SHOOT SID
3:30 PM	SHOOT TOMMY
4:00 PM	
4:30 PM	SHOOT FRANKIE
5:00 PM	SHOOT JOY
5:30 PM	
6:00 PM	Finish shooting, process files, wrap out
6:30 PM	
7:00 PM	Out of studio

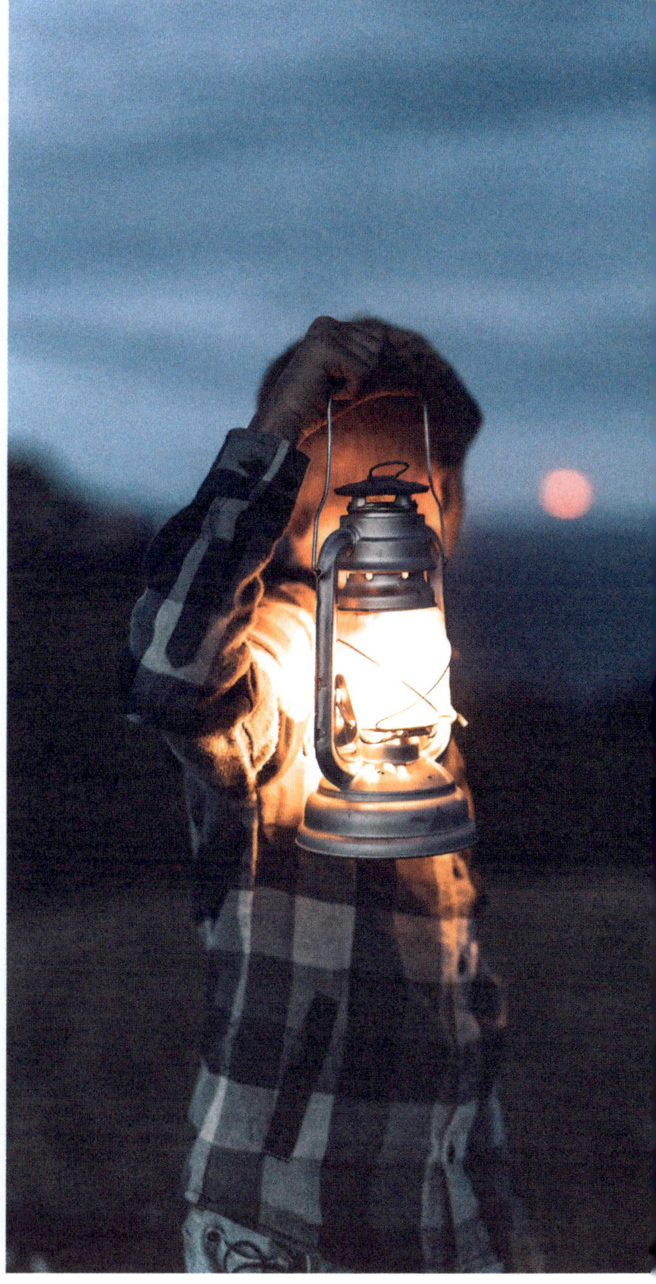

Step 3: Shoot

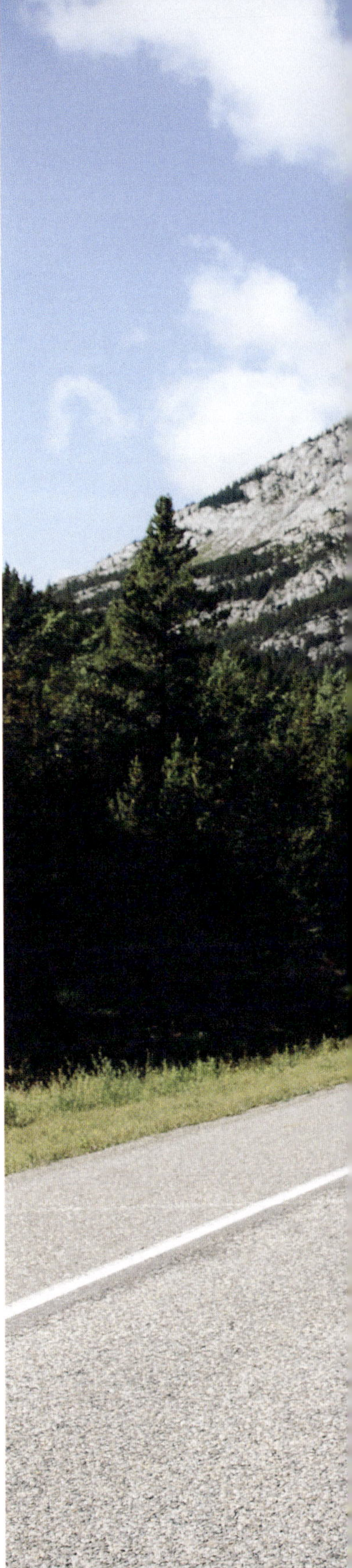

Shoot day has arrived! All your planning and creative preparation have led to today. In this chapter, I'll offer tips for working with models and talent, detail the type of lenses and camera settings I use, and provide some tried-and-tested lighting strategies. I'll also run through a range of shooting techniques for you to experiment with.

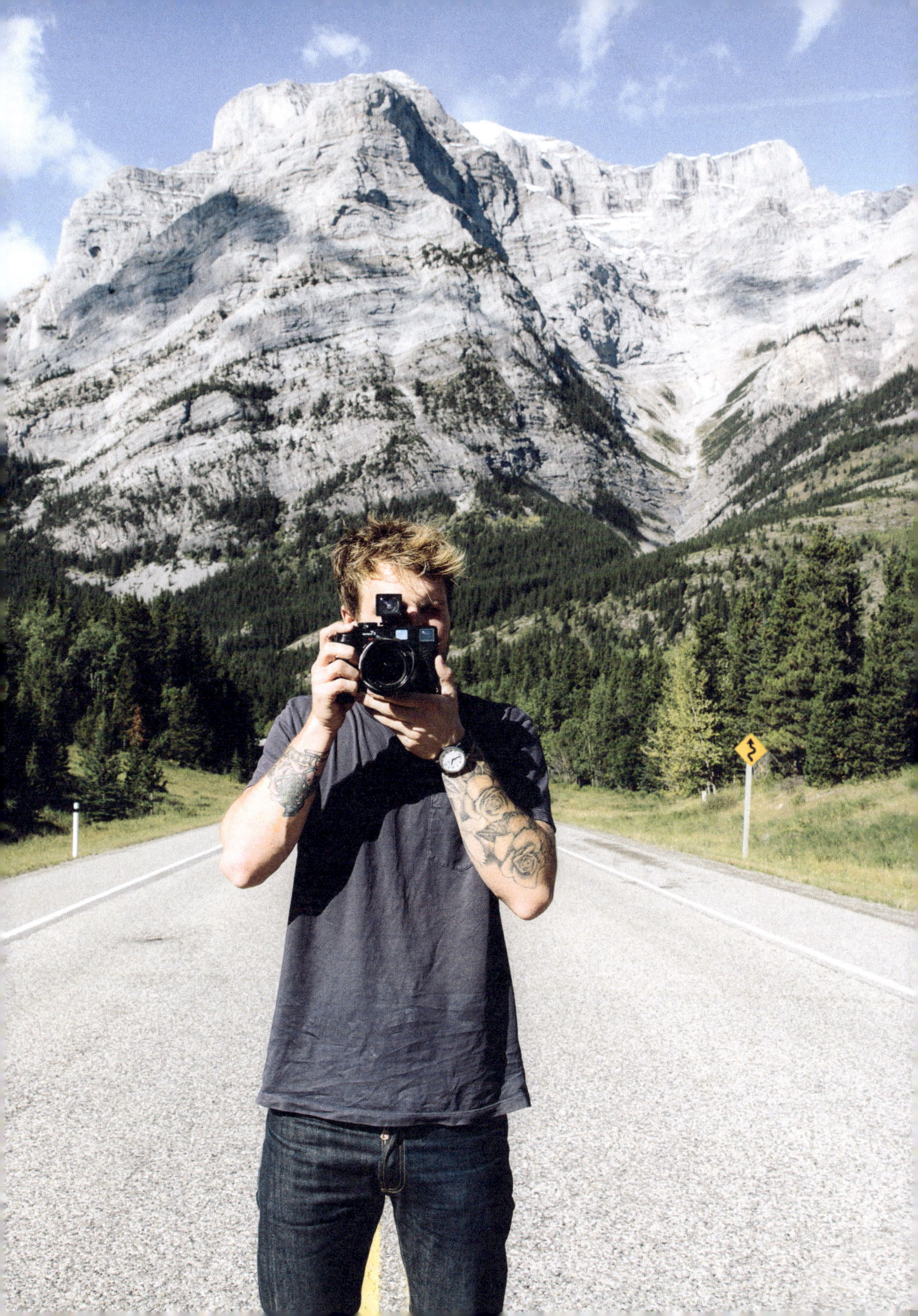

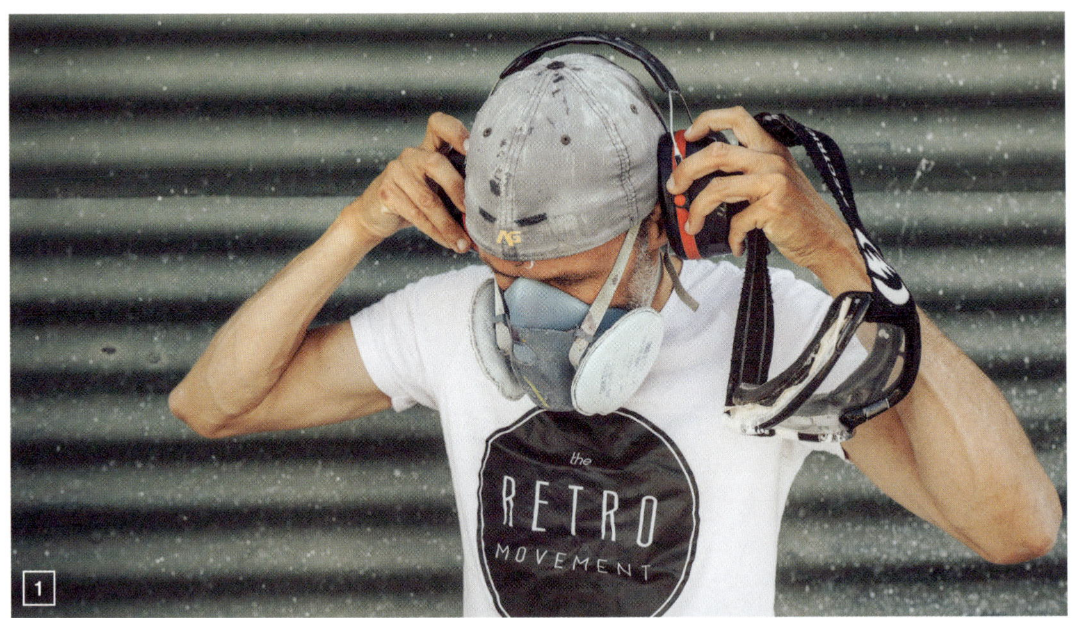

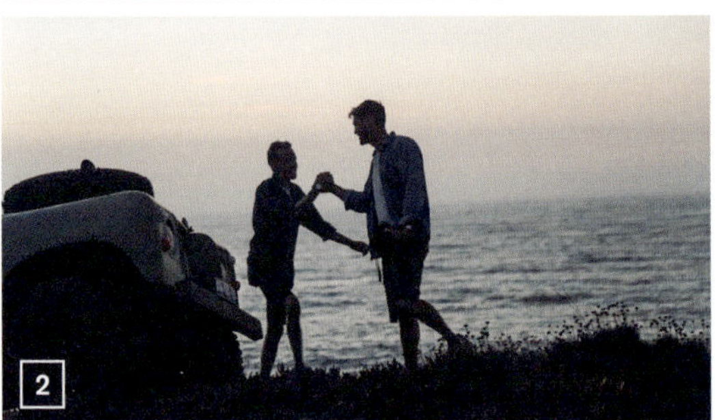

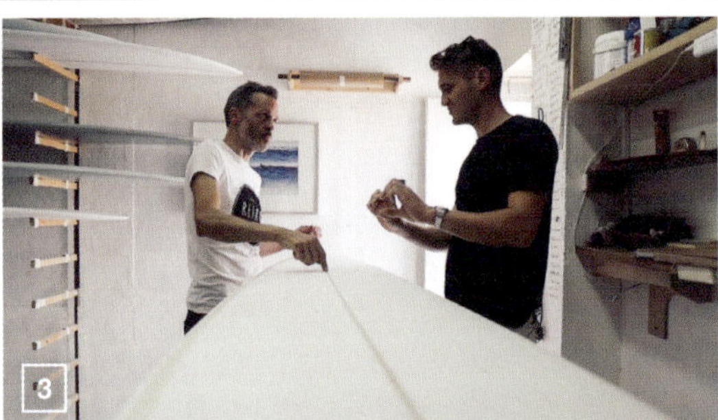

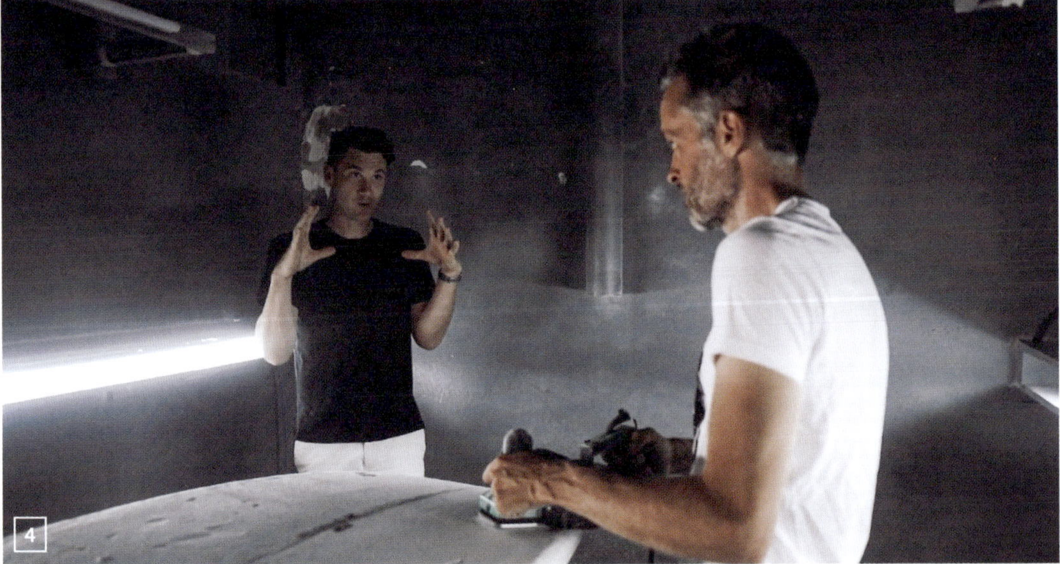

MEETING YOUR SUBJECTS

Before meeting a person I'm due to photograph, I'll always do a little bit of research to see if I can find a common connection unrelated to the shoot.

RESEARCH

In the case of my Cool & Vintage shoot, the surfer I was due to photograph had posted a YouTube video online. He talks about his life, his philosophy and what things mean to him. I learned he was a father, and considering I'm also a dad, it seemed like an excellent meeting point.

RELATE TO YOUR SUBJECT

Having your photograph taken can be relatively intimidating, and it's understandable why many people freeze up as soon as the camera comes into view. If you're looking for natural imagery, you want your subjects to feel as comfortable as possible. It's good practice to find something in common with your model, so you can connect on a relatable, human level first and not solely as photographer and subject.

DITCH THE CAMERA

Leave your camera in the car when you meet for the first time. Don't faze your subject from the outset by waving a big DSLR around. Once you're comfortable with each other, you can introduce the camera and begin discussing the shoot.

REHEARSE

Rehearse with your subject. If you're shooting a person doing their job or something they do regularly, ask them to show you the actions involved. It will be second nature to them, but it will all be new to you. Some minor direction might be required to help you capture the images you need. I prefer to give guidance in a rehearsal, that way there are no surprises when it comes to the actual shoot.

1 *Dan Costa, my subject for the surf shoot, is a professional board-shaper and surfer.*

2 *Shaking Dan's hand after wrapping our shoot. The end of a good day.*

3 + 4 *Talking through the board-shaping sequence with Dan. Here, I'm telling him what type of image I'm looking to capture, but also asking him to run through his usual process so I know what to expect and there are no surprises when it comes to capturing the sequence on camera.*

SEE THE LIGHT

The word 'photography' comes from the Greek word *phōtos*, which means 'light', and *graphé*, 'drawing', so to photograph literally means to 'draw with light'. Light is fundamental to making good pictures – more important than anything else, in fact – so it's imperative you learn to *see* it.

TIMING

Light changes throughout the day as the position of the sun moves through the sky. At midday, it falls vertically downwards, just like those super-unflattering ceiling lights. Ever stood under one of those and shot a selfie? Try it. Horrible results. It's the same with the midday sun. There is minimal diffusion from the atmosphere, so it makes for an uncompromising, high-contrast light that is usually too harsh to work with.

Conversely, when the sun is closer to the horizon (in the morning and evening), the light is softer due to the angle at which the sunlight passes through the earth's atmosphere. I'm sure you'll have heard the term 'golden hour', which describes that beautiful morning/evening light.

LOCATION AND ATMOSPHERE

Now, if you want to make dreamy, pastel-coloured photos and you live in a habitually sunny part of the world like California, all you need to do is schedule your shoots at golden hour, and everyone's a winner. However, not all of us live in such a consistently 'lit' part of the world, and sometimes it's not possible to restrict shooting times to the morning or evening. Also, what if you want a different vibe for your photo? Perhaps something moodier like the image opposite that was made for the watch brand Breitling?

Understanding the effect light has on a photograph is the single most important step you can take to improve your photography. There are several factors to consider, starting with the type of image you are looking to make. What is your subject matter? People, landscape, architecture? If it's people, a cloudy day would work better than full sun as the contrast won't be so harsh, but for landscape scenes, you'll want to shoot at golden hour (see page 103).

Is there a time or environmental constraint? If you live in the heart of the city and want to make dreamy golden pictures, you're probably going to have to travel to shoot or artificially light your scene. It's possible, of course, but such approaches are expensive and beyond the remit of this book. I'd instead advise you to start thinking about working with what you have and adapting your strategy accordingly.

EXAMPLE

I live in Wales, where it is almost invariably cloudy and grey. I used to bemoan such weather, but over the years I have learned to work with it. Indeed, I've built a personal style that leans heavily on the type of light experienced under such leaden skies. On a grey day, the clouds act like a giant diffuser, spreading and softening sunlight. The contrast is low, meaning landscapes can be shot throughout the day, and it also makes for easier portraiture as there is no need for artificial diffusion.

Unfortunately, these conditions can feel a little flat and lack atmosphere, but this is where your creativity as an artist comes in. The image opposite was made on a super-flat, grey day and the entire scene felt dull.

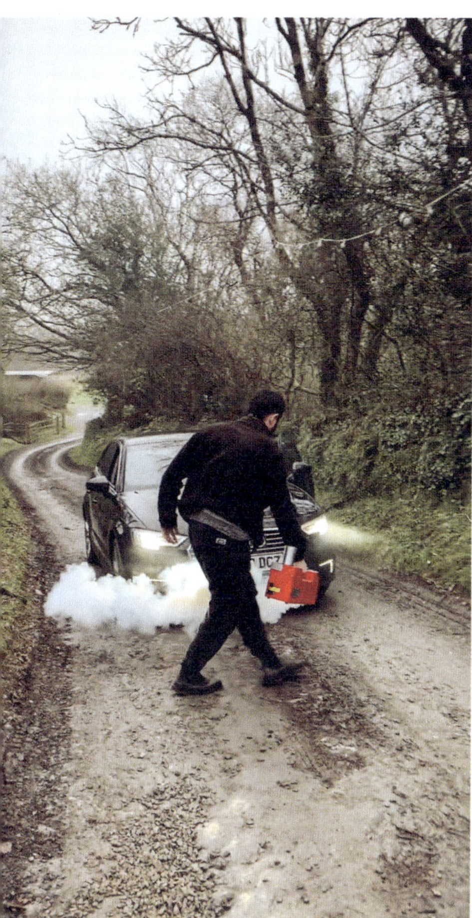

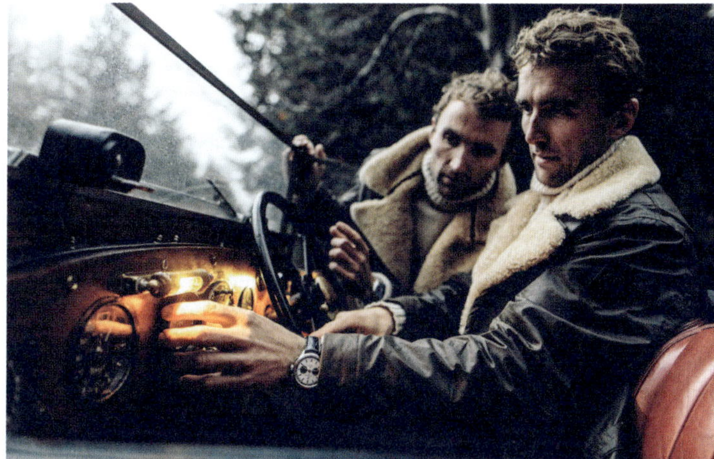

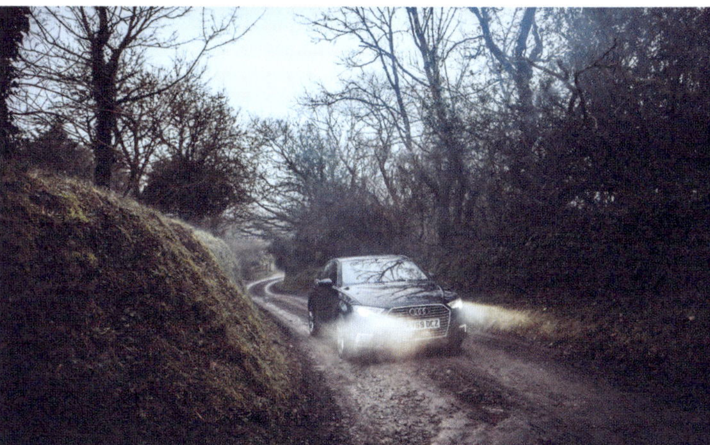

How could I create the hero shot my client required without it feeling artificially lit?

After a chat with the client and my team we decided to introduce the light we lacked from the sun by shining the vehicle's headlights through some artificial haze. This added depth and atmosphere and when combined with a blue/grey colour grade, and a fairly heavy vignette, we achieved the image my client desired. You can read more about this technique on page 128.

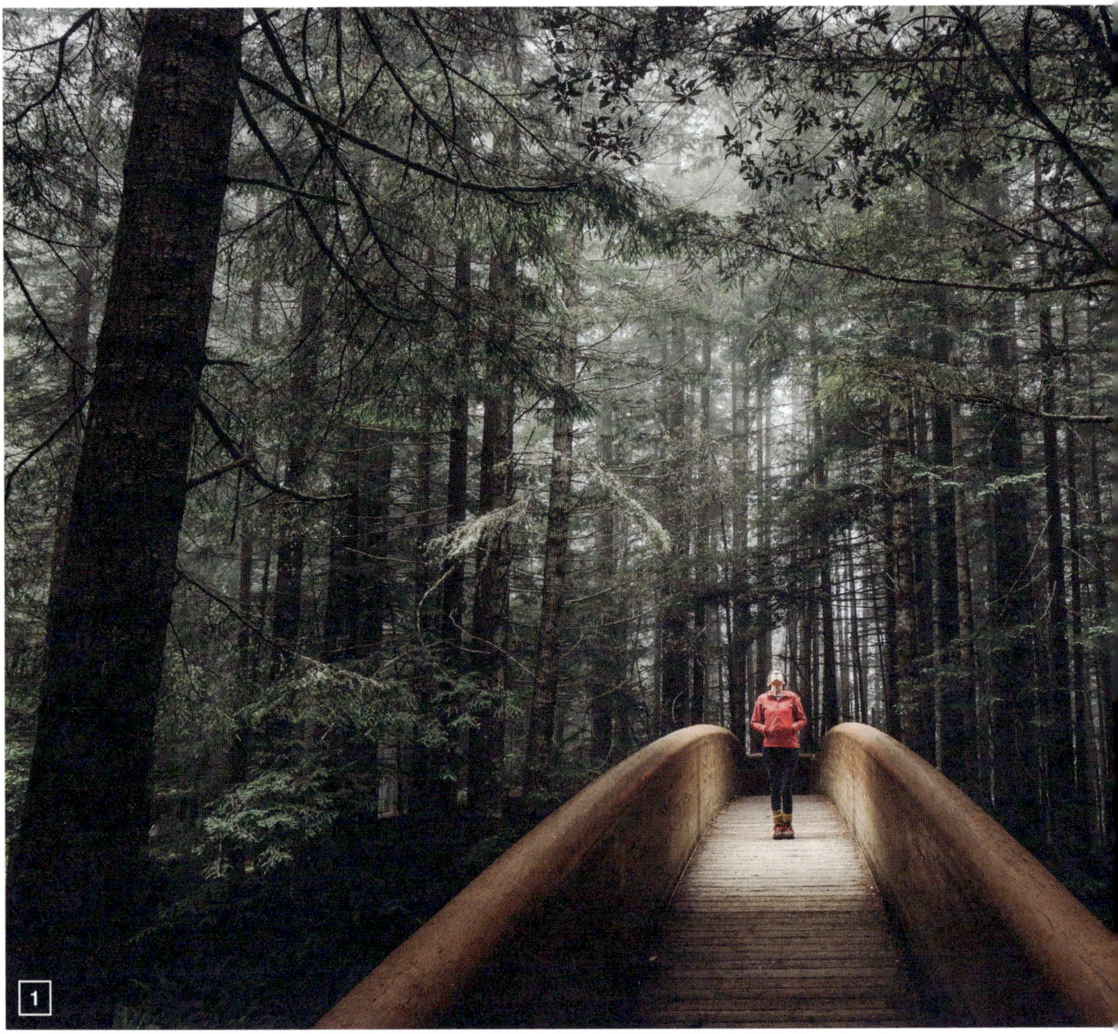

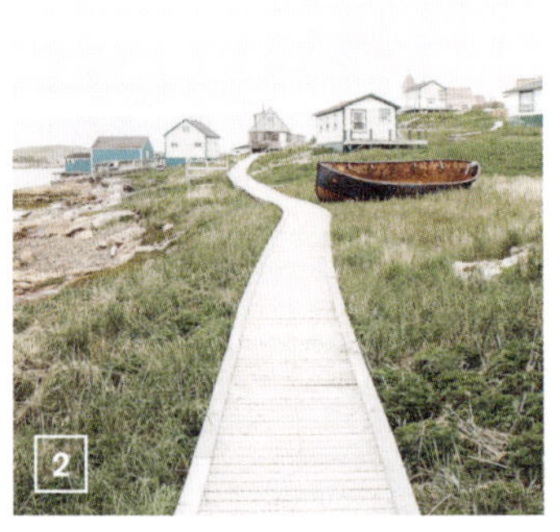

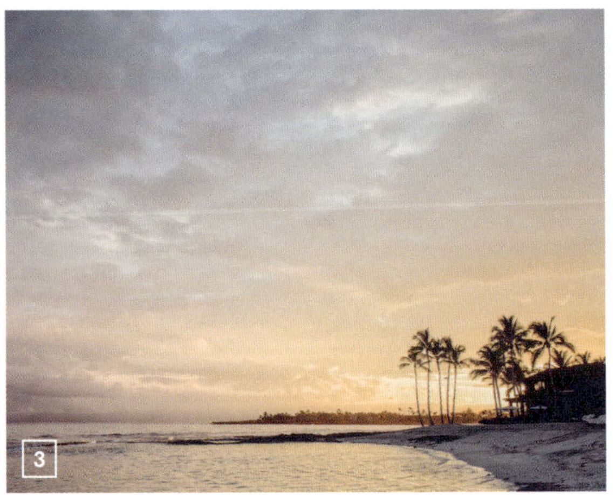

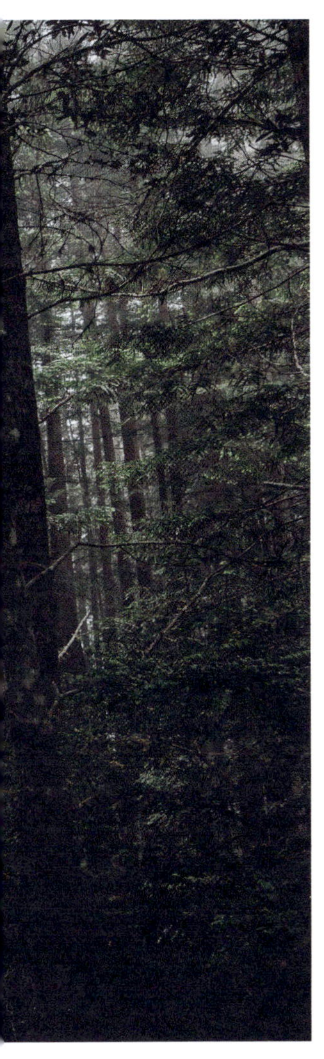

TYPES OF SUNLIGHT

DIRECT SUNLIGHT

Harsh and uncompromising, direct sunlight is often considered the worst type of light to shoot in. Sharp shadows and high contrast make it tricky to photograph flattering portraits. Reflections are a nightmare, plus you get blown highlights and colours that are all washed out. However, with some clever use of shadows, or by bouncing light with reflectors or diffusing it with silks, direct light can lead to some satisfying results. It can also work well for modern architecture.

DIFFUSED LIGHT

Cloudy days are your friends. That might seem counterintuitive, but believe me, once you understand the flexibility they offer, you'll get where I'm coming from. Acting like a giant softbox over the sun, a thin veil of cloud softens the harsh sun, meaning you can shoot all day. They reduce contrast, which puts more detail in the highlights and shadows of your photograph and delivers more even tones.

GOLDEN HOUR

Sometimes referred to as 'magic hour', this is the period just after sunrise and just before sunset. It's a great time to shoot, as everything is washed in a beautiful low-contrast wave of light. There are no harsh shadows, reflections are minimal and pretty much any subject shot at this time will look great. Note: the magic 'hour' is actually more like 20–30 minutes in duration; it passes quickly, so make sure you're in the right place at the right time!

BLUE HOUR

The blue hour is a period of twilight when the sun is just below the horizon and residual, indirect sunlight takes on a predominantly blue shade. Typically the 'hour' begins around 30–45 minutes after sunset or before sunrise. It's a great light to shoot campfire scenes in, or cityscapes, because the orange light given off by a fire or street light will perfectly complement the deep blue sky. Make sure you have a fast prime lens fixed to your camera as light levels will be pretty low at this time of day.

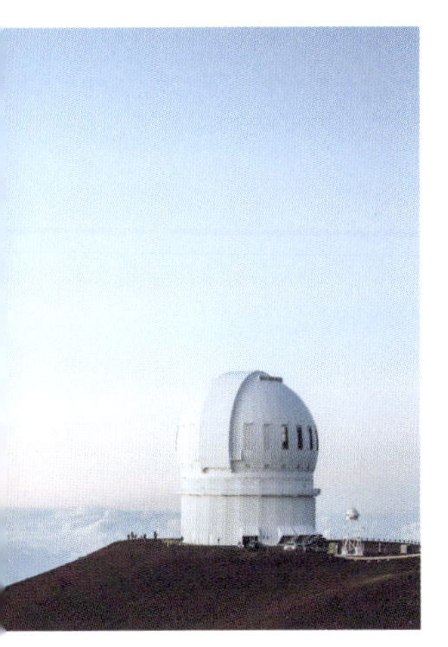

1 *The clever use of shadow in a forest helps to make use of the direct sun above.*

2 *Cloud cover presents an even, low-contrast light that is good for a range of subjects.*

3 *Golden hour.*

4 *Blue hour is worth getting up early or waiting around for.*

Project /

Capturing Mystery: **Shooting Silhouettes**

BRIEF

+ Create drama or a sense of mystery by shooting a silhouette of your subject.

REQUIREMENTS

+ A strong light source behind your subject.

+ Your subject should ideally be a well-defined shape that is easily identifiable.

OBJECTIVE

+ To expose for the background light, as opposed to your subject, which can seem counterintuitive at first!

Silhouettes are a great way to add a little drama or mystery to a scene, and due to their simplicity, they often stand out in a set of images. I love using them towards the end of a series, because a silhouette doesn't present the viewer with a clear picture. Remember what I said about leaving gaps in the narrative? Silhouettes are a relatively easy way to inject that sense of 'wonder' into your work.

STEP 1 / **BACKLIGHTING**

To capture a silhouette you need to backlight your subject and make sure there is little, or no light hitting them from the front. Ensure your subject is between you and a bright sky or artificial light. Backlighting your subject will drop them into the shadows and only their outline will be visible against the background.

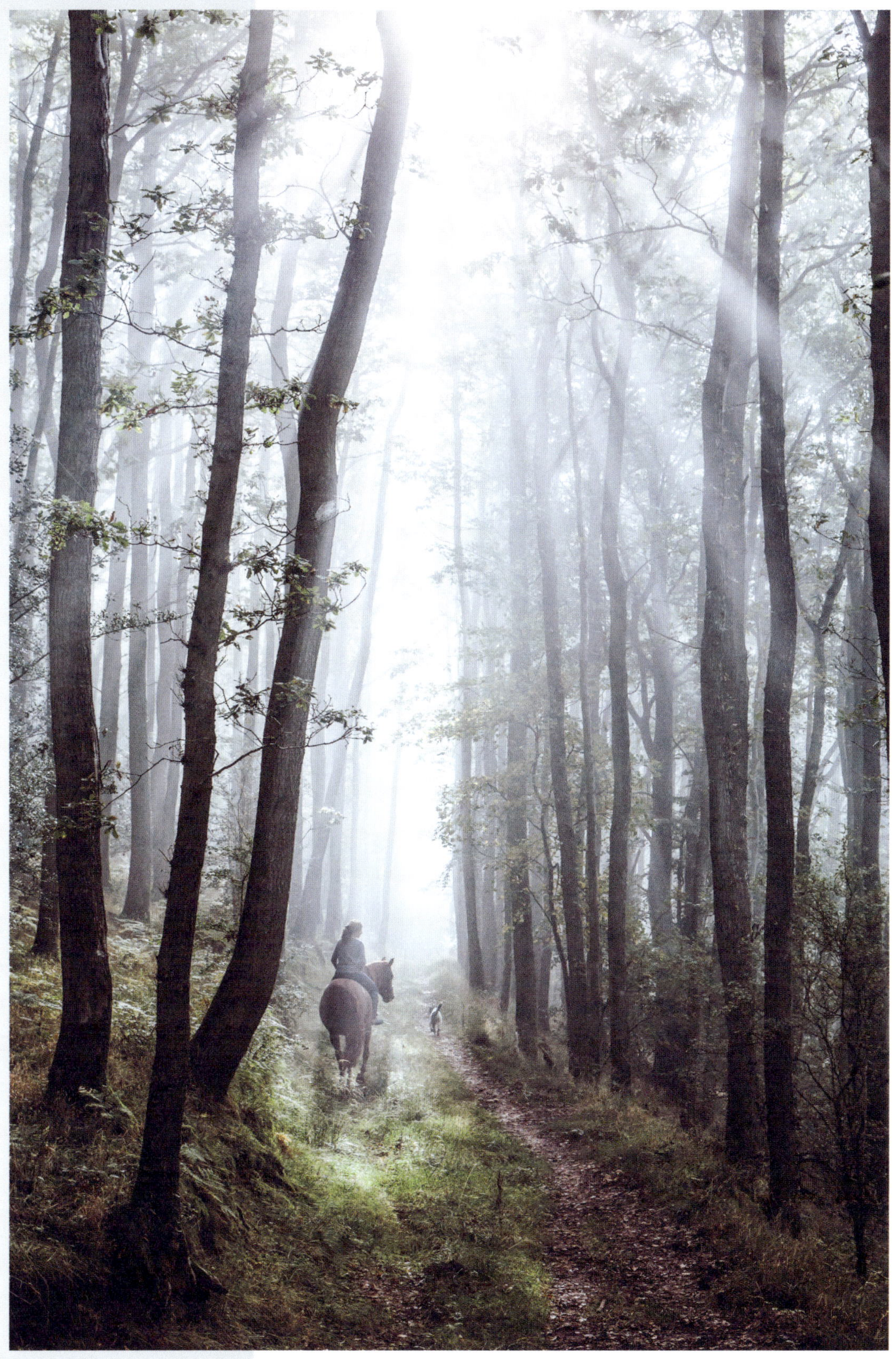

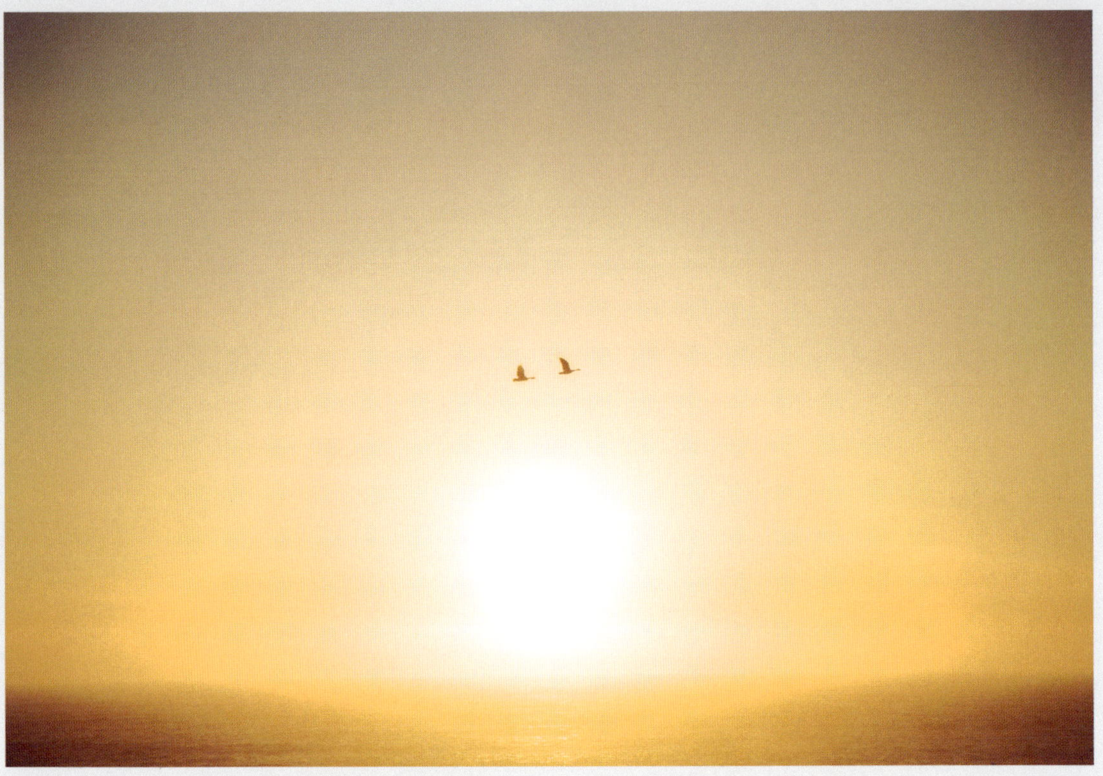

STEP 2 / **METERING**

Next, you need to expose for the bright background, and not for the subject, which is a little counterintuitive as far as your camera is concerned. Your camera is always trying to help you make well-exposed pictures, and if you are shooting in evaluative mode, the camera will try to even out the image and lift the shadows of your subject. However, for a silhouette, you want the subject to be underexposed. Give your camera a helping hand and switch to spot metering, which tells the camera to expose just a small portion of the frame.

STEP 3 / **EXPOSE**

Look for the brightest area in the background and set your exposure by aiming your camera's metering point towards it.

For a DSLR, the metering point is the active focal point which is usually the square or circle in the middle of the viewfinder. Use the Exposure Lock button to 'hold' the exposure while you reframe your shot.

If you're shooting with a phone, you just need to touch the brightest point in the sky with your finger and the phone will automatically adjust the exposure.

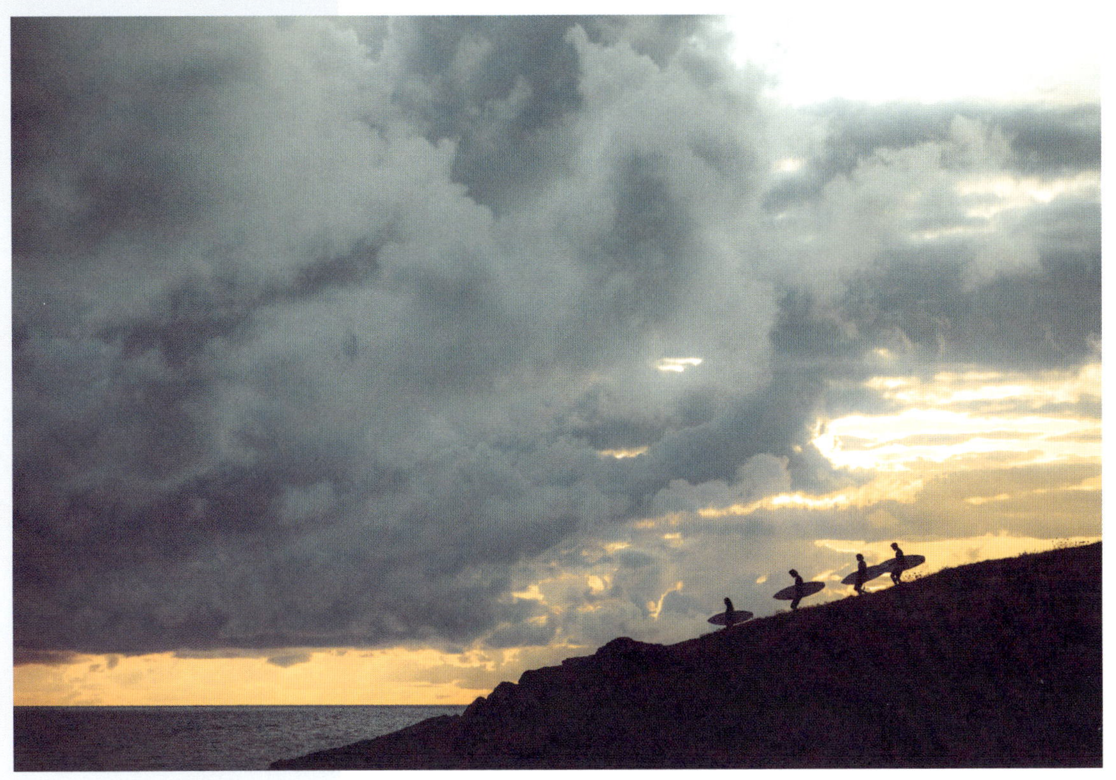

STEP 4 / **SHAPE THE SCENE**

Because you're not illuminating your subject from the front, a viewer is only going to see the outline, so it's important to keep elements clearly defined. Keep subjects separate from each other and think about their shape to help relay the story – see above.

STEP 5 / **KEEP LOW**

The background – as opposed to your subject – is the hero when it comes to a silhouette, so you'll want to keep as much of it in frame as possible. When composing the image, get low down, below your subject. Lie down, or maybe ask your subject to jump in the air – anything to prevent them merging with the horizon.

CAMERA SETTINGS

Have you ever looked at the menu system for your DSLR? It's a deep rabbit hole! I shoot with a Canon DSLR, but most settings are standard across all of the other major camera manufacturers. Here is a simple guide to understanding your camera settings, starting with the three pillars of photography: aperture, shutter speed and ISO.

APERTURE

Think of aperture like the pupil in your eye. As you move from a light to a dark environment, your pupil gets wider, letting more light into your eye and helping you see in the dark. Changing the aperture on your camera works similarly. By widening the aperture (lowering your f-stop), you can change the exposure of your image (make it brighter) and vice versa. Aperture also plays a significant aesthetic role in controlling depth of field – the wider your aperture, the more blurred the background.

SHUTTER SPEED

Using the eye example again, think of the shutter speed as like your eyelids. In bright sunshine, you squint or blink to reduce the amount of light entering your eye; in the dark, you will open your eyes wide and blink less to let more light in. Shutter speed on a camera is no different. Use a fast shutter speed in bright sun, and a lower speed in low light. As with aperture, the shutter speed also plays an aesthetic role – lower shutter speeds combined with moving subjects create motion blur (see pages 120–127).

ISO

In basic terms, ISO is another method for brightening or darkening a photo. The higher the ISO, the brighter the image. So, if you are shooting in very dark conditions, you might want to boost your ISO in conjunction with a slow shutter speed and a wide aperture to capture a well-exposed image. However, shooting at a high ISO will introduce grain or noise, so there is some trade-off in boosting it. To combat this you can use a tripod to keep the camera still so that any motion blur associated with the slow shutter speed is reduced.

Aperture, shutter speed and ISO are intrinsically linked and it can be hard to get your head around them at first, but the more you practice, the more you will understand the effect they have on your images.

Here are some example settings for different subjects.

- Cloudy day portrait with background blur:
  1/640 sec   f/2.8   ISO 800
- Sunny day portrait with background in focus:
  1/320 sec   f/8.0   ISO 160
- Golden hour landscape:
  1/160 sec   f/11   ISO 400
- Blue hour scene:
  1/50 sec   f/1.4   ISO 2000

IMAGE FORMAT

Always shoot Raw images, as opposed to JPEGs. Raw files deliver superior image quality. You can make JPEGs from Raw files, but you cannot work the other way around (see pages 164–165).

RELEASE SHUTTER WITHOUT CARD

This prevents your camera from shooting if a memory card is not present. Turn it off!

AUTO FOCUS METHOD

Use Single Point or Zone Focusing. This will bring up a grid of focus points in the viewfinder so you can specify the point at which the camera will focus. For example, if you are shooting a portrait with a shallow depth of field, you can tell the camera to focus on the eyes of your subject and ensure they stay sharp.

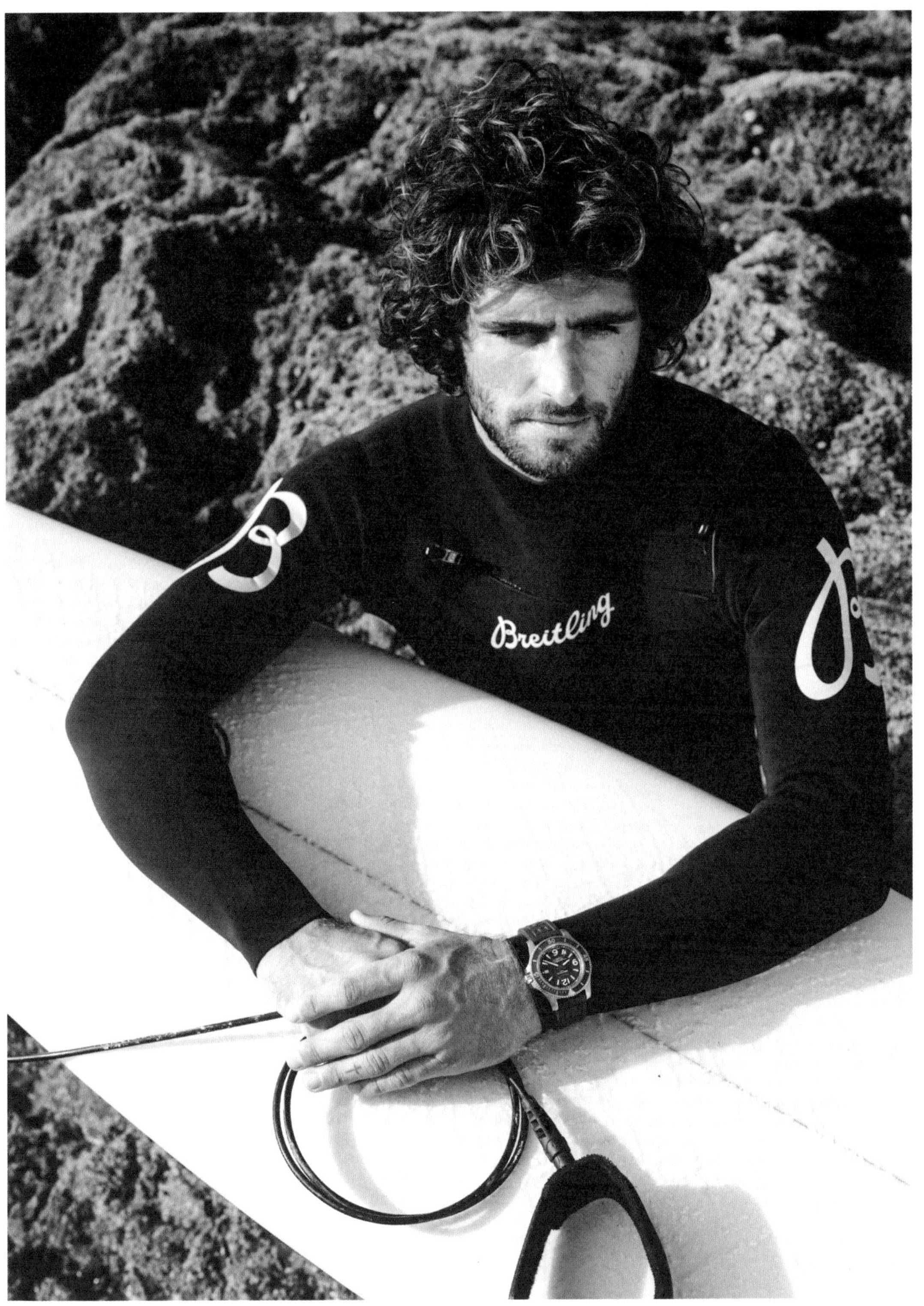

SHOOTING WITH PRIME LENSES

I only shoot with prime lenses and I do that for a few reasons.

MORE LIGHT

A huge benefit of prime lenses is that they have wider maximum apertures. So if I'm shooting in low light situations, a prime is going to allow me to get the exposure I need without having to increase my ISO or lower my shutter speed.

SHALLOW DEPTH OF FIELD

Another benefit of a wide aperture is that it allows for a shallower depth of field. That means I can keep subjects sharp while blurring the background. It means I can isolate a subject in their environment.

QUALITY

On the whole, prime lenses are sharper than zoom lenses and produce a better quality image. From a design perspective, it's easier to create glass for one focal length, and there's generally less distortion and less chromatic aberration in the images they capture.

FIXED FOCAL LENGTHS

Learn to love the constraints associated with shooting at a fixed focal length. It will make you a better photographer because it forces you to compose with your feet as opposed to a zoom ring. I understand why, when starting out, you might think you need a good zoom to get closer to the action, but good composition often makes for more impressive images than proximity. Zooms make for lazy photographers.

A fixed focal length will prevent you from standing still – a terrible habit – so instead of standing still and adjusting that zoom ring, I'm always moving. I have to because I can't get a variety of shots unless I'm walking (or running!) around.

Shooting at a fixed focal length will also help you 'see' photographs in the world around you. When you can *see* a scene at a particular focal length, you have a much better idea of how your final shot will look.

It also helps in the edit when pairing images. If a sequence is shot using a range of different focal lengths (by zooming in and zooming out), it can be harder to match pictures together. It's possible, but it takes longer and doesn't always feel that natural. Sticking to a series of set focal lengths can make the editing process much quicker.

TIPS

/ Prime lenses are renowned for producing sharp images even at low f-stops, so don't be afraid to open your aperture wide.

/ If you only have a telephoto prime, it's still possible to shoot wide-angle images. Check out the '50 & Stitch' technique on page 118.

/ Zoom lenses can be stopped down to f/20 or smaller apertures, but their performance begins to deteriorate at around f/8. Prime lenses offer less diffraction across a range of apertures.

/ Zoom with your feet as opposed to your lens. You'll end up with better images and ultimately become a better photographer!

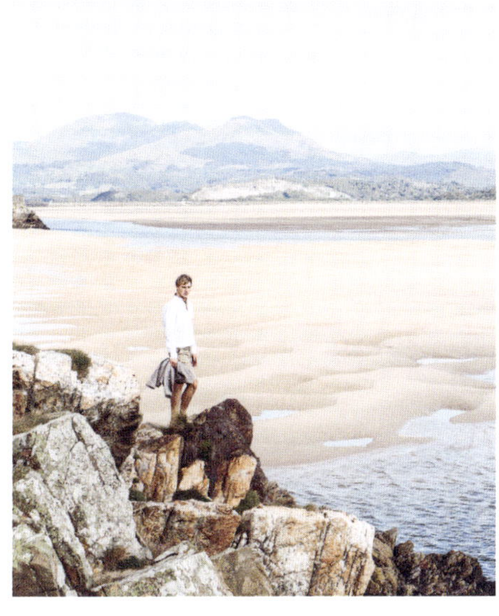

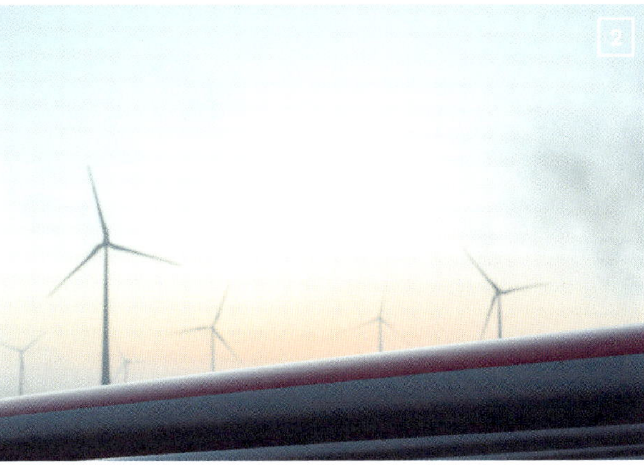

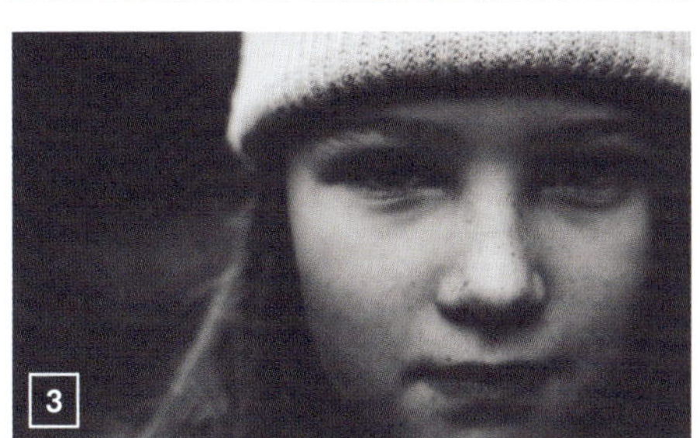

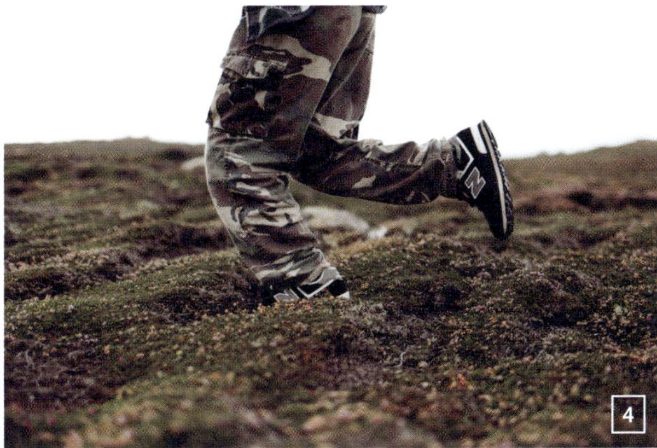

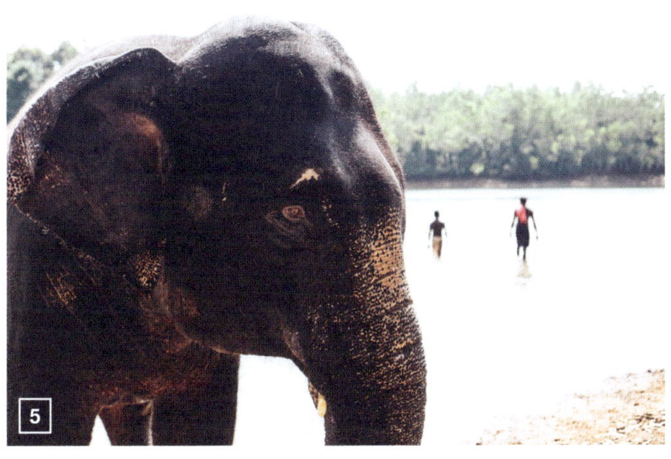

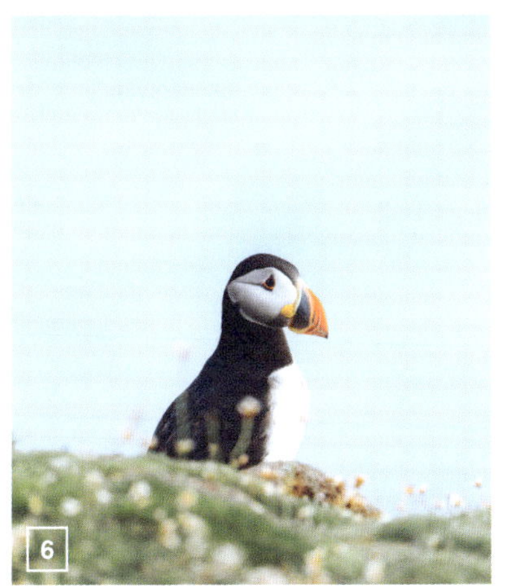

1 *1/1400 sec at f/9   ISO 160   50mm*

2 *1/200 sec at f/5.0   ISO 800   85mm*

3 *1/320 sec at f/3.2   ISO 320   40mm*

4 *1/4000 sec at f/1.4   ISO 50   35mm*

5 *1/125 sec at f/3.5   ISO 125   35mm*

6 *1/320 sec at f/5.6   ISO 400   400mm*

Exercise /

Phone Portraits

Achieving a shallow depth of field that makes your subject pop from its background used to be something that required expensive prime lenses, but now it is possible to achieve a similar effect with your phone.

The iPhone's Portrait mode allows you to shoot portraits with beautifully blurred backgrounds, so you can emphasise the subject by reducing distractions in the rest of the frame. If you don't have an iPhone, use the Aviary or LightFX apps to achieve this affect.

**How to use Portrait mode
on a smartphone**

1 Open the Camera app and swipe to Portrait mode, which is between 'photo' and 'square', just above the shutter button

2 Aim your phone at your subject, which needs to be between two and eight feet from your camera. The Camera app lets you know when you're too close or too far away, or if the area is too dark.

3 When Portrait mode is ready, the lighting effect, such as Natural Light, turns yellow. Once you're happy with the lighting, simply tap the shutter button to take the photo.

4 If you'd like to experiment with different portrait lighting, swipe the Natural Light box above the shutter. You can choose from various options, including Studio Light, Contour Light, Stage Light and Stage Light mono.

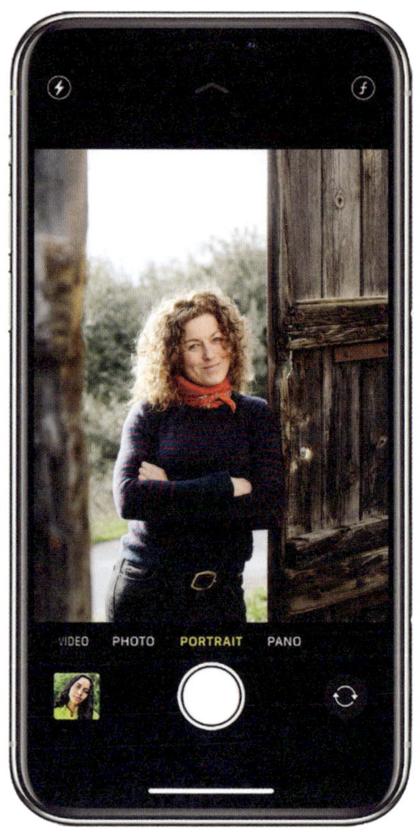

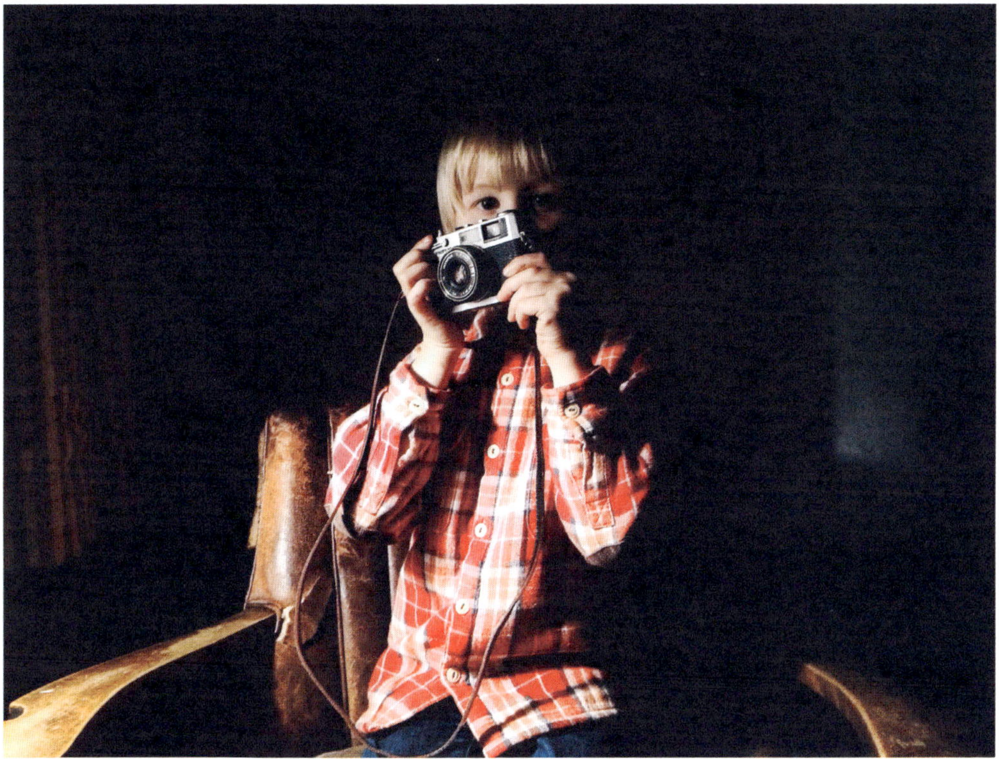

iPhone 3S using window light in a dark room. Here, I'm isolating my subject using light and dark.

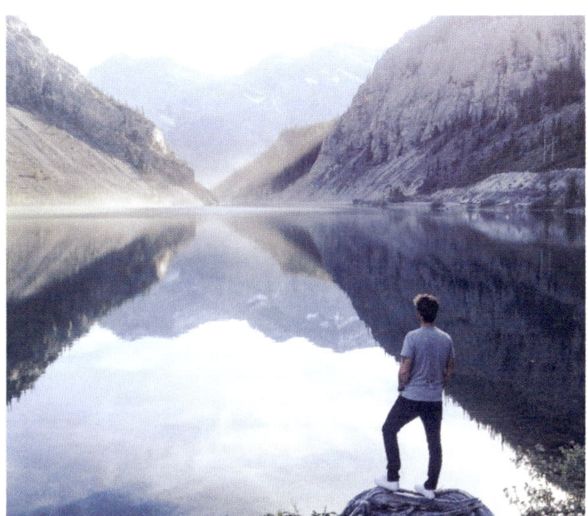

Taken with an iPhone 4s. Here the subject is isolated against a lake with fog and light.

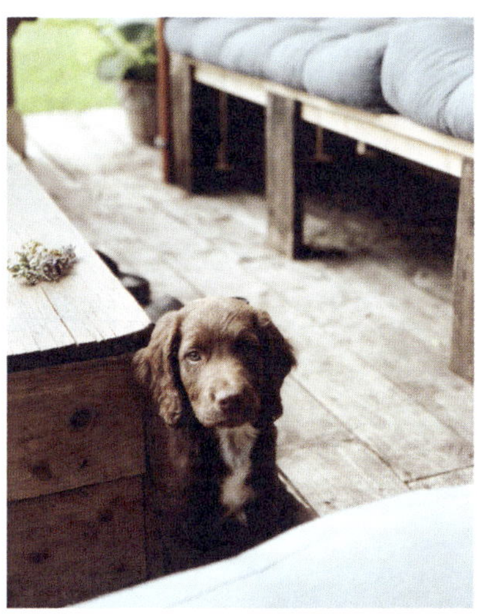

Shot using an iPhone XS with Portrait mode activated. Note the blurred background.

SHOOTING TECHNIQUE: REMBRANDT

There are many ways to create atmosphere and mood in an image without using an injection of artificial mist. The aim of the smoke in the example on page 101 was to 'shape' the light emitting from the headlights of the car, and 'shaping' light is what we'll look at here.

SHAPING LIGHT

Shaping light and taming its rebellious nature is a crucial skill to master. There are a couple of techniques you can use to level up the atmosphere in your portraits. First up is the 'Rembrandt Triangle' and in the next section we'll discuss catchlights.

REMBRANDT LIGHTING

Rembrandt lighting takes its name from the Dutch draughtsman, painter and printmaker. An innovative and prolific master in three media, he is generally considered one of the greatest visual artists of all time. He used a dramatic form of lighting in his paintings that is moody and atmospheric. It's also relatively easy to construct once you know what you are looking for. Take a look at the picture shown here, and, in particular, note the small triangle of light under the model's eye on the right side of his face. It's a signal that the primary light source is coming from the opposite side of the face.

TECHNIQUE

If you light your subject's face from one side, the opposite side will be an interaction of shadow and light. With Rembrandt lighting you are looking to create a triangle of light on the opposite cheek. If you find the shadow effect too dark, you can use a reflector to 'fill' in the shadow according to your preference. This lighting effect does not require expensive equipment or a fancy camera – you simply need one light source.

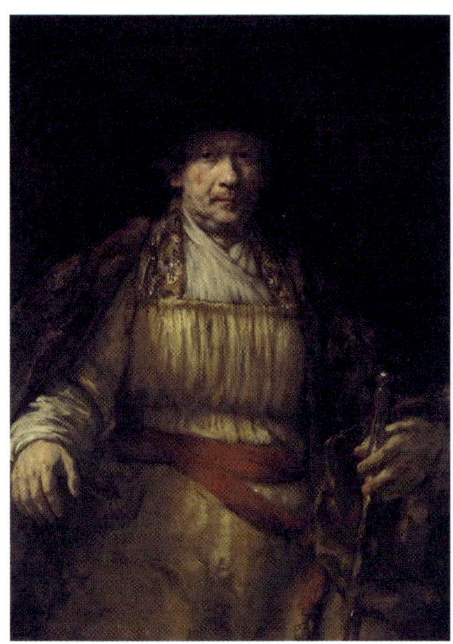

Courtesy of Wikimedia

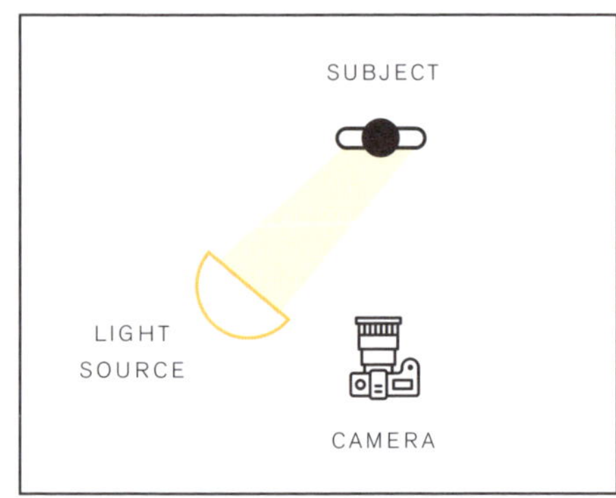

Try your hand at lighting a portrait using Rembrandt lighting – it's a fairly easy effect to master, only requiring a single light source. It will help you 'see the light' and inject mood into your photographs.

Exercise /
Rembrandt Lighting

Try it at home

1 Find a room in your house that has a north-facing window to give you a beautiful, even light, regardless of the time of day.

2 Ensure any other windows in the room are blacked out. Merely drawing the curtains should do the trick.

3 Position your model just below the north window with their face at a 45-degree angle to it. Window light should illuminate the side of the face next to the window and the opposite side should be plunged into shadow. Keep adjusting the position of your model until you see the telltale triangle. Look too for the shadow on the side of and slightly below the nose.

4 The intensity of the effect can be changed by altering the distance between the model and the light. Do this by moving them closer or further away from the window.

Having practised the effect on a friend, you'll know what to look for and can begin to get creative when shooting portraits, as shown here.

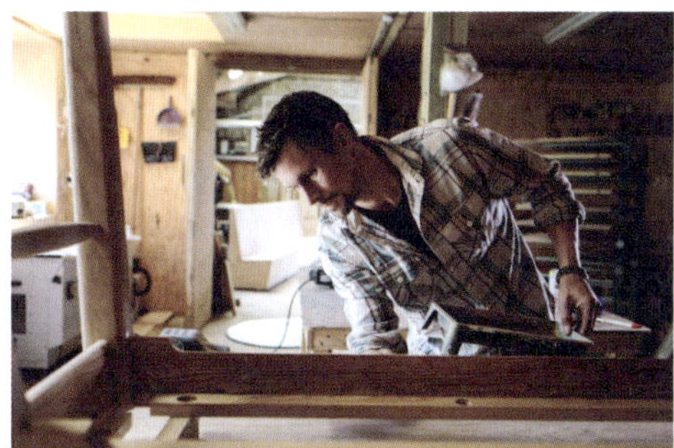

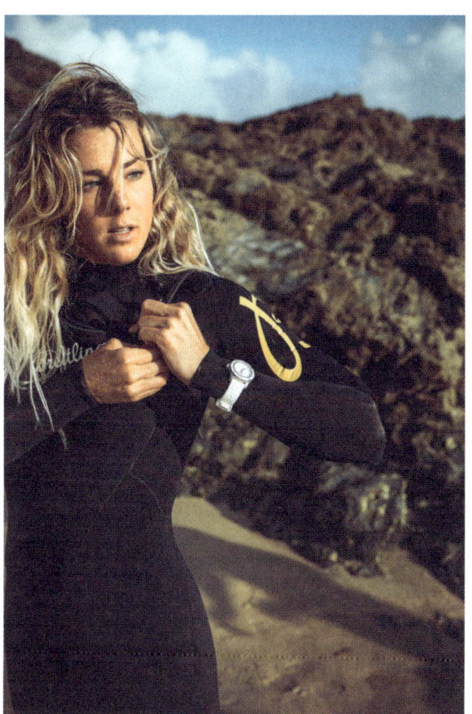

SHOOTING TECHNIQUE: CATCHLIGHTS

Shakespeare once said *'the eyes are the window to your soul'*. And it's true – the eyes provide heaps of information about someone's emotional state. Since we're in the business of shaping emotions through the photographs we make, it pays to carefully consider the eyes of our subjects – the aim of this technique is to bring them to life.

A small speck of white light reflected in the eyes of your subject will make a huge difference. Referred to as catchlights, they're important because without them a portrait can look dull and lifeless. Compare the portrait below, which doesn't have a catchlight, with the image opposite, which does.

This is a reasonably easy 'light' to 'catch,' and you need no special or expensive equipment. All you need is a light source to reflect in your subject's eyes. This can be artificial, like a camera flash, or natural light from the sun. A reliable option when working indoors is to limit the direction of natural daylight by positioning your subject near a window or door.

TECHNIQUE

Try to find a north-facing window to give you that nice even light across the face regardless of the time of day. Your subject does not have to look directly into the source: eyes are spherical, and a light source positioned to the left or right will be visible as a reflection in the subject's eyes.

The closer your subject is to the window, the larger the catchlight will appear. Look for it in the eyes of your subject and ask them to move their head or body position left or right until you are happy with the look.

ALTERNATIVE TECHNIQUE

I often use a circular reflector to add a catchlight. Eyes are round, so a circular catchlight is more pleasing than the small square you get from a window.

Simply position your subject in front of a window and bounce light back into the face and eyes using a round, silver reflector. This is often referred to as 'fill' light. The window light is backlighting the scene and will provide a pleasing 'rim' or 'hair' light around your subject's head that can pop them out of the shadow.

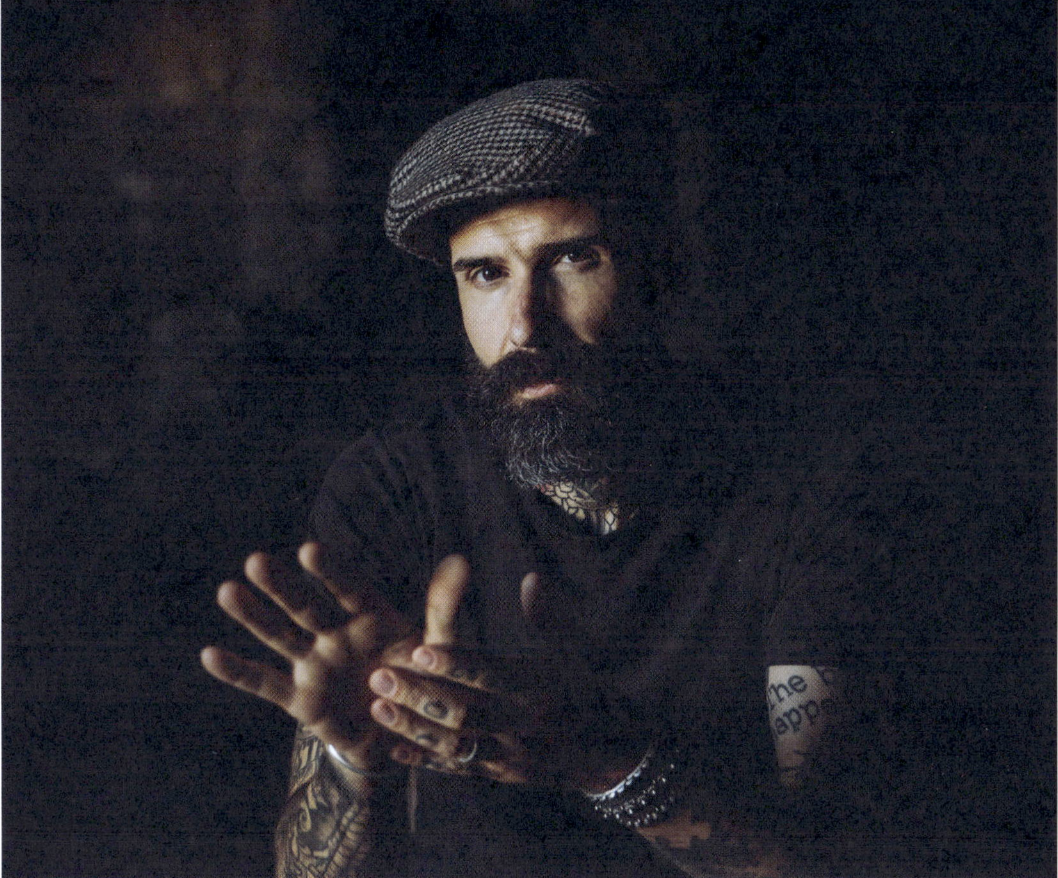

Exercise /

Experimenting with Catchlights

Try heading out with a friend and experiment with catching the light in their eyes.

Compare images with and without a catchlight present and you'll soon understand their importance. Don't be afraid of moving your subject around in order to change the effect – this is a form of direction and can help with rapport. Here are a few lighting setups that you can follow, each of which delivers a different shape/intensity of light.

- Subject backlit by window with a round reflector in front and to one side. The window light bounces off the reflector, illuminates the face and creates a circular catchlight.

- Subject side lit by window. Rotate their head and body to catch more or less light in their eyes.

- Flash with reflector. You can also create catchlights using an off-camera flash, or even a torch. Position the light to the side or behind your subject and bounce it back into the eyes of your subject using the reflector.

SHOOTING TECHNIQUE:
50 & STITCH (THE BRENIZER METHOD)

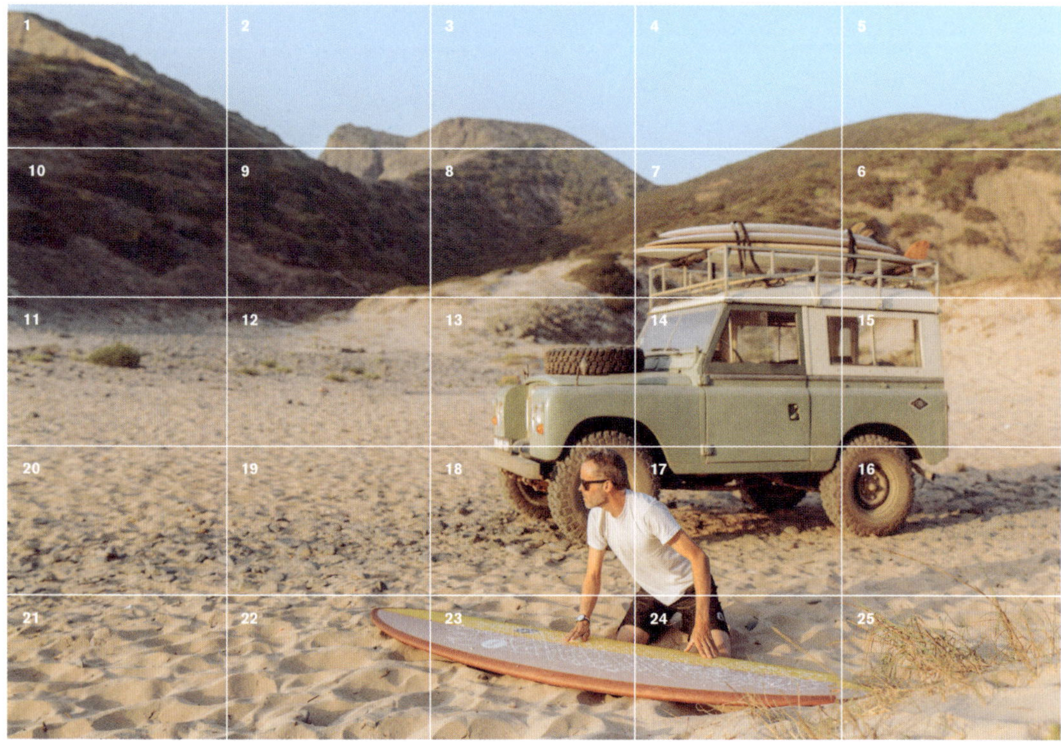

I often keep a 50mm lens on my camera, as I prefer that focal length over all others. It's light and fast, and the wide aperture provides a beautiful depth of field. I love the look.

However, it's not very wide, which makes it more challenging to capture extreme or long shots and tell a more complete story. I could switch lenses, but instead I often keep the 50mm attached and use a stitching technique that allows me to mimic the look of large-format film photography with a digital camera.

To do this, I shoot multiple images of a scene while panning my camera, and then in post, I stitch the images together to create a panorama. There are numerous benefits of working in this way.

HIGH RESOLUTION

By stitching together multiple images, you're effectively creating a very high-resolution image which means you can make massive prints or crop into a picture without losing image quality.

DEPTH OF FIELD

Shooting with a wide aperture at this focal length will throw the background out of focus to a far greater extent than a wide-angle lens, making your subject pop.

DEPTH PERCEPTION

Telephoto lenses compress distance, bringing background elements closer to foreground elements. A wide-angle lens has the opposite effect.

Have a go at shooting a wide-angle portrait using the '50 & stitch' method. It's a fairly straightforward technique and fun to play with. You can keep pushing this technique too – I have a friend who made a single composition from hundreds of images!

Exercise /

Stitching

1 Choose a wide aperture, something like f/3.2 or below. The wider you shoot, the more pronounced the effect.

2 Frame your subject in the centre. Half depress your shutter button, and either lock focus or switch to manual focus. Then shoot across the scene from left to right, top to bottom, making a series of images in an organised layout – see the image opposite. Ensure you are slightly overlapping each take.

3 When you've finished shooting, switch your lens to manual focus and take a picture of your hand. This will help when you import all of these images into Lightroom. By shooting a picture of your hand you create a cut between stitches and make a blank frame in your Lightroom filmstrip, helping you see where your stitch starts and ends in the edit.

4 When you import your card, everything's going to come in sequential order according to capture time. The blank frame shows us that everything before this frame is part of the same stitch, so all I need to do is select them all and hit Control-M, which tells Lightroom to create a panoramic image from all of those separate frames.

5 Use Lightroom's Photo Merge tool to stitch the images together. You may need to try different projection methods to render the best-looking stitch.

RECAP

/ Using the technique of '50 & stitch' is another way to take a wide-angle photograph if you only have a telephoto lens on your camera.

/ Create a massive-resolution file with great depth of field. Backgrounds are really thrown out of focus in a more dramatic fashion than a wide-angle lens can render.

/ Have fun with it. Send me some examples, I'd love to see them.

SHOOTING TECHNIQUE: BEGINNER PANNING SHOT

When I'm shooting transitional images that involve cars, bikes or other vehicles, I like my audience to feel like they are travelling through the landscape. I want to evoke the sensation of something passing by, and I use a couple of techniques to achieve this.

We'll start with the more accessible technique of the two, called a panning shot. 'Panning' involves following a moving subject along the horizontal plane of motion and combines a slow shutter speed with camera motion to create a sense of momentum. It is a resonably straightforward method of keeping your subject in focus while blurring your background: slow your shutter speed and pan your camera with the

subject before snapping the picture. However, there are a bunch of moving variables at play, and you'll need to carefully consider each individually. The project on page 122–125 breaks down the process into steps. Give it a go!

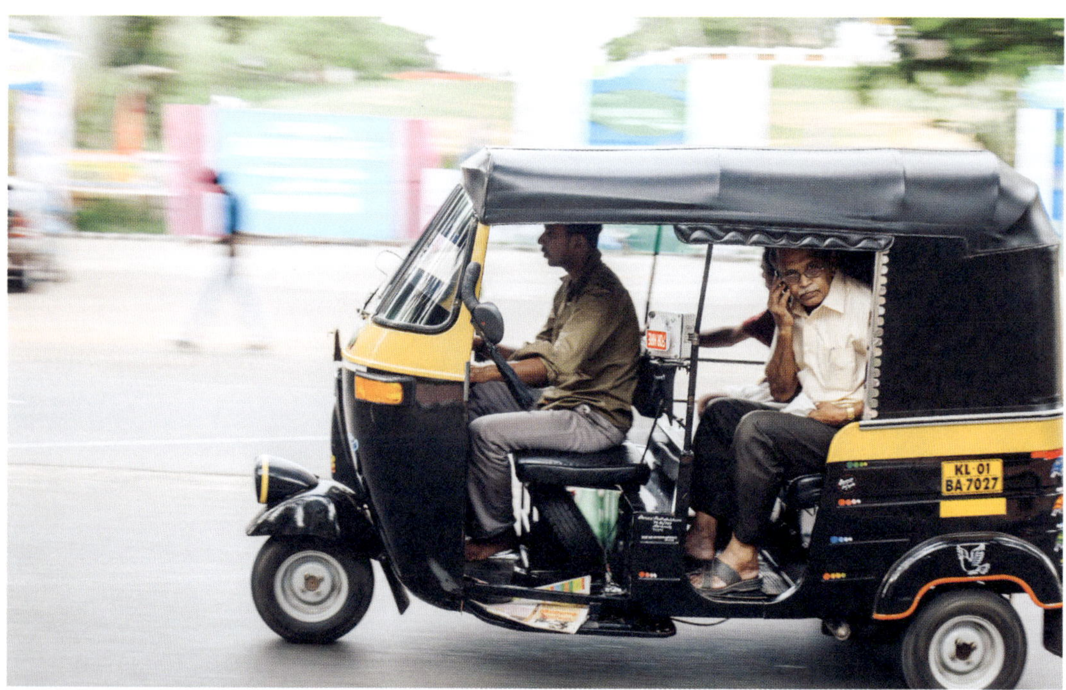

1/60 sec at f/7.1, ISO 100

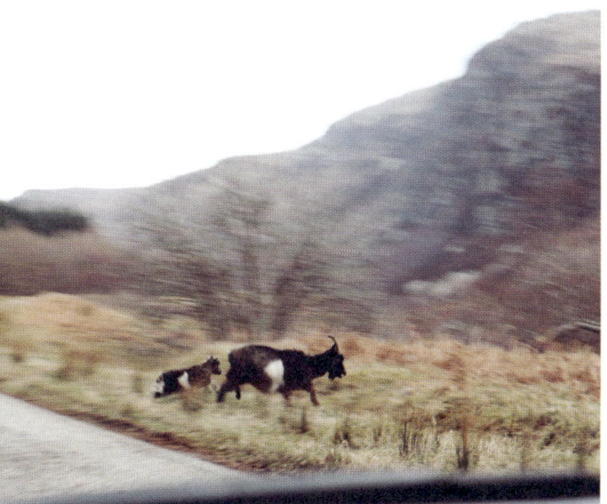

1/40 sec at f/5.0, ISO 400

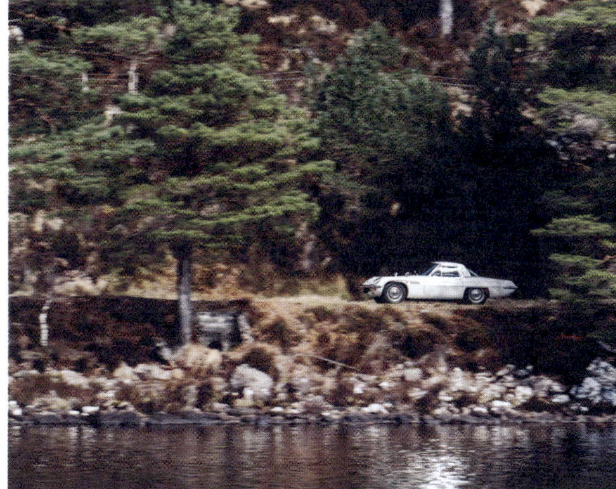

1/600 sec at f/8.0, ISO 400

Exercise /

Panning with a Smartphone

Traditionally the preserve of DSLR cameras, it is now possible to create panning shots using your phone. There are no hard and fast rules for this technique – trial and error is a part of the process. Experiment and have fun. See the following pages for more detailed instructions for using a DSLR.

1 Position yourself so that you can pan left to right, or vice versa, and put some distance between yourself and your subject. It's important to remember that the background is playing as much of a part in this shot as your subject, despite it being out of focus and blurred! If you're too close to your subject they will fill the frame and the effect the background has on the feeling of the overall image will be less pronounced.

2 You'll need to set the phone camera to Manual mode. With some models you might need to shoot with an app – try the Moment camera app, which is available for iOS and Android.

3 Set the focusing to Continuous and select a shutter speed between 1/30 sec and 1/60 sec. If you are shooting during the day, keep the ISO as low as possible.

4 Most phones will track a subject as it moves across the frame and lock the focus accordingly. Simply tap and hold on your focal point until you see an AE/AF Lock banner appear at the top of the screen. If you're not happy with the exposure, you can adjust by swiping up or down on the screen.

Project /

Keep Moving: **Motion Blur**

BRIEF

+ Capture motion blur to
  instil a sense of movement
  in an image.

REQUIREMENTS

+ Steady hands.

+ Shutter Priority mode.

+ A slow shutter speed.

+ An ND filter if it's bright outside.

OBJECTIVE

+ Learn to move your body as your
  subject approaches. Capturing a
  good panning image depends as
  much on the way you move as it
  does on your camera settings.

Photographs are, by nature, still images, but
what if we want to communicate a sense of
movement? Some of my favourite pictures
use motion blur to convey a sense of speed or
travel. It's a great way of injecting a sense of
pace or of the passing of time into your work
and such images sit well when viewed against
static or 'still' pictures of the same subject.

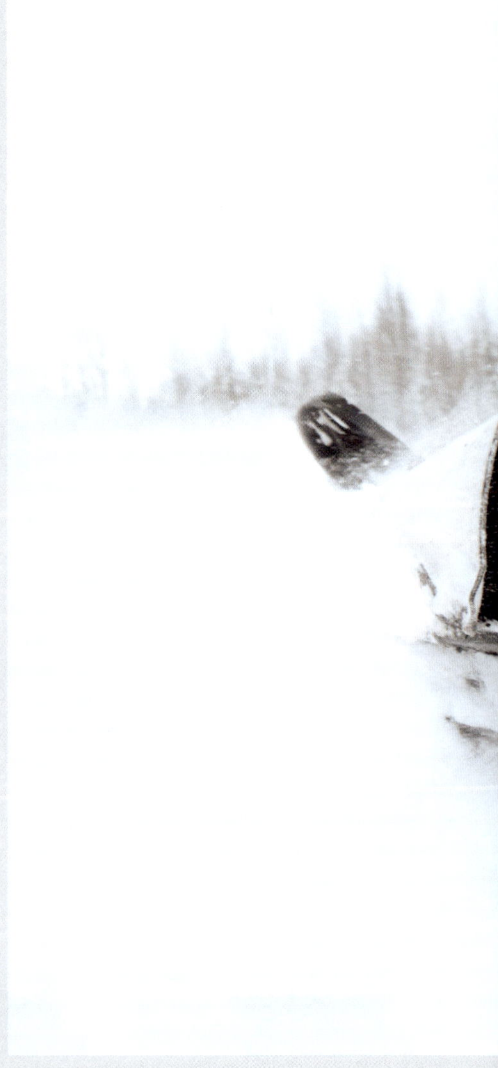

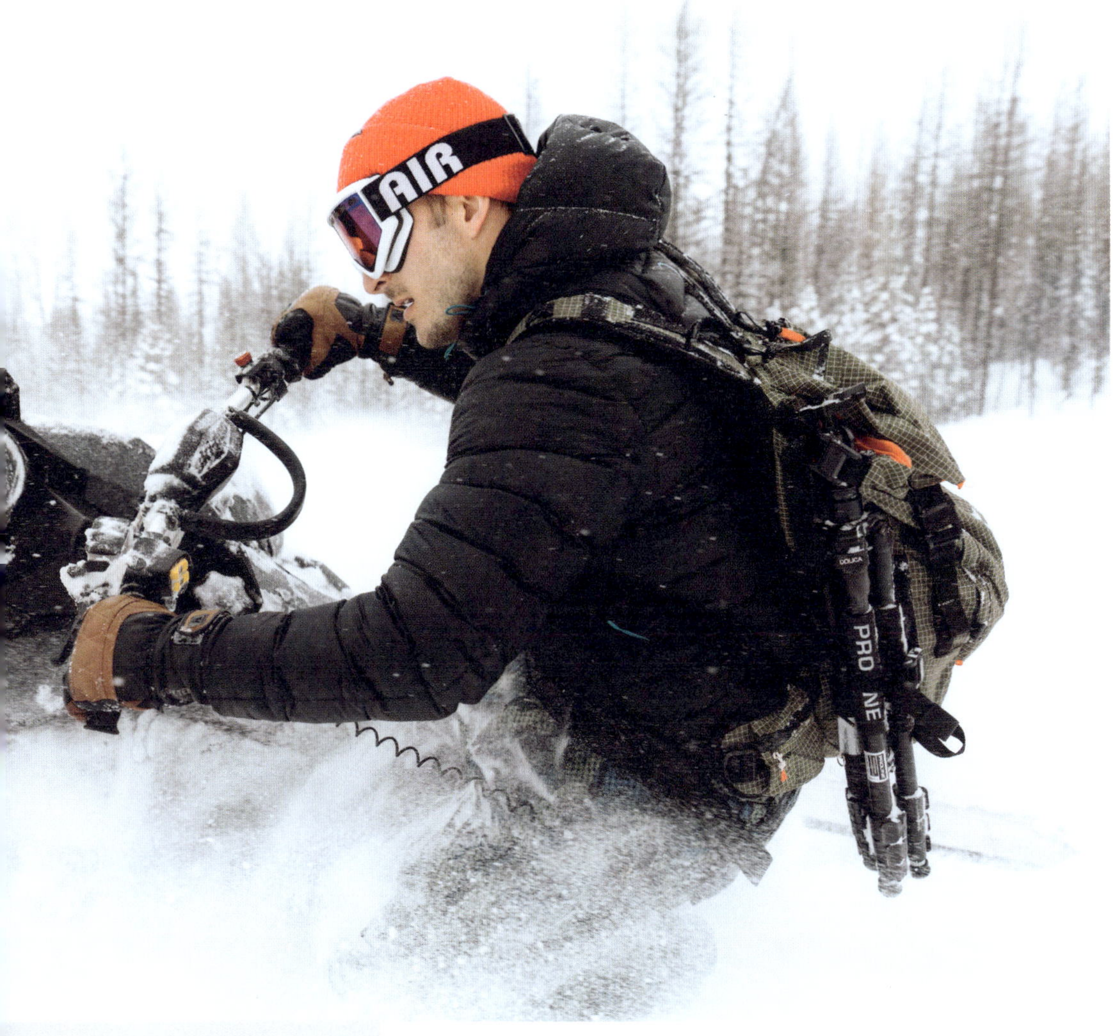

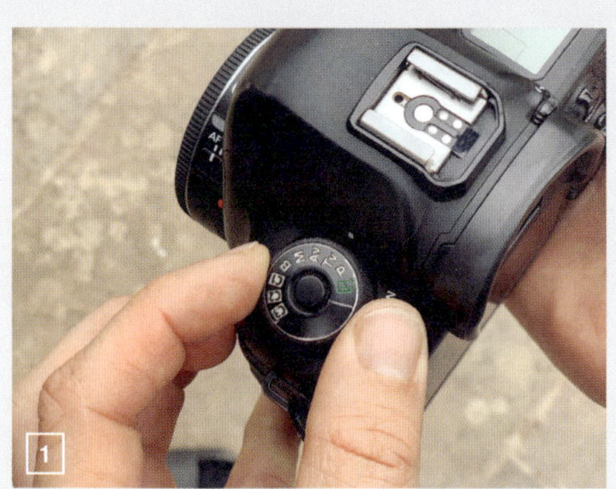

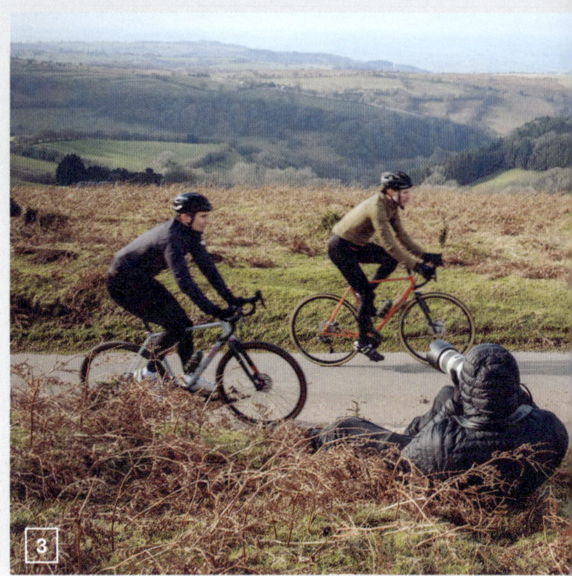

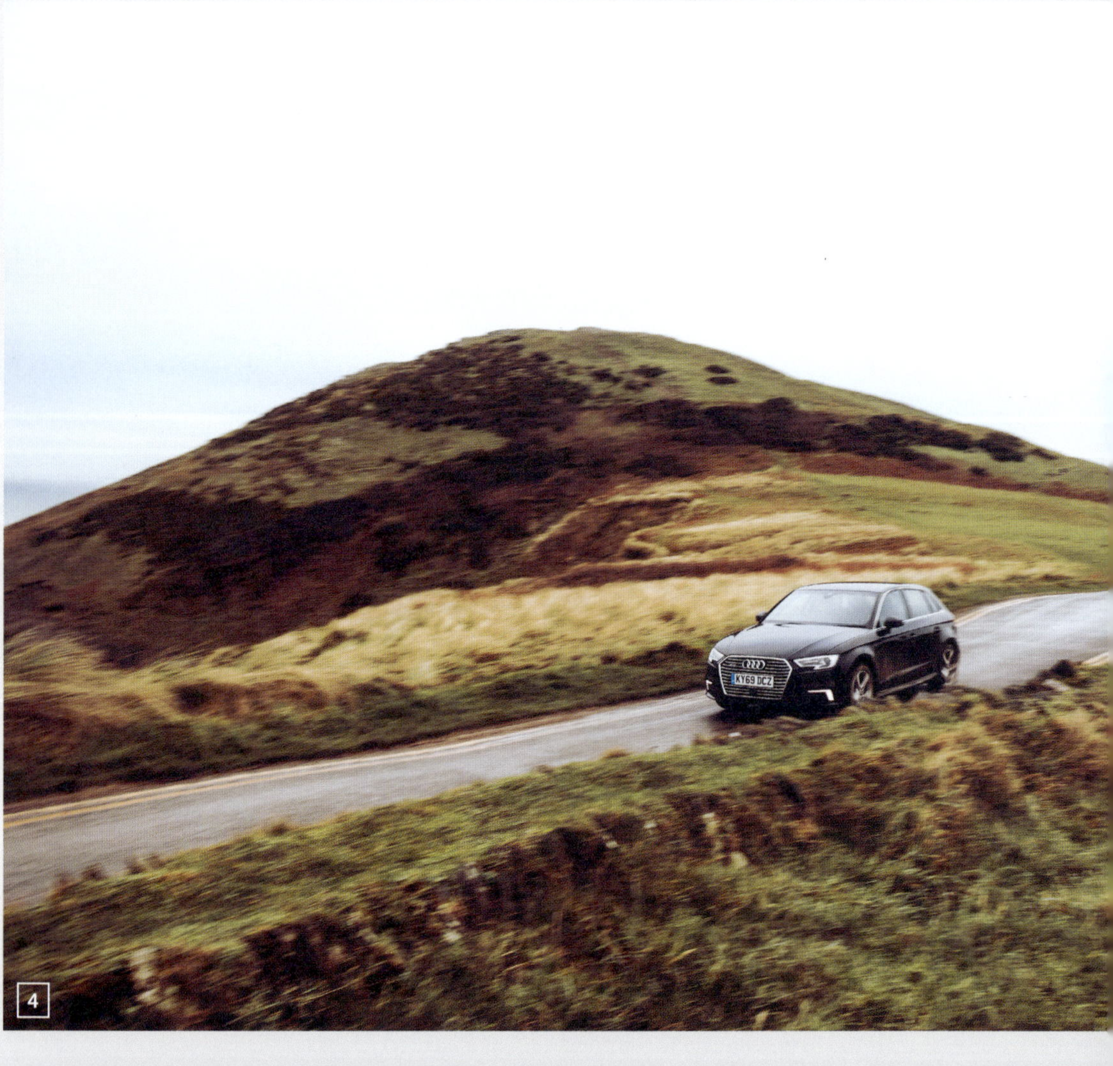

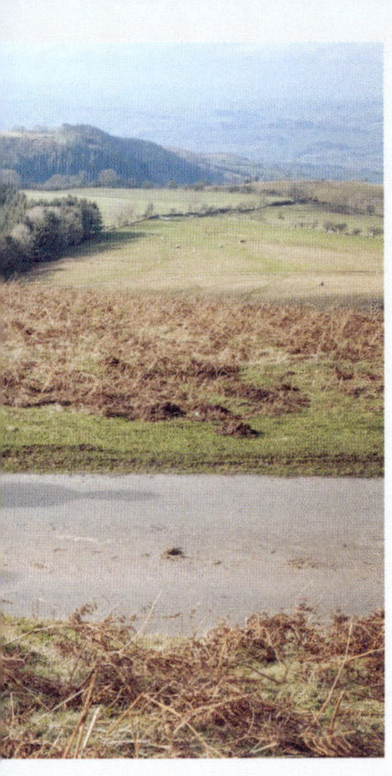

STEP 1 / **CAMERA SETTINGS**

Motion blur requires a longer exposure time, so you'll need to slow your shutter speed to realise the effect. Switch your camera to Shutter Priority mode. This will instruct your camera to look after the aperture settings as you make shutter speed changes.

If you're shooting in the middle of the day and the sun is high, you'll be letting a lot of light reach the sensor because you've slowed your shutter. As such, you may need to compensate with a neutral-density (ND) filter so as not to overexpose the image. Alternatively, try shooting at either end of the day when there is less light in the sky.

STEP 2 / **SPEED**

How fast your subject is moving, and how pronounced an effect you want will determine your shutter speed. It's a matter of trial and error. However, let's assume we are making a panning shot of a moving vehicle. Start with a shutter speed of 1/100 sec or less. This should keep the vehicle sharp while blurring the background.

STEP 3 / **KEEP IT STEADY**

Start in a standing position with your feet firmly planted and a slight flex in your knees; I sometimes sit or squat on the ground. You should feel relaxed but stable. Holding your camera in both hands, firmly press your elbows into your sides and practice rotating your entire upper body, while panning from left to right in a smooth fashion. When you're happy, try the shot on a moving target. As the subject approaches, begin panning with it and hit the shutter, shooting in Continuous mode.

STEP 4 / **FOLLOW THROUGH**

Similar to a golf or tennis swing, it's essential to continue to pan with the subject even after you have released the shutter. This will ensure the motion blur is smooth from start to finish.

SHOOTING TECHNIQUE: ADVANCED TRACKING SHOT

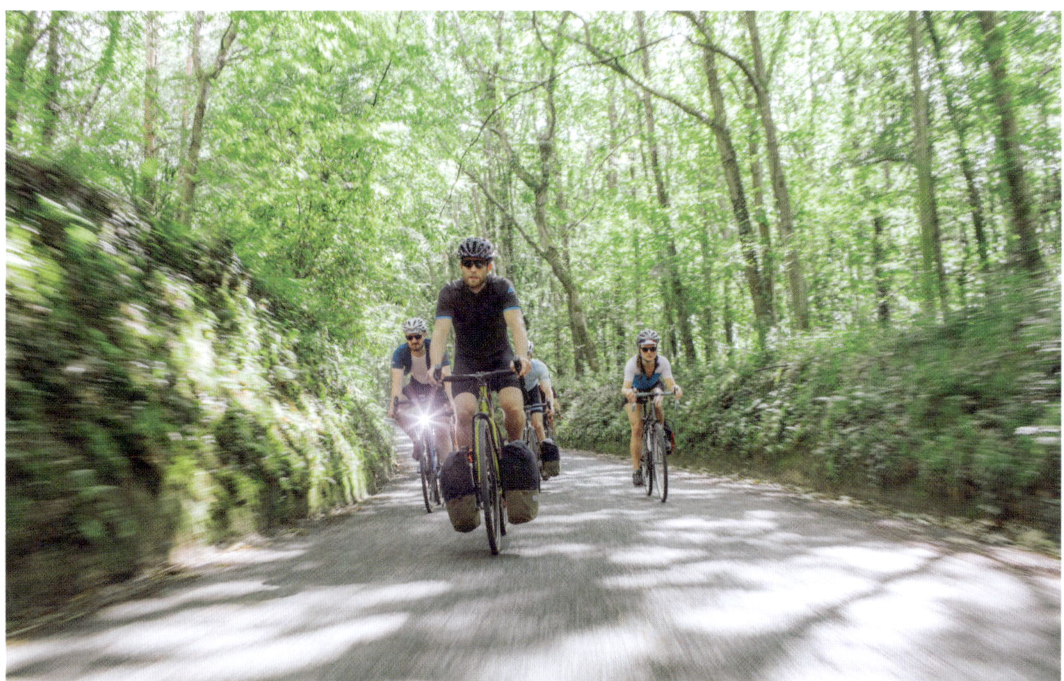

We've looked at panning, now I'll describe the second technique I use to evoke a sense of movement in my images.

To create this type of image, you'll need to shoot from a lead car travelling just in front of your subject, for example, another vehicle. Both vehicles need to be moving at the same speed along the road to ensure the subject stays sharp and the background blurs. The blurring effect provides a feeling of movement.

This technique works with any moving vehicle. The example above uses road bikes, but it's the same concept – a lead vehicle is travelling at the same speed and just ahead of the cyclists.

EXPERIMENT

There are a lot of variables at play with this technique, and you will need to tweak your camera settings, as well as adjust your driving speed and camera position until you get to the right place creatively. Approach it with an experimental attitude – it can be quite frustrating, but also a lot of fun.

Keep in mind that your main subject may never be completely sharp and in focus. This technique is more about generating a 'feeling' of movement and some blurring of your main subject can actually add to that feeling. It's a trial-and-error technique and you will undoubtedly start out with a bunch of poor shots, but the more you practice, the better you get.

Tracking shots are great for dropping your audience into the story and allowing them to feel a sense of speed or urgency. They work just as well if you're following a vehicle and shooting from behind, and in many ways this angle actually feels more natural for the viewer.

Exercise /

Tracking

1 Choose a wide-angle lens. The longer your lens, the more pronounced any camera shake will be – and when you're in the back of a car, you shake! Start at 24mm or 35mm.

2 Begin by matching your shutter speed with the speed you intend to travel, so if you're travelling at 40 miles an hour, try 1/40 sec. Put your camera into Shutter Priority mode, so your camera looks after your aperture settings should you change the shutter speed whilst tracking.

3 When in the back of the car, try to keep your camera as steady and low as possible. The lower you are to the road, the faster it will move past the camera and the more pronounced the blur. This is called 'road rush' in the business.

4 Adjust as you go. I find it helpful to work with walkie talkies so I can easily direct the driver in the subject vehicle – *'ease off the pedal please'* or *'drive 10 miles an hour faster'* and so on.

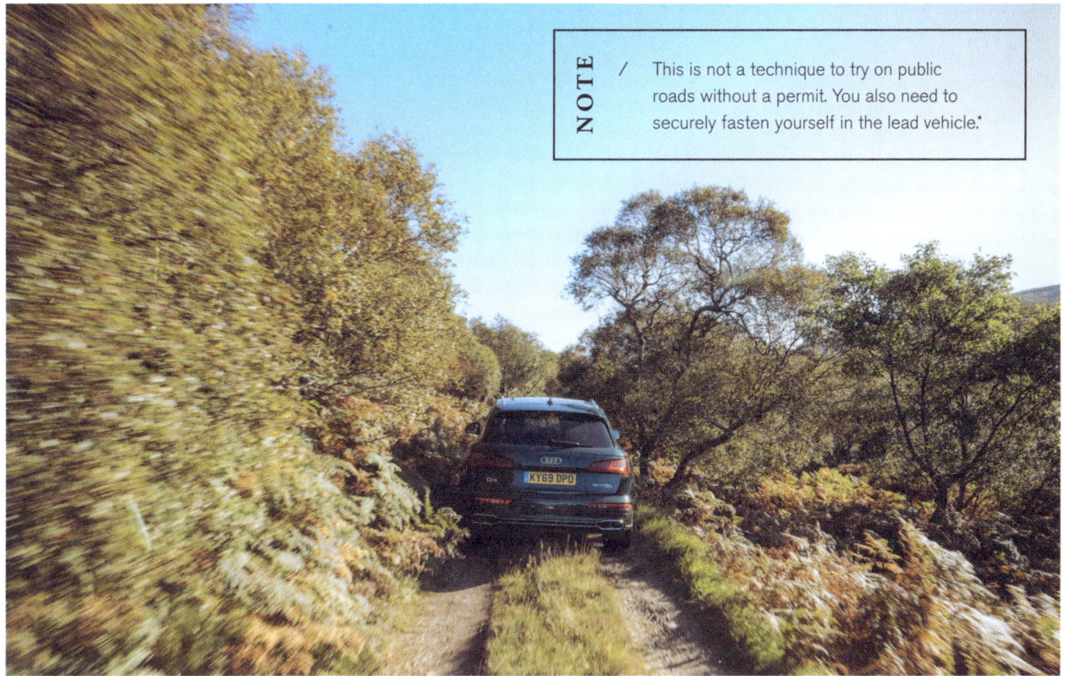

Do not fall out of a car. It won't end well.

SHOOTING TECHNIQUE: CINEMATIC

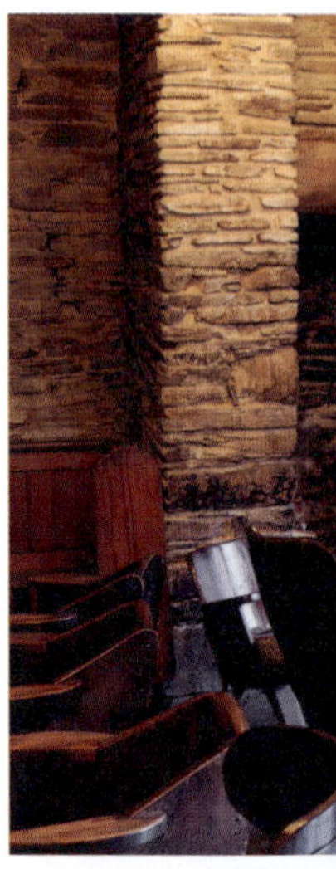

Let's talk about 'cinematics' for a second. What does it mean to you? The dictionary describes it as 'the atmosphere of watching a film, like in the cinema'. For me, the key word in that definition is 'atmosphere'.

Is it possible to bring movie-like atmosphere – and the depth of emotion that comes with it – into a still image? Of course it is. In this section I'm going to look at smoke, or haze; how it creates depth, how to make it and why it's one of my favourite techniques for bringing cinematics to a photograph.

HAZE

Compare the 'before and after' scenes on the the opposite page, which show the interior of a small pub I photographed in West Wales. I wanted to create a cosy vibe and asked the owners to light the fire and candles, but the scene still lacked atmosphere. We introduced a small amount of haze into the room before shining a light through the window from outside. I wanted to simulate the effect of the sun shining through the window, creating an 'end of the day' feeling. The introduction of haze diffuses the window light, softening it as though it were golden hour (see page 103). It also has a three-dimensional effect via the streaks or visible light rays. The audience can 'see the light', giving the image more depth, atmosphere and emotion.

EQUIPMENT

Adding a layer of haze to the interior of a building is a fun place to start if you're new to the technique. You don't need costly equipment because you are working in a relatively small space and won't require a massive amount of haze to benefit from its effect. Professional haze machines are expensive, but you can get similar results using lower budget fog machines. These tend to pump out a lot of smoke (initially too thick to shoot through), but a bit of 'wafting' from a friend will disperse the smoke and give you the effect you need.

Another approach is to buy haze in a can. Search online for 'synthetic smoke in an aerosol can' and you will find plenty of options from various manufactures.

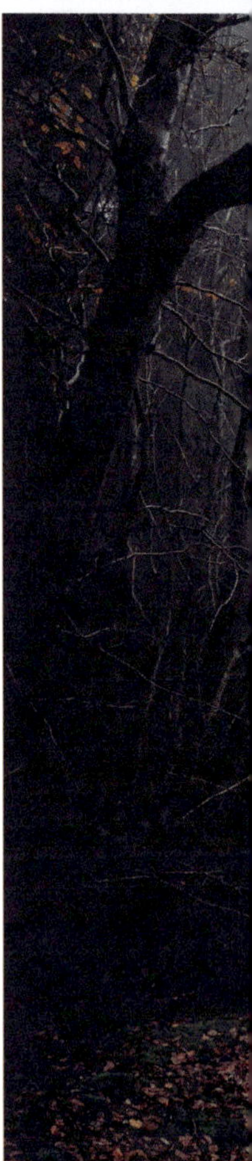

TIP / Hazing brings a new physical element to a scene, adding texture and depth. Hanging in the air, the particles act as a diffuser, spreading light and softening the image recorded by a camera's sensor. You can also use haze to show a viewer where a light source is coming from.

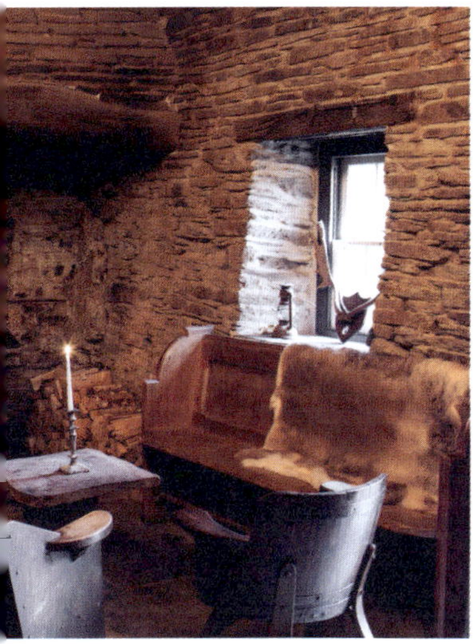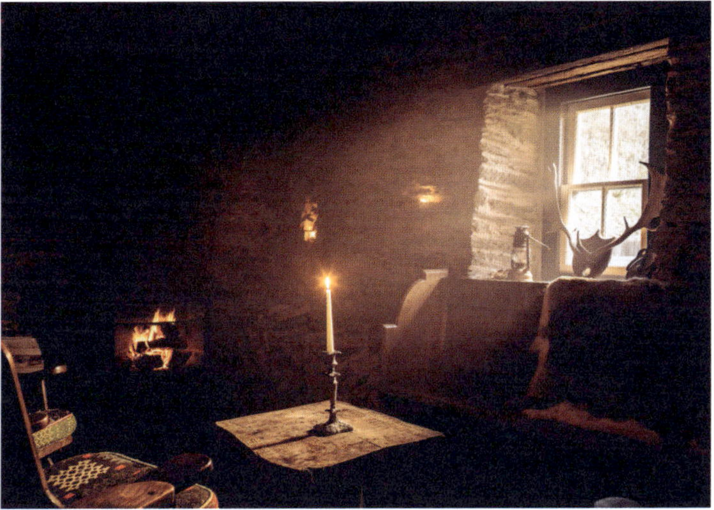

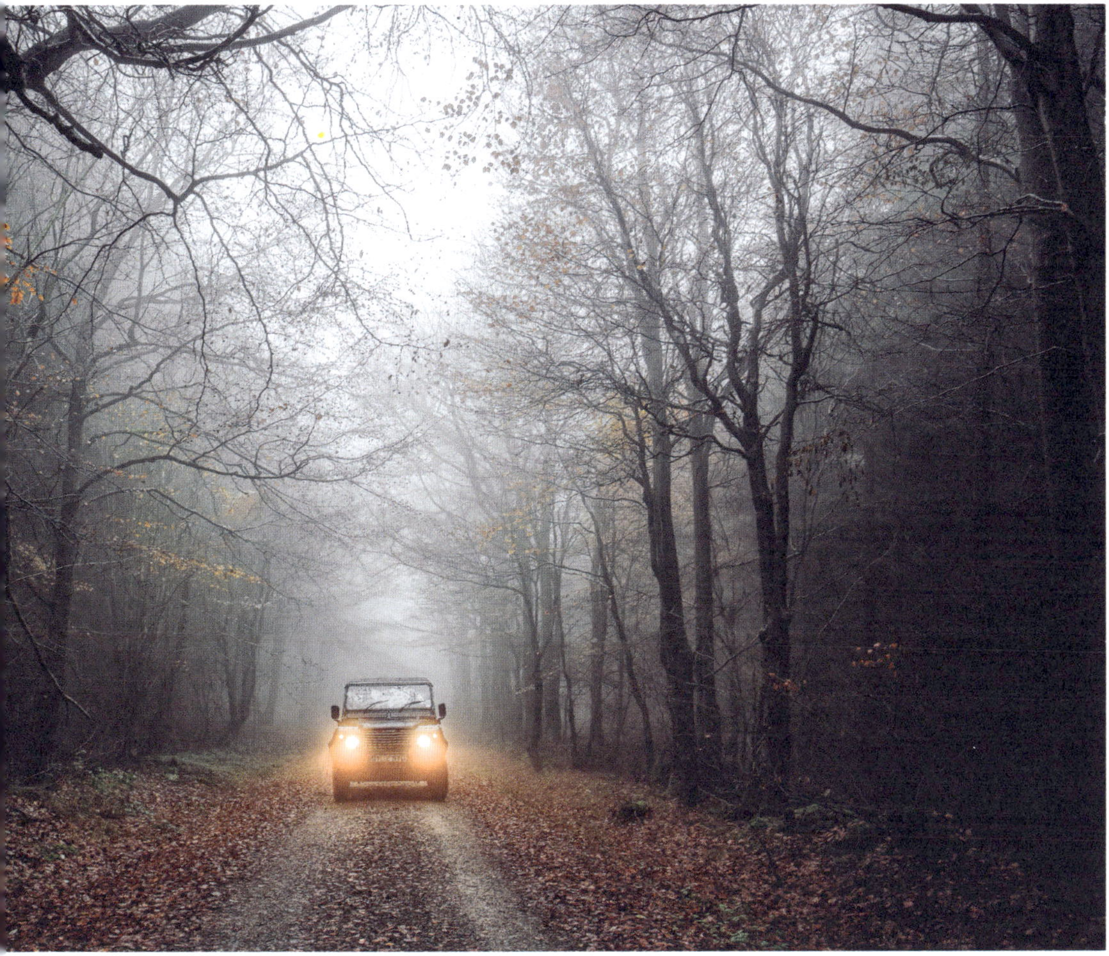

Project /

Dreamlike Scenes with Lens Flare

+ Capture lens flare to give a hazy, dreamlike feel to your image.

+ A strong light source e.g. sunlight, street lights or flash.

+ A wide-angle zoom lens.

+ Old lenses without anti-reflective coatings.

+ Objects in front of the lens to obsure the light source.

+ Learn to control lens flare and use the effect creatively to enhance your images.

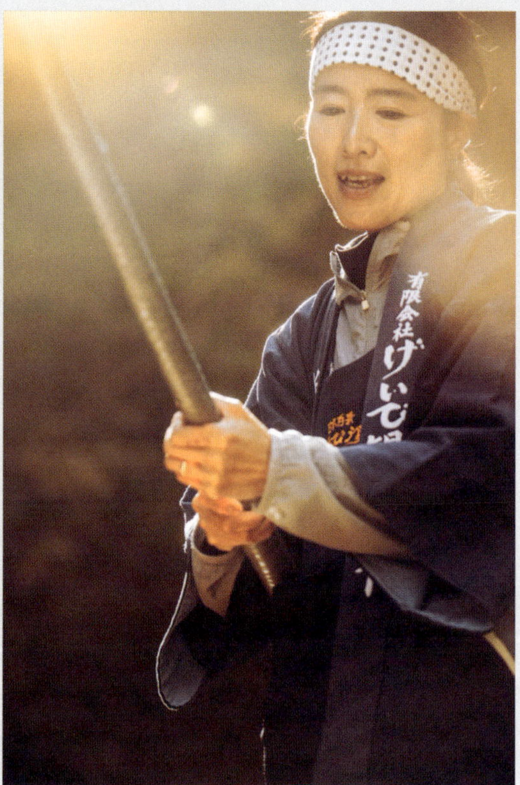

Lens flare portrait with a magical quality

Lens flare is usually created when either non-image-forming light hits the front of the lens and reaches the film or sensor, or you have a strong light source in the frame. The result can be distinct, bright polygons appearing across an image and/or an overall reduction in contrast. Lens flare is usually considered a flaw, but can also be used intentionally to bring a distinct feeling to an image.

You need a reliable light source, and the sun is the obvious choice here, but it is also possible to create flares using streetlights or even a candle in a low-lit room. This is one of the rare occasions when I would recommend a zoom lens over a prime because a fixed focal length is less susceptible to the effect. Zooms are complicated internally and have more surfaces from which light can reflect and bounce.

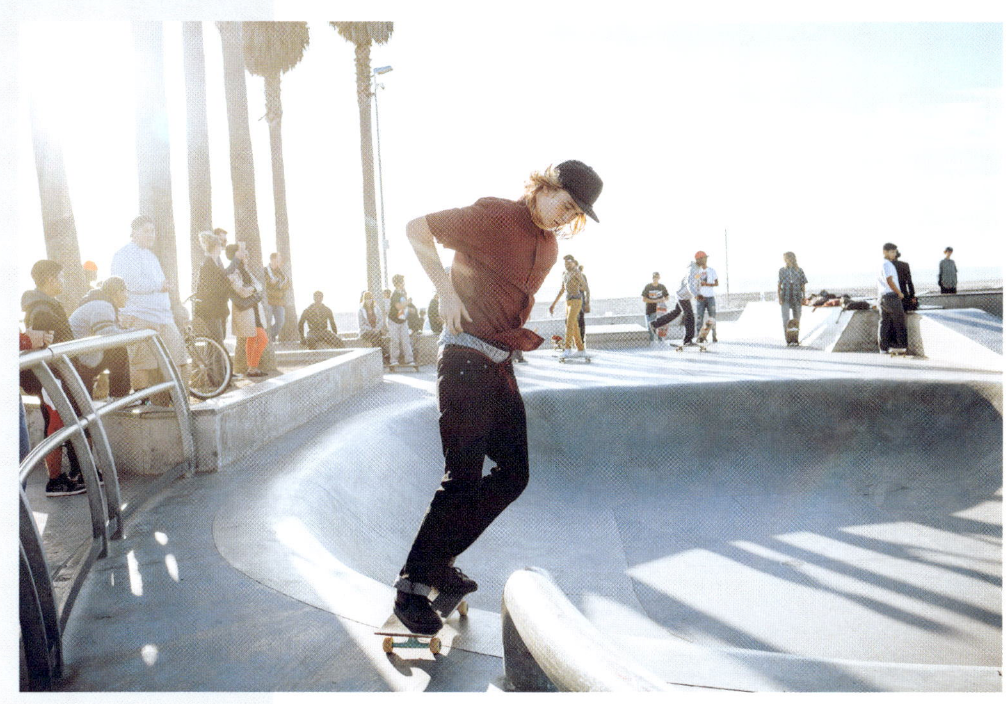

Hazy effect and subtle artefacts produced by shooting into the sun.

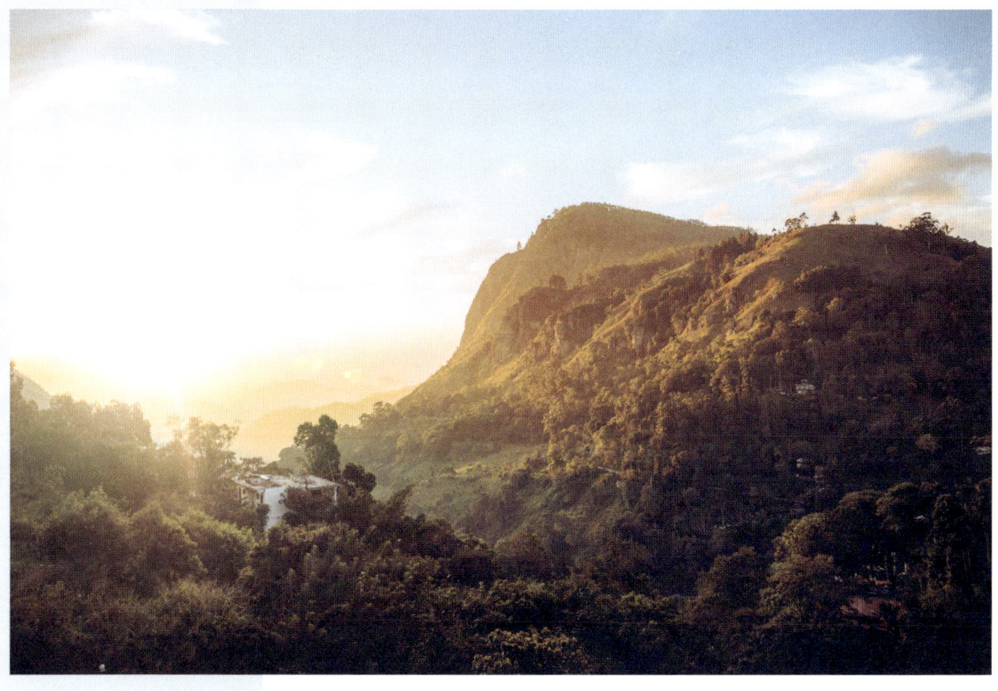

Starburst shape created by shooting into the sun with a small aperture.

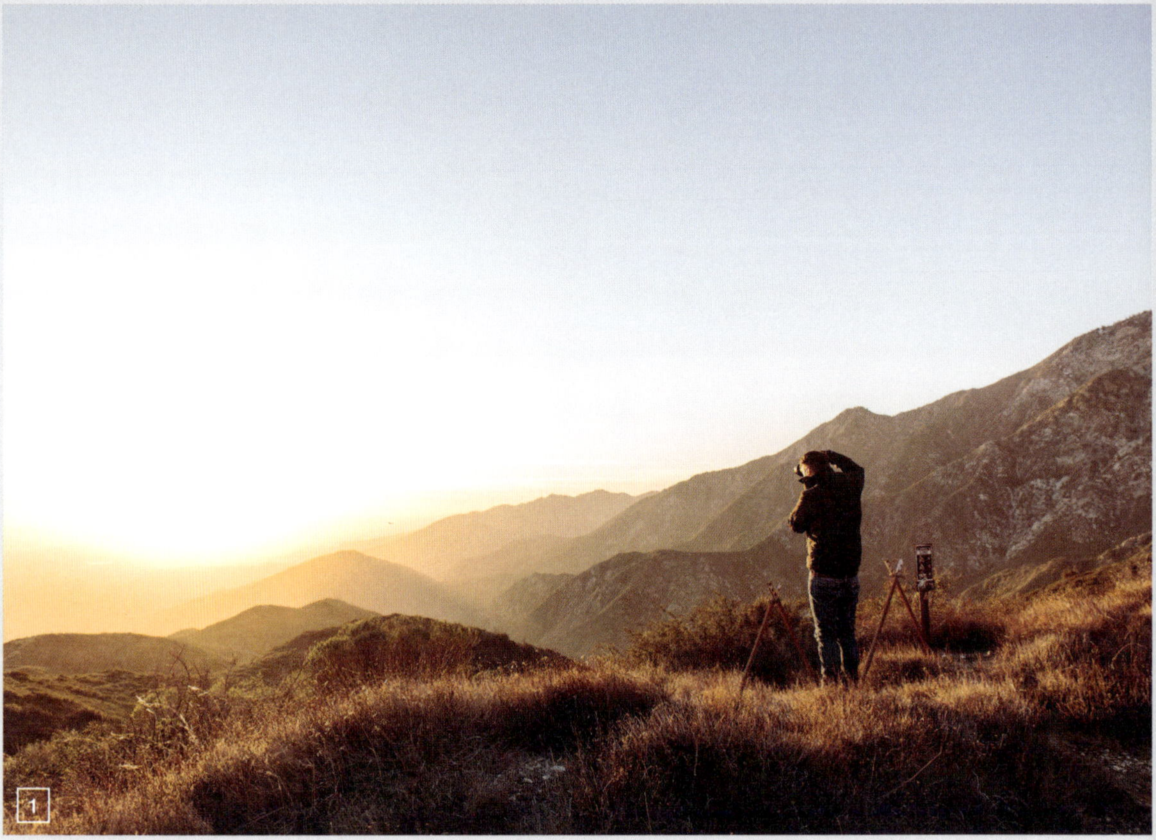

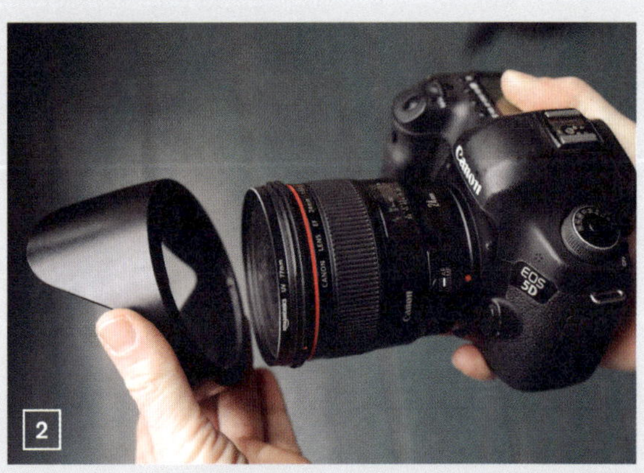

STEP 1 / **POSITION**

Shoot directly towards the light source, but be careful if you're shooting towards the sun. I think the best effects are to be had when the sun is low in the sky; this also minimises the risk of blindness!

STEP 2 / **CAMERA**

Remove the lens hood, as this is designed specifically to reduce flare caused by stray light entering the lens from outside the angle of view.

STEP 3 / **LENS**

Use a wide-angle lens. An older lens without anti-reflective coatings can deliver better effects.

STEP 4 / **APERTURE**

To create starbursts, close down your aperture. The smaller you make your aperture, the more pronounced the starburst effect. Try setting your aperture to f/22.

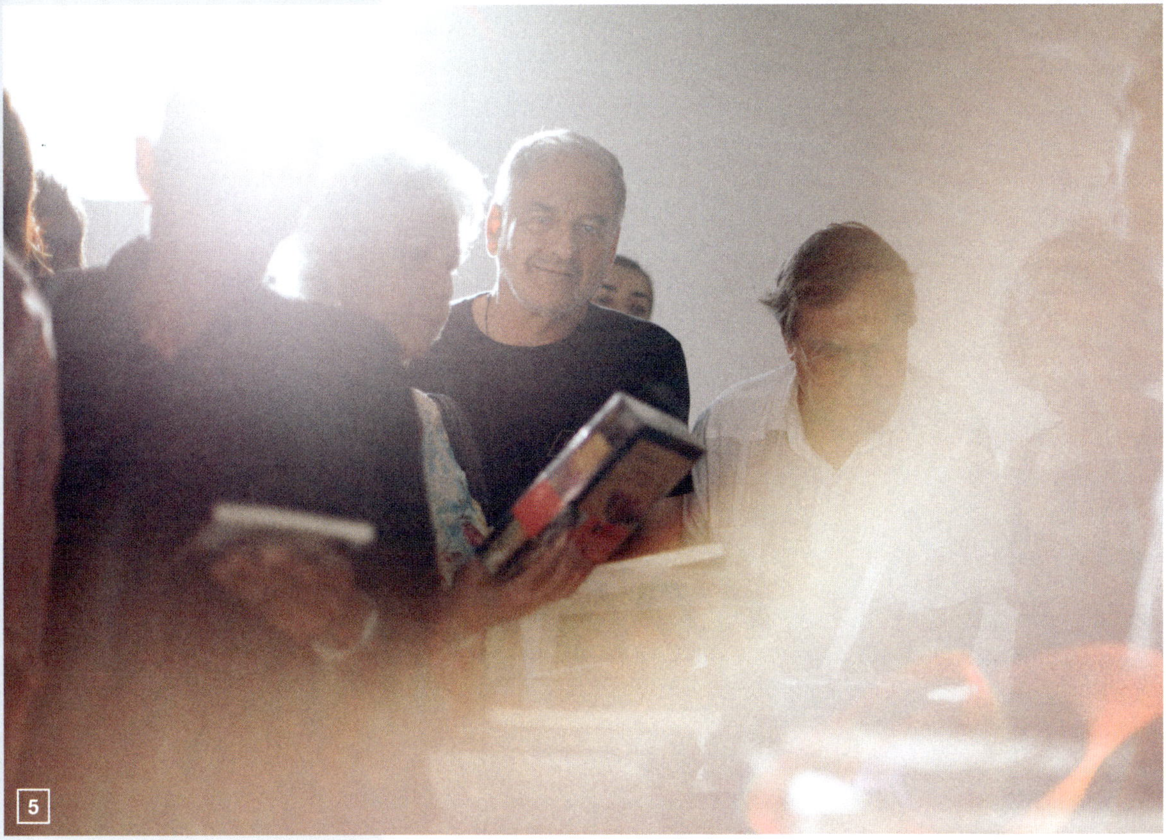

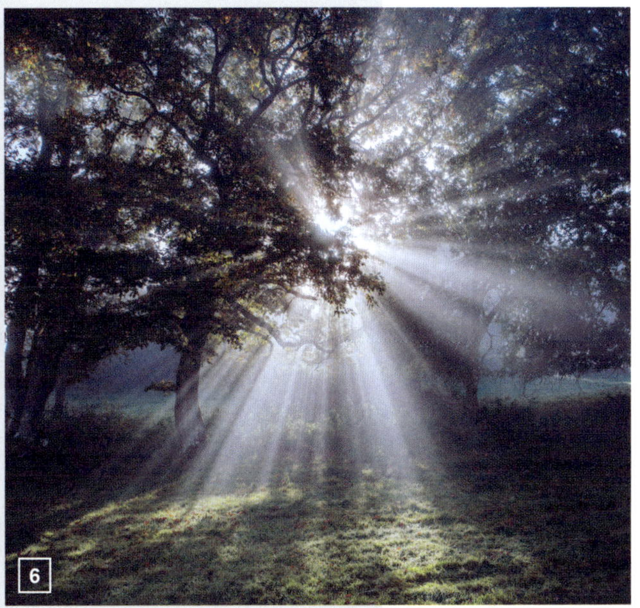

STEP 5 / **HAZE**

You will need to use a wide aperture to create a dreamlike haze. Something like f/3.2 will keep the subject in focus while hazing out background details.

STEP 6 / **FLARE**

The amount of flare is ultimately based on where the lens is pointed and what is included within the frame. Try partially blocking the light source with your subject for more creative compositions.

STEP 7 / **FOCUS**

Switch to manual focus. When shooting into a bright source your camera can have trouble focusing. Trust your eyes instead.

SHOOTING TECHNIQUE: DIRTY FOREGROUND

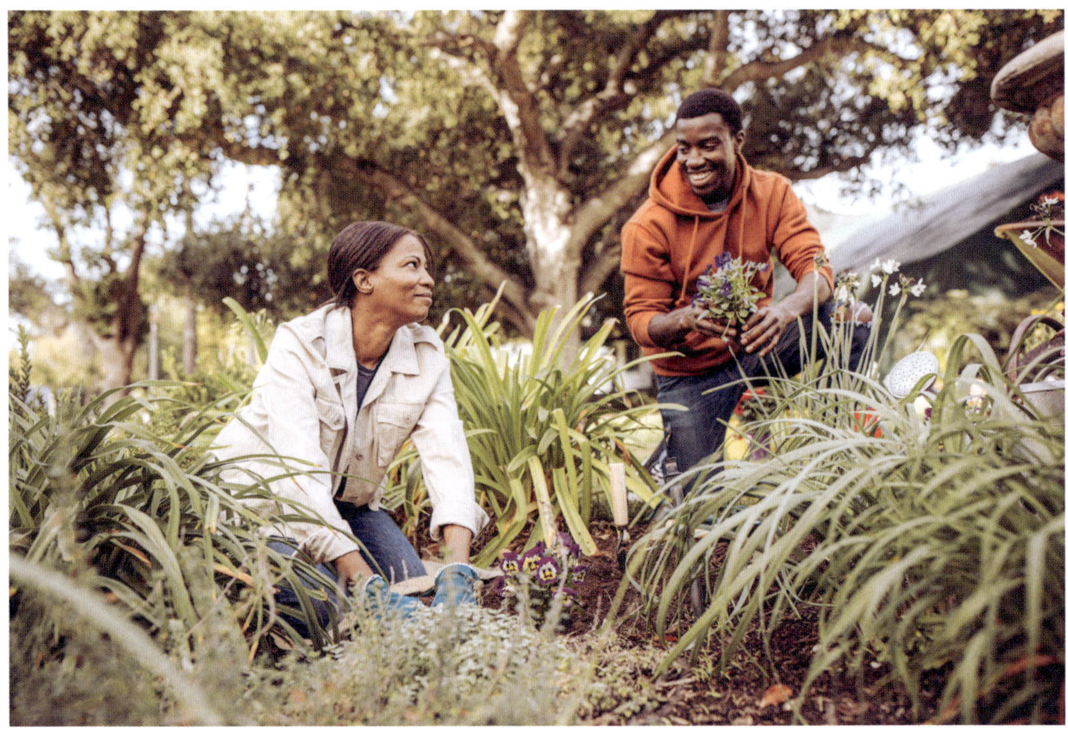

Photographs are two-dimensional – they have an _x_ and a _y_ axis – so I'm always looking for leading lines that create a third axis, or dimension. In a landscape, this might be a river, road, shoreline or the edge of a forest that leads the eye into the image. But how do you add depth to a tighter frame, such as those involving people? Enter the 'dirty foreground'.

My first lesson in photography was from my grandfather when I was eight years old, and it was in 'dirtying the frame'. He taught me that adding something in the foreground is a great way to make a two-dimensional image appear more three-dimensional, as well as creating a 'fly on the wall' effect. It gives the viewer the impression they are looking in on a scene, helping to raise the sense of realism.

Shooting a scene with a wide aperture will help throw foreground elements out of focus and ensure they don't distract from the main subject. I like to shoot at f/3.5 and bring foreground elements very close to the lens – to capture the image above of a mother and son gardening, I lay in the vegetation and shot through it.

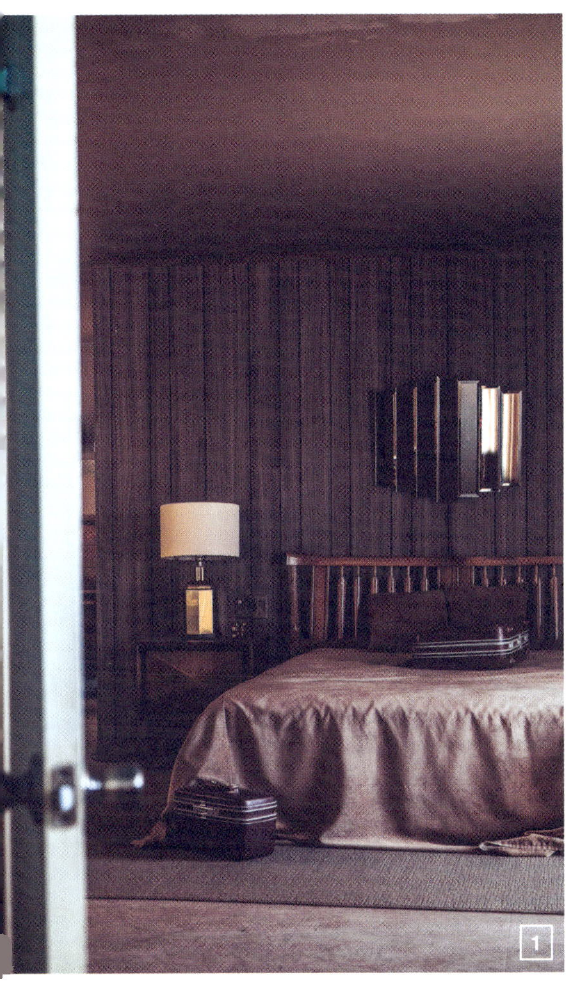

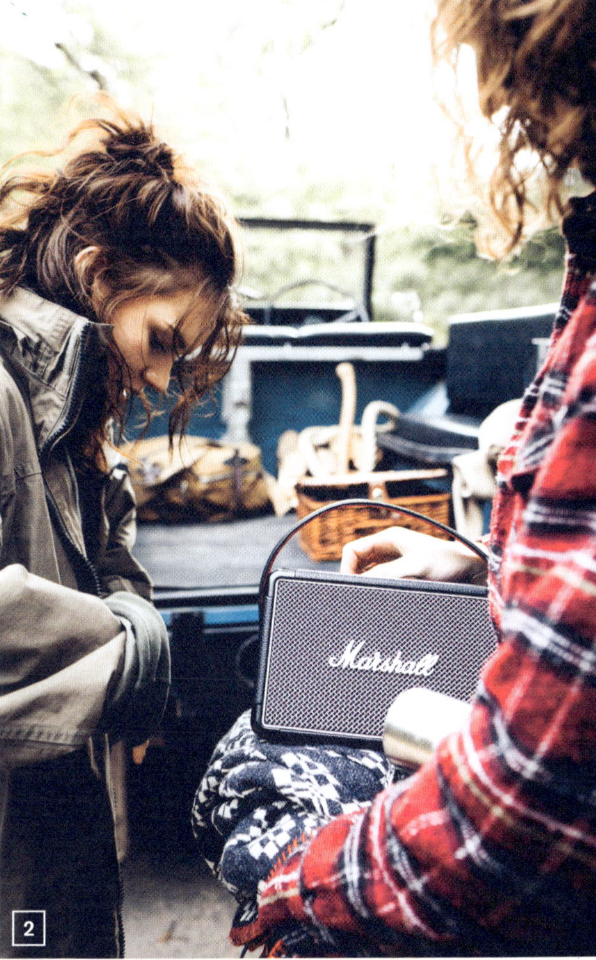

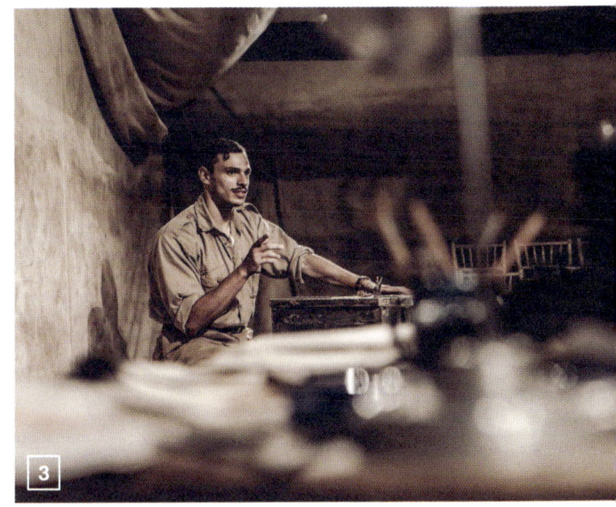

Here are some more examples where the foreground element brings something to each image.

1 *Shooting through a doorway gives the viewer a sense that they are being 'let into a secret' or seeing something that perhaps they shouldn't. It has a voyeuristic effect.*

2 *Shooting over a person's shoulder places the viewer into a scene, and leads the eye. In this image I chose to dirty the frame with my model's arm, which at the same time leads the eye to the product. Guess who the client was!*

3 *Here, blurred foreground imagery frames the subject, providing a frame within a frame.*

Step 4: Edit

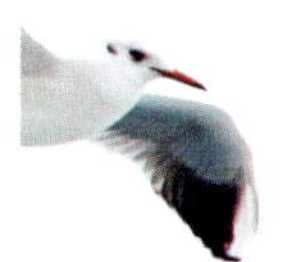

Welcome to the edit suite! I really love this part of my job, as it's where I get to actually work with the photographs captured on shoot day and really begin to pull a story together.

In this chapter, we'll run through the basics, like importing images from your card into Lightroom, establishing naming conventions, folder structures and using rating systems. We'll also touch on colour grading within Lightroom, creating presets and adding film-inspired imperfections. We'll then finish with a relatively detailed and crucial section on backing up your images.

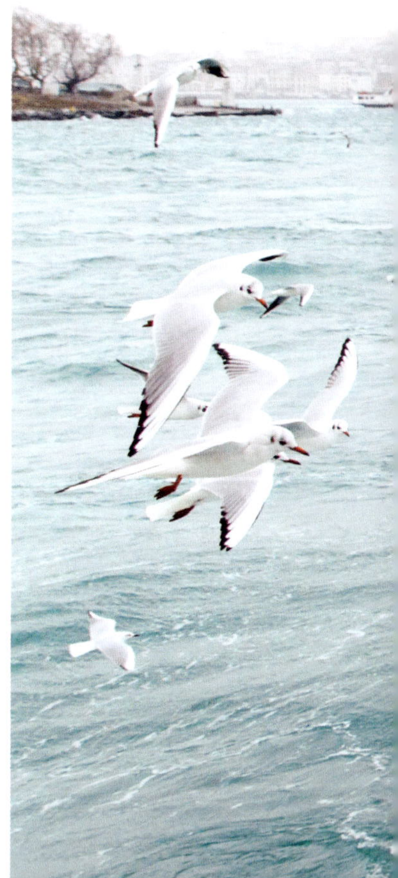

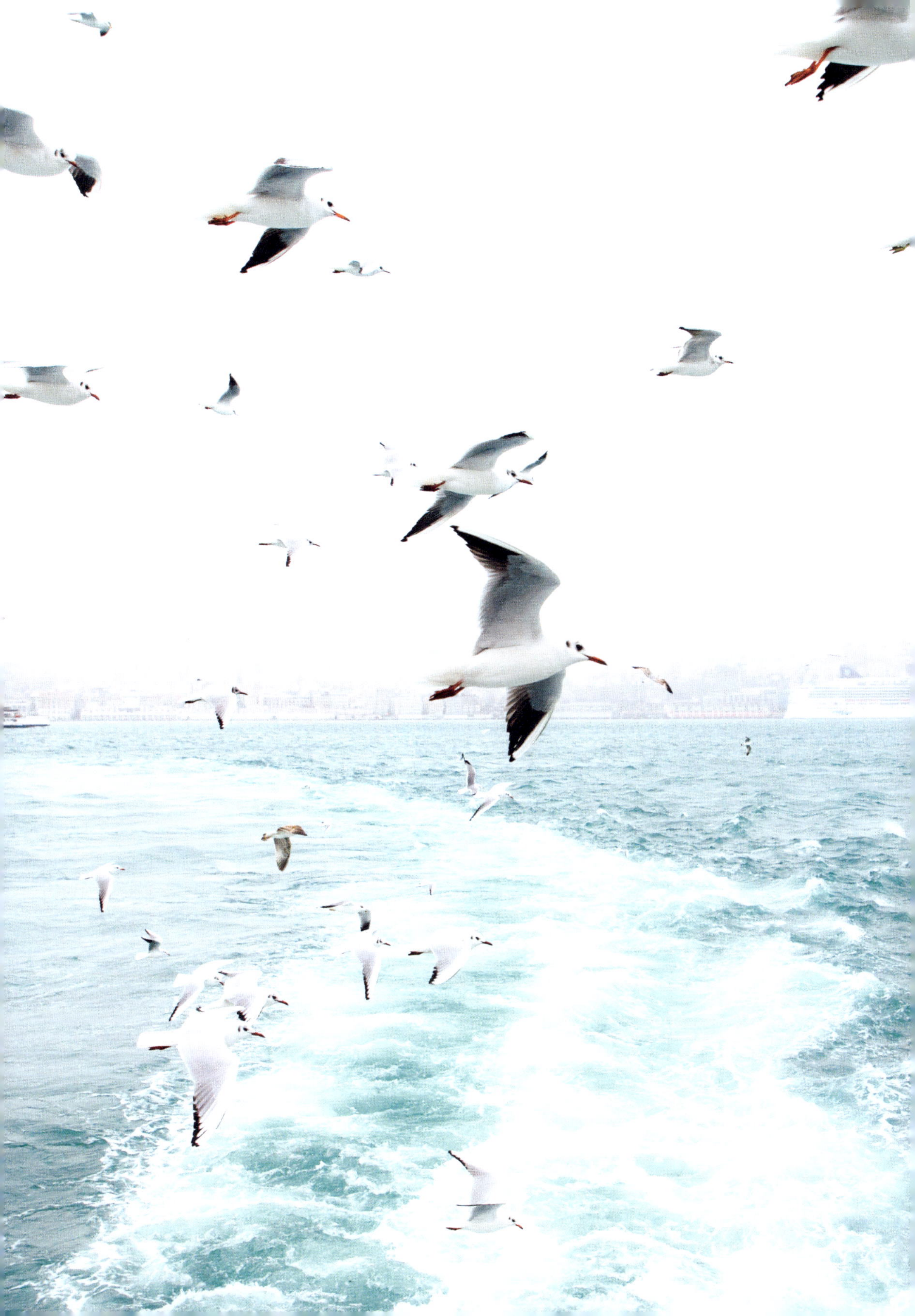

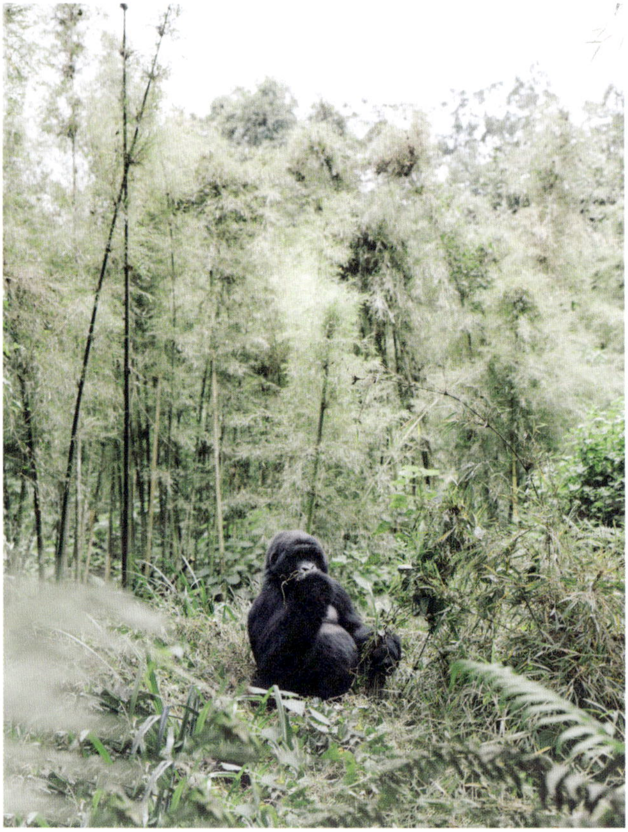

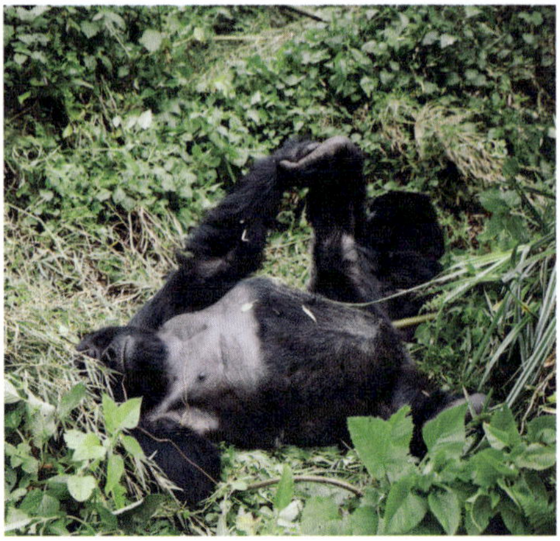

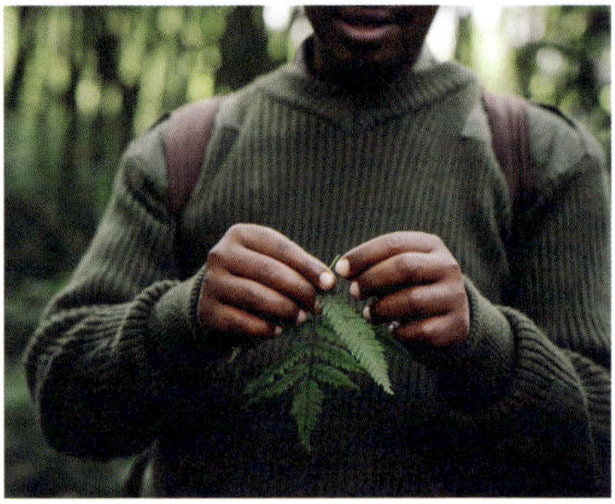

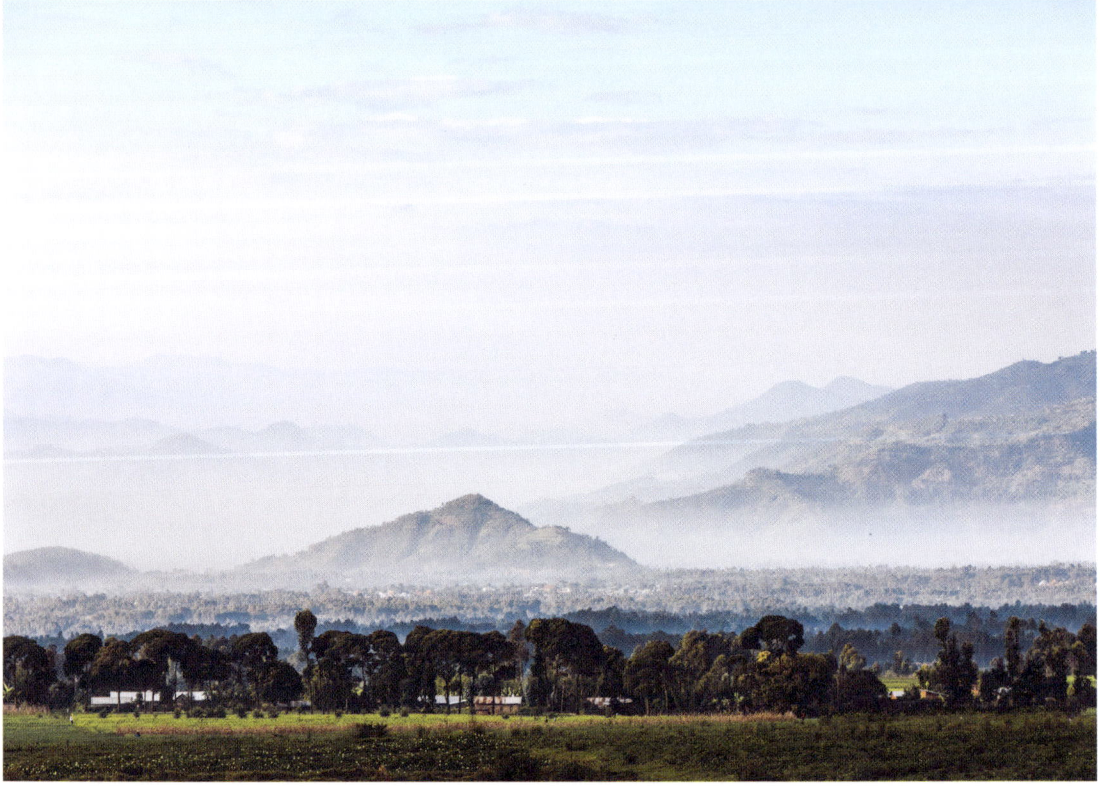

SAVE TIME:
ORGANISE YOUR IMAGES

Before you can do anything with your images, you need to pull them off your camera or phone and get them into your computer.

LIGHTROOM

Let's walk through the process I use for importing images from my card into my favourite image catalogue software called Adobe Lightroom. It is the best software I have found to view, maintain and edit images from a shoot, and it works hand-in-hand with Photoshop for more advanced retouching.

Split into seven different modules – Library, Develop, Map, Book, Slideshow, Print and Web – it's a powerful piece of software, but if I'm honest, I only ever use the first two!

LIBRARY

The Library module is where you manage your archive and is the first port of call when importing images from a camera or phone. There is no limit to the number of images you can import into a catalogue, so it's tempting to use one catalogue for your entire archive. However, I recommend using a separate catalogue for each shoot, as I have experienced speed issues with the one-catalogue approach in the past. Plus, if it corrupts it could take down your entire archive.

SAVING CATALOGUES

I create a new catalogue per shoot and I save it in two places: first in a Dropbox folder, which keeps a copy on my hard drive, and then as a backup in the Cloud. This allows me to work across multiple computers and keep the catalogue in sync, regardless of which computer or location I'm working from. Any changes made on my iMac at the office will sync to my MacBook at home because the catalogue is stored in the Cloud.

NAMING CONVENTIONS

I keep a consistent naming convention for each catalogue:

WORK-YEARMONTH-CLIENT-CAMPAIGN

For example:

WORK-201805-AUDI-RWANDA

I follow the same naming convention for storing the Raw assets (images) which sit on an external hard drive called a NAS, which automatically uploads them to Amazon Cloud Drive – (more on this on page 159).

Within each shoot folder, I also make four or five other folders for storing the original Raw files and retouched assets for quick retrieval at a later date.

CAPTURE – where I will import all of my raw files.
DRONE – for any images or video shot from the sky.
2500px – for any retouched JPEGs output at that size.
4000px – for any retouched JPEGs output at that size.

Start by importing your images from your memory card or phone into the Capture folder so you can begin editing in Lightroom. It's worth renaming your files at this point using the same naming convention as above:

YEARMONTH-CLIENTNAME-NAMEOFSHOOT-01.JPG
YEARMONTH-CLIENTNAME-NAMEOFSHOOT-02.JPG
YEARMONTH-CLIENTNAME-NAMEOFSHOOT-03.JPG

A tidy ship is a happy ship!

MAKING YOUR SELECTS

Before we begin retouching or colour grading images, we need to narrow down our selection to the very best images from the shoot. This is called 'making selects' and I use a three-pass approach to filter down the pictures from a shoot.

FIRST PASS

Put Lightroom into Loupe mode ('E' on the keyboard) and use the arrow keys to make the first pass through the Capture folder. This first pass should be fairly intuitive – don't think too hard, just a simple yes/no approach at this stage. Does the composition work? Yes. Is it out of focus? No. Barrel through and use the 'P' key to make your 'picks'. Anything that doesn't make the grade (misfires, out-of-focus shots and so on) can be rejected using the 'X' key.

SECOND PASS

Next, click the small flag symbol to filter the catalogue according to your picks. Lightroom will show only the images you flagged as a pick. Work through the catalogue again, this time giving images you like best one star. You might find you flagged multiple photos of the same subject in the same pass but now you're taking a closer look, so choose which of the variations you like best.

THIRD PASS

Once you've gone through the catalogue and rated everything worthy of one star, return to the Grid view ('G' on the keyboard) and filter the library to a more manageable size. Make a third pass through your selects, paying even closer attention to them. Filter out duplicates and rate the best images with two stars.

COLOUR LABELS

At this point I'll introduce a colour labelling system which I use to filter all my two-star photos into specific shot types, as discussed on pages 40–45.

- **Red** denotes a cutaway – 6 on the keyboard.
- **Yellow** denotes a close-up shot – 7 on the keyboard.
- **Green** denotes a medium or a medium close shot – 8 on the keyboard.
- **Blue** denotes a long shot – 9 on the keyboard.

Now, when I'm building my story and I need a cutaway scene, I can filter the entire catalogue based on that type of shot.

SAVING TIME

Although this might feel like a lot of work up front, when you're working with a lot of images and you want to retrieve things quickly, it's invaluable in terms of time management, especially if you're coming back to a catalogue months down the line.

Often, clients or magazines will be looking for a specific style of image and will do a call out to photographers. Having a system in place that allows you to open up a catalogue months after a shoot has been archived and retrieve images very, very quickly will save you time. Remember: time is money when you work as a freelancer.

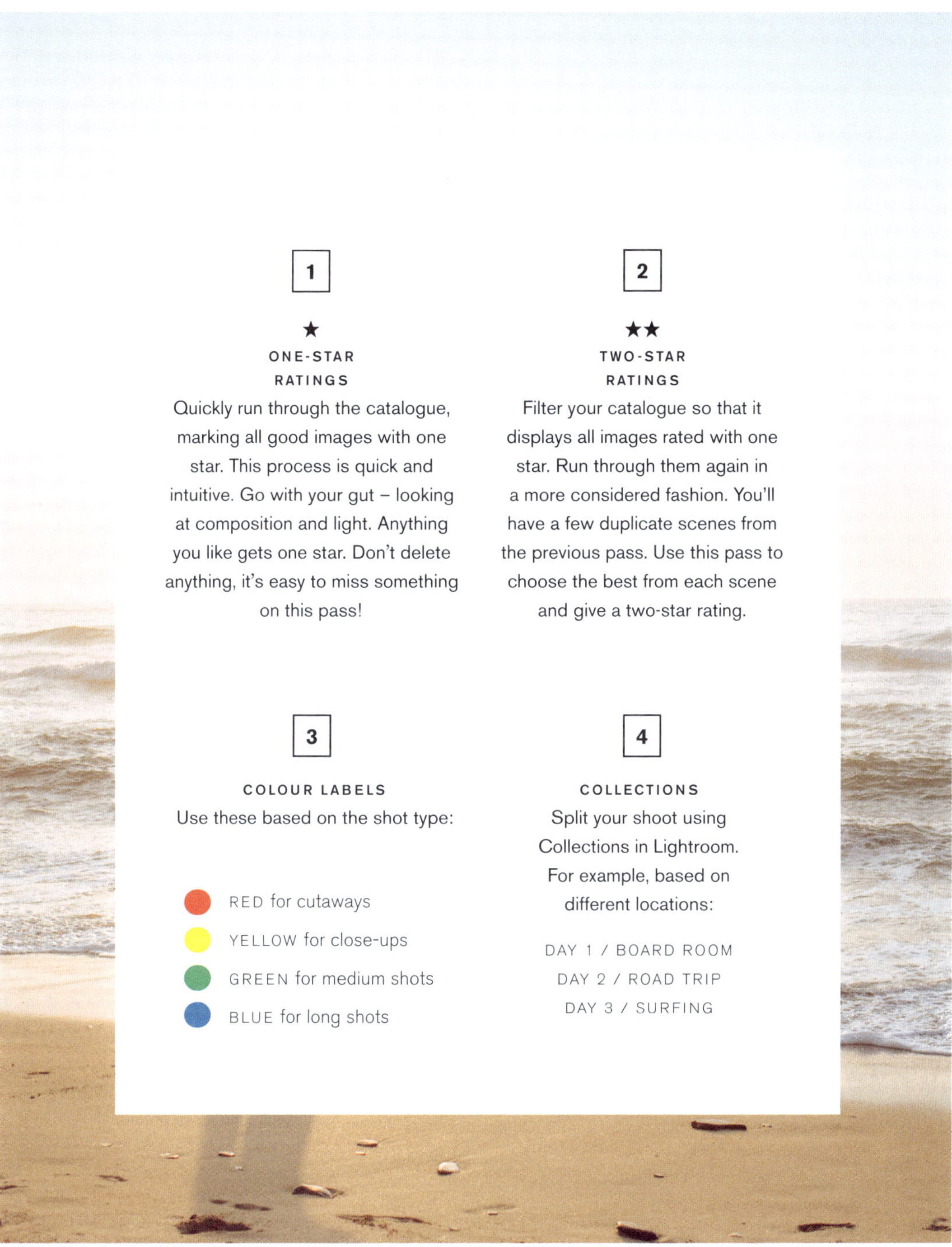

1

★

**ONE-STAR
RATINGS**

Quickly run through the catalogue,
marking all good images with one
star. This process is quick and
intuitive. Go with your gut – looking
at composition and light. Anything
you like gets one star. Don't delete
anything, it's easy to miss something
on this pass!

2

★★

**TWO-STAR
RATINGS**

Filter your catalogue so that it
displays all images rated with one
star. Run through them again in
a more considered fashion. You'll
have a few duplicate scenes from
the previous pass. Use this pass to
choose the best from each scene
and give a two-star rating.

3

COLOUR LABELS
Use these based on the shot type:

RED for cutaways

YELLOW for close-ups

GREEN for medium shots

BLUE for long shots

4

COLLECTIONS
Split your shoot using
Collections in Lightroom.
For example, based on
different locations:

DAY 1 / BOARD ROOM

DAY 2 / ROAD TRIP

DAY 3 / SURFING

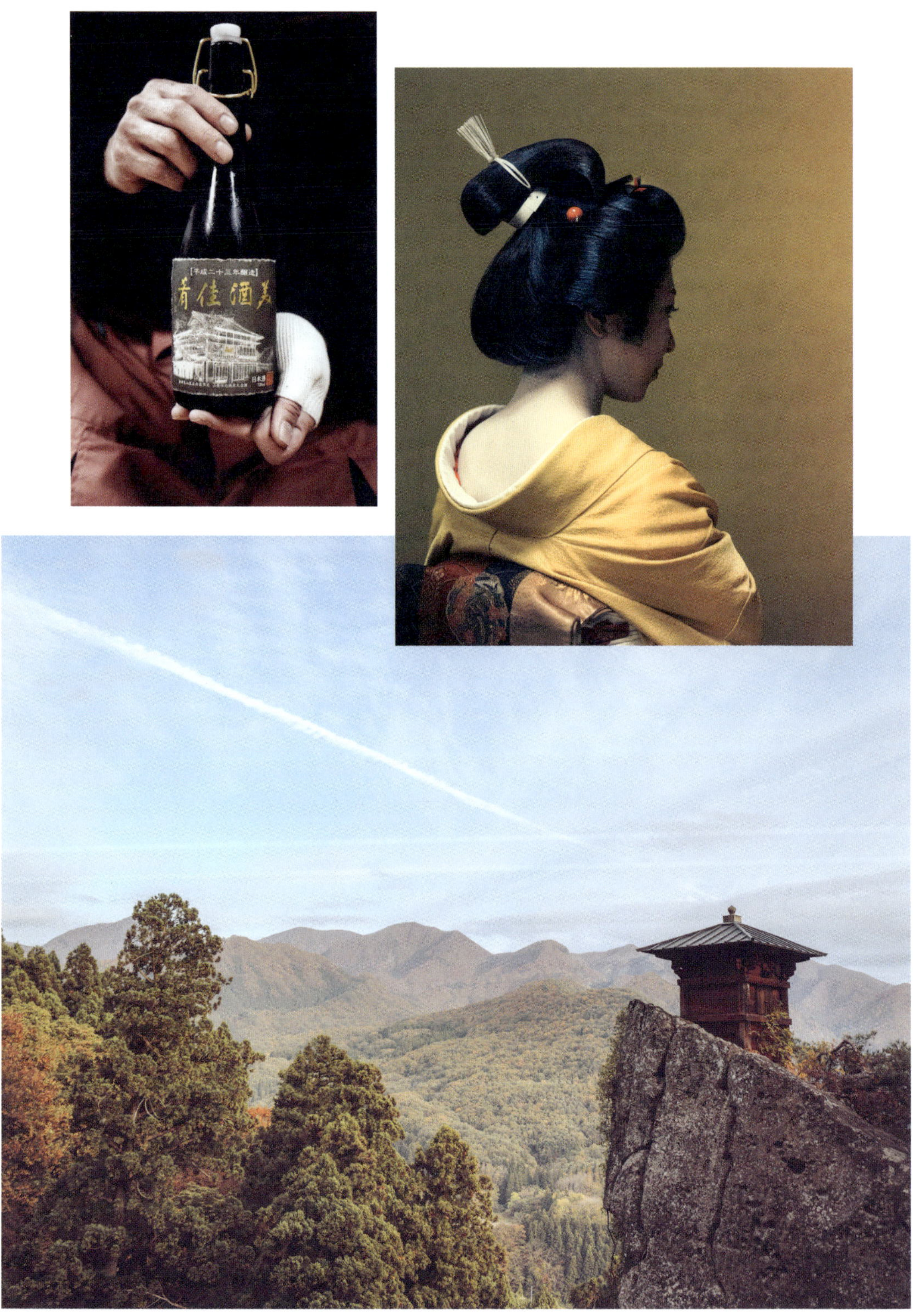

LIGHTROOM COLLECTIONS

Once you have rated and colour-coded your images, you can use Lightroom's Collections feature to group images together without moving them on your hard drive.

Collections are virtual folders, which can be super useful for pulling out images from a shoot for clients, social channels or your website.

It's also worth quickly mentioning Smart Collections here. These are collections automatically populated according to specified criteria. I use them in tandem with my colour-labelling system to pool images from a catalogue according to shot type. I store Smart Collections inside a Collection Set called, you guessed it, 'Shot Types'.

Exercise /
Making Collections

1 Click on 'Collections +' to create a new collection and give it a name (Website selects, Facebook post, etc.).

2 Check the 'Set as target collection' box and return to Loupe mode ('E'), adding images to your newly created collection using the 'B' key. Press Shift + Tab to hide all the panels and maximise the viewing area.

3 Select all images (Cmd + A) while in Grid mode and hit 'N' to show your selection in Survey mode.

4 You can now drag the images around, creating a new order, and you'll begin to understand how images will look when paired against each other. I like to knock out the background by turning the lights out – hit the 'L' key twice.

5 Remove any images you don't want using the X in the bottom right corner of an image. Don't worry, they are only removed from this view, not from Lightroom and not from your disk.

6 Move images around and see what works best, filtering down your selects according to the task in hand. The example opposite is a Facebook post, and I decided to go with three images – one wide, one close-up and one medium shot. When viewed together at a glance they tell an intriguing story that should pull in viewers to find out more.

GRADING:
BASIC ADJUSTMENTS

Once you've narrowed down your catalogue, you can begin processing images within Lightroom using the Develop module. Before I go anywhere with my edit, I like to have an idea of my endpoint, rather than just flinging sliders around, and that's based on a couple of factors:

- **Where the image is going to sit within the story.**
- **The lighting conditions in the scene.**

As an example, I'm going to use an image from the board-shaping room from the Cool & Vintage shoot. It was lit by fluorescent light and I think it's a good one to start with because the lighting conditions are far from ideal. The fluorescent bulbs give out an icy glow. The whole scene feels quite industrial, almost sci-fi in nature, so it makes sense to play on that when it comes to the colour grade.

Let's also think about where this image is going to sit within my photo story. I know from storyboarding that the endpoint will be on a beach at the close of the day, which is going to be really beautiful because of the orange and pinks of the sunset. So, how can I oppose that orange and pink colourway?

If we look at a colour wheel, the opposite colour to orange is blue – the hue of fluorescent light. Blue and orange are complementary colours, so I know they're going to work well together.

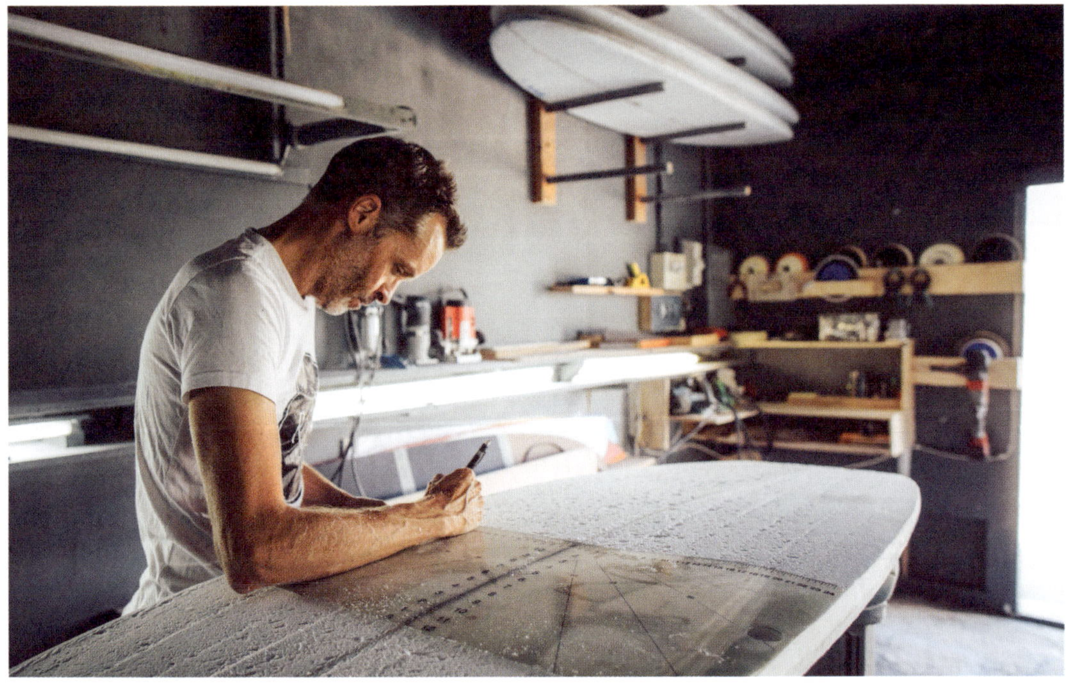

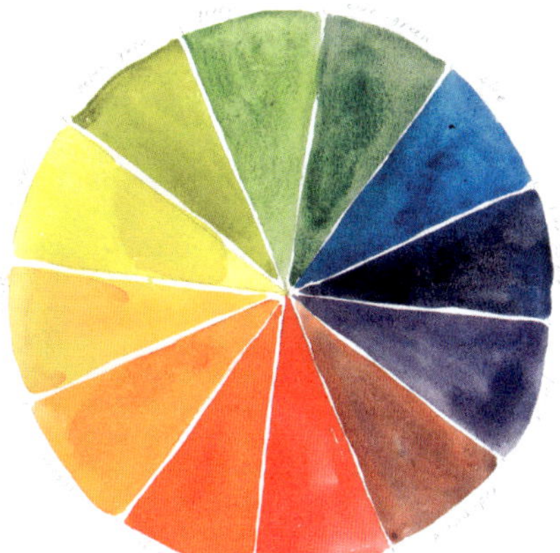

Complementary colours sit opposite each other on the colour wheel.

Let's begin at the top of the panel and work through the tools at hand:

1 Histogram

2 Basic

3 Tone Curve

4 HSL

5 Split Toning

HISTOGRAM

The Histogram panel is essentially a graph depicting the brightness levels of a photograph. The left side of the histogram shows the dark areas of the image all the way to black, the right side shows the lightest areas all the way to white and the middle shows the mid-tones.

I can see from the histogram (below right) that although this is a fairly dark image (most of the graph is weighted to the left) the highlights were 'clipped' because they bleed off the edge of the graph. In Lighroom, click 'Show highlight clipping' by hitting the triangle to the right of the histogram and you can see precisely where on the image it's happening. In the image opposite, it's caused by a fluorescent strip light running through the middle of the frame.

Clipping means that due to the intensity of light (or lack of it for clipped shadows), there is no image information left to display. It often occurs in highlights when the photograph has been overexposed. It's a problem because it can lead to a lack of detail across large areas of the image.

In the example, middle right, the sky has been clipped to white. Thankfully the Raw file format is forgiving and it is often possible to bring detail back to an image by using the highlights slider.

BASIC

I make most colour tweaks using the Tone Curve and HSL panel, so the Basic panel is reserved for levelling out the shadows, bringing back the highlights, bringing up the blacks, dropping the clarity down, and also, dropping the saturation.

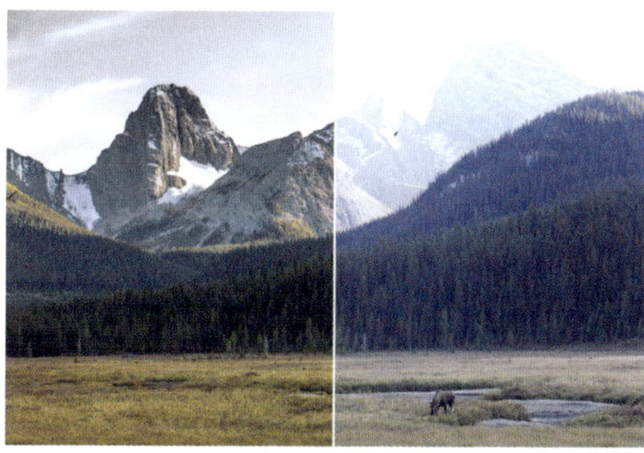

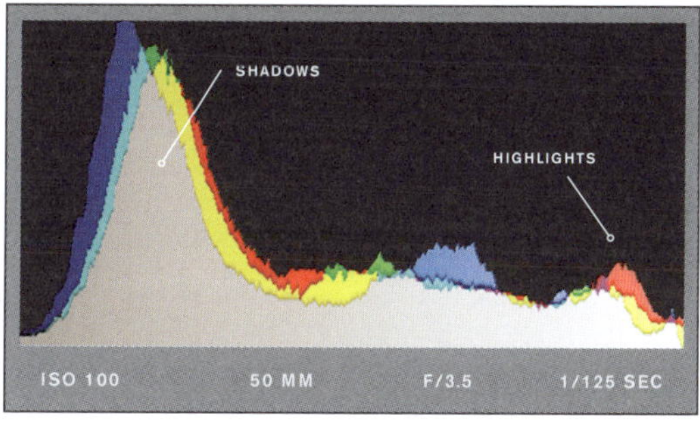

The Tone Curve panel is where most of the colour grade is applied. The curve can be thought of as an advanced contrast slider. It allows you to make micro-adjustments to the brightness of specific tones within an image.

I also use the RGB curve to fade darker areas of an image. When images are printed on uncoated paper stock, shaded areas can look a little faded as the paper soaks up the ink. I like the effect. However, if an image is destined for screen only, I need to simulate the effect and can do so using the tone curve.

Another common technique is to apply an S-curve. This is where you manipulate the shape of the curve to replicate the letter 'S'. Drag the lower third of the line down and raise the upper third. This intensifies the shadows and lightens the brighter areas of the image. It essentially adds contrast to the image and helps it pop, as shown opposite.

Changes to the bottom half of the curve will affect the shadows of an image and changes to the top half of the curve will affect the highlights.

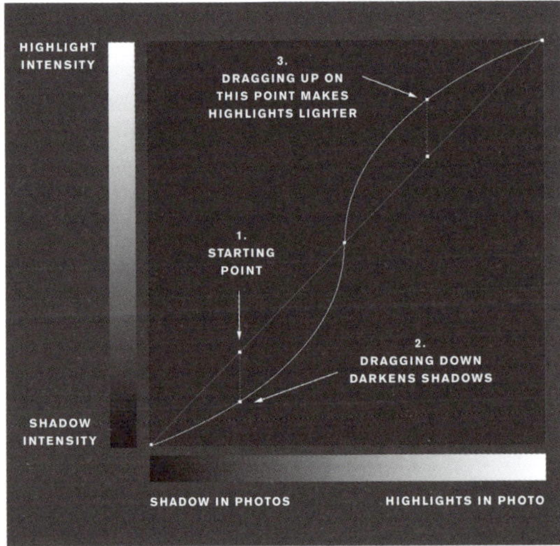

Applying an S-curve.

The HSL (Hue, Saturation, Luminance) panel allows you to control different colours independently, which makes it very powerful and a lot of fun.

HUE
Adjusting this slider will allow you to make subtle changes to colour along a gradient. Use it for turning green grass yellow or perhaps to fix a portrait by removing an orange cast from skin tones (caused by tungsten lightbulbs) by changing instances of orange in an image to pink.

SATURATION
Saturation is the intensity of colour and it can play an influential role in controlling the emotions experienced by viewers of a photograph. Highly saturated colours generally convey brighter emotions, whereas muted, desaturated colour can lend a sense of brooding or sadness.

LUMINANCE
Luminance refers to the brightness of colours and this slider – along with the Saturation slider – is the one that I use most when looking to 'pop' the colours in an image.

In the example opposite, I'm changing the hue and luminance of the flesh tones to pop my character out of the background. In the photo on the left, you can see his skin has turned a little bit blue because of changes made across the image with the Tone Curve. Increasing the luminance of any instances of orange and yellow and minor adjustments to the hue helps to restore our surfer to his normal colour and pull him out of the background which stays blue.

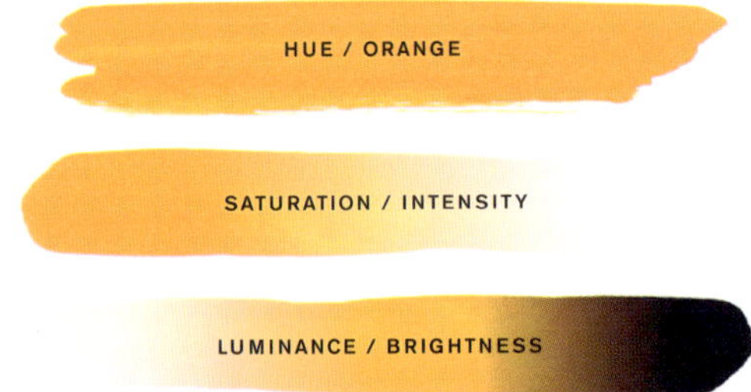

The Split Toning panel, buried between the HSL and Detail panels, is often overlooked by many photographers. It's understandable, because, as we've just discussed, there are a bunch of other ways to change the colours of an image in Lightroom; why do we need another option?

In essence, split toning is simply the addition of different colours to the highlights and shadows of a photograph and is used to add a tone to an image. Changing the tone of a picture changes the mood, which goes a long way to changing how your audience will feel when they look at your image (see pages 80–83).

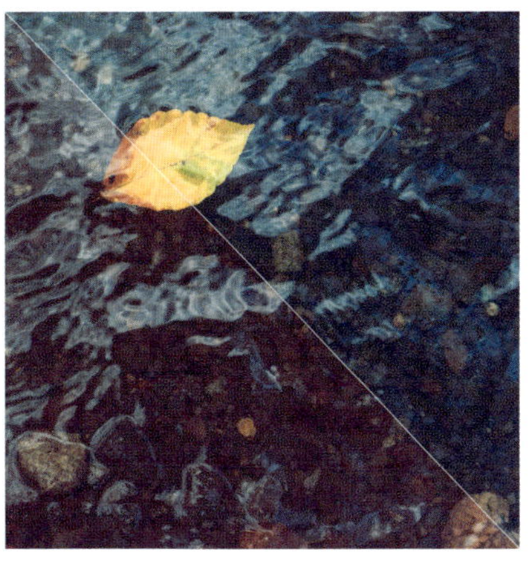

Split toning: note the colour difference between the split toned top half of this leaf image and the bottom half. Cooling blues have been added to the shadows which turns the water a different shade.

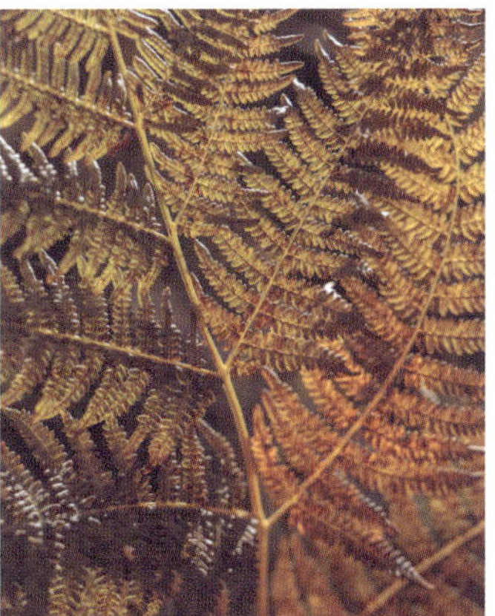

Original image lacks contrast.

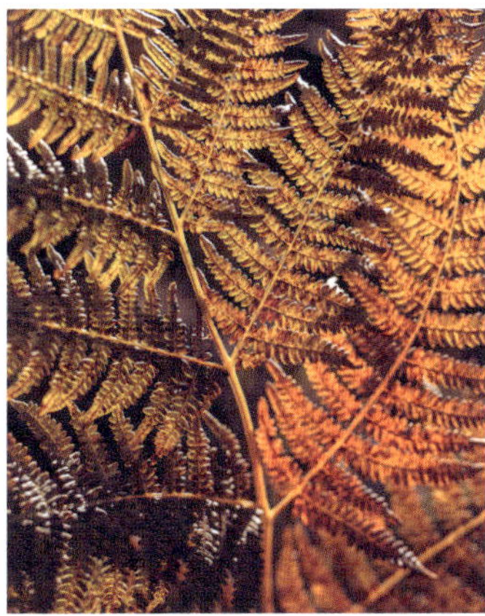

S-curve applied to make the image pop!

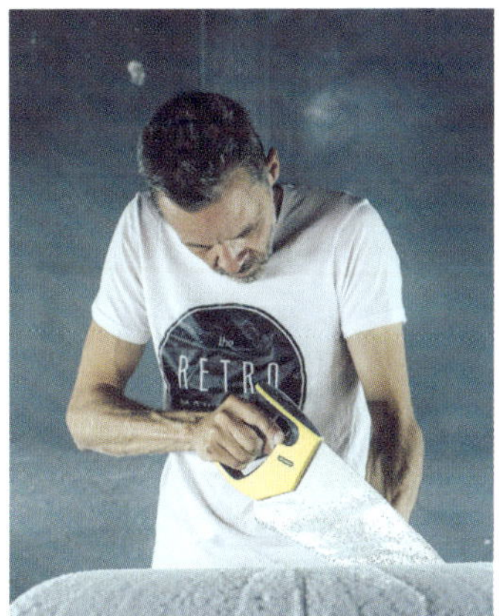

Skin colour looks blue and unnatural.

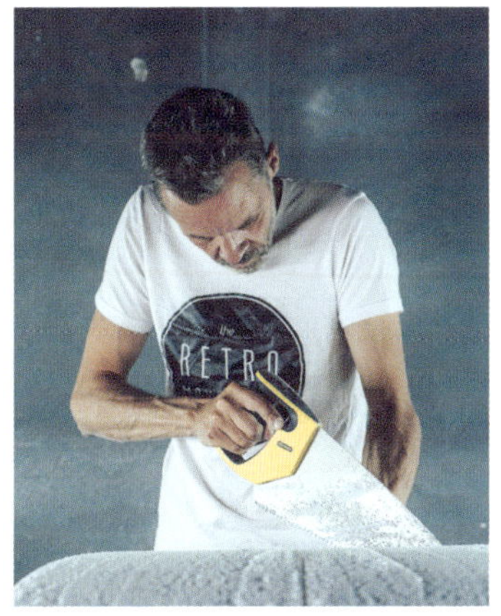

Skin colour normalised using adjustments to hue and luminance.

SHORTCUT KEYS

/ Tab: hides/reveals the side panels giving you a larger work area.

/ L: Dims the surrounding image area. I change the default background colour from black to white, because I often print images with a white border, so it helps me to see the image against a white background.

/ F: Full-screen preview.

/ I: Toggle through image info (title and metadata) at the top left of the image.

Project /

Shoot with Film to Influence Your Grade

BRIEF

+ Shoot with film and study the analogue effects and inconsistencies.

REQUIREMENTS

+ Film camera and a roll of film – think about your choice in relation to your subject.

+ An open mind. Experiement and embrace imperfections.

OBJECTIVE

+ To experiment with film stocks and learn to appreciate the inconsistencies of film photography so that you can create unique grades for your images when editing digital files.

Let's quickly duck out of the technical aspects of editing digital images and talk about the importance of shooting 'old fashioned' rolls of film for a second. It might seem counterintuitive in this day and age, but I have no doubt that shooting film will improve your work behind a DSLR, as well as in the digital darkroom.

When editing, you don't want to rely on the one-stop-shop presets that everyone else is using. Shoot a few rolls of film, study the results and build on what you find when editing your digital images. We'll look at emulating analogue film effects overleaf.

STEP 1 / **CHOOSE A FILM STOCK**
When you choose a roll of film, you're effectively setting the ISO speed (which affects the level of grain and detail in your developed images), as well as the colour and tone before you've even taken a shot. For example, Kodak Portra is often favoured for portraits because of its ability to reproduce realistic skin tones, whereas something like Kodak Ektar 100 gives out beautiful vibrant hues, especially in red and blue tones, making it a go-to film for landscape and architecture photography.

STEP 2 / **WORK WITH IMPERFECTIONS**
You're likely to experience analogue inconsistencies when shooting with film, especially if you're using a cranky old camera where the winder doesn't work correctly, or there are holes in the casing. Light 'leaking' onto your film will introduce marks and imperfections. Sometimes they work and sometimes they don't, but that's what I love about shooting film. There's an element of unpredictability. It feels organic and real. It's worth noting that the 'imperfect' look I'm describing has influenced many of the popular filters found today on Instagram.

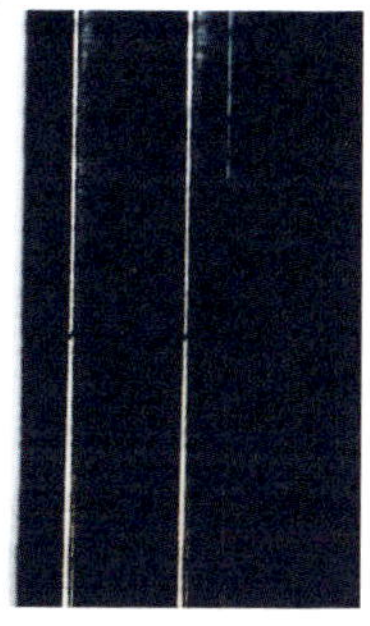
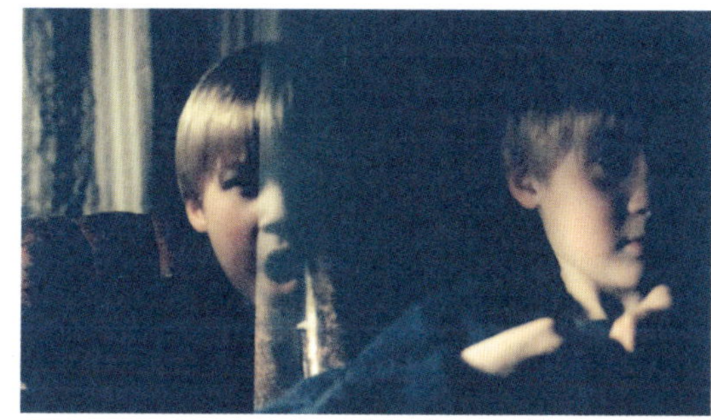
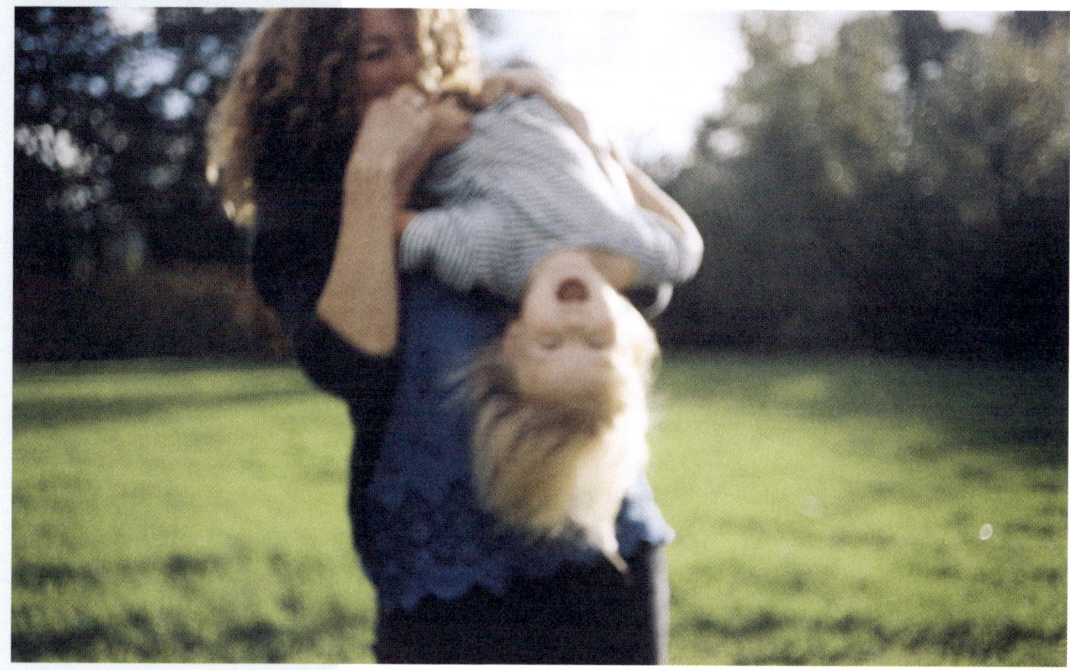
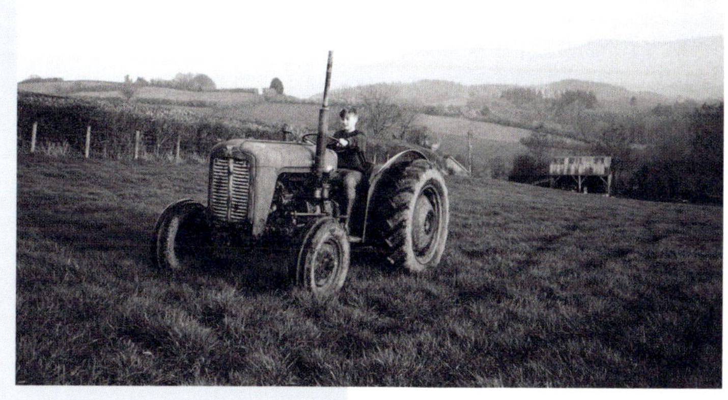
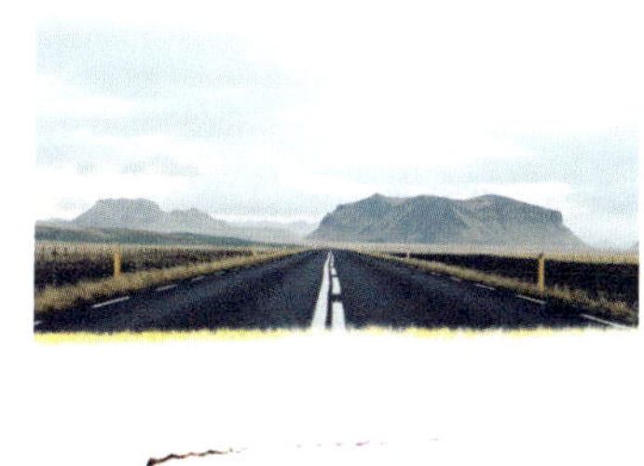

INTRODUCING FILM GRAIN & EFFECTS

Building on the previous project, let's take a look at a program called Exposure from Exposure Software. I use it to add analogue film elements, such as light leaks or film grain, to a digital file.

The proliferation of smartphones and digital cameras has put photography at the fingertips of us all, but these new digital tools often do the job *too* well. The images they create lack the fuzziness, blurriness and inconsistencies that analogue photography can give us. They lack feeling.

Lightroom has a 'grain' slider in the Develop module of course, but I find it applies grain across the whole image too evenly. It looks fake, and it can also make the image look noisy.

If you look at the image opposite, which was shot on Kodak 400TX film, you will notice that film grain is more apparent in the shadows and mid-tones than in the highlights.

Exposure allows you to emulate analogue film more realistically by adding grain to different parts of the image according to the tonal range, so you can add grain to the shadows without affecting the highlights, and vice versa.

Exposure is also great for introducing light leak effects into digital files. The following exercise will run you through that panel within the program.

Exercise /
Adding Light Leaks

1 Create a new layer in Photoshop and fill it with black using the Paint Bucket tool.

2 Open the file in Exposure and turn off all panels.

3 Open up the Overlays panel and select the light effect. This will give you a whole bunch of different light leak effects, most of which are a bit heavy for my liking, but I do like the 'Side' ones.

4 Choose one to your liking and apply it to the black layer.

5 Back in Photoshop, select the light leak layer and choose Image > Adjustments > Desaturate, and then change the layer effect to 'Screen'. This will remove the colour and the background so that only the light leak is affecting the image.

6 Placing the effects on separate Photoshop layers means you have more flexibility in terms of placement. You can move them around, flip them, reduce the opacity, and so on.

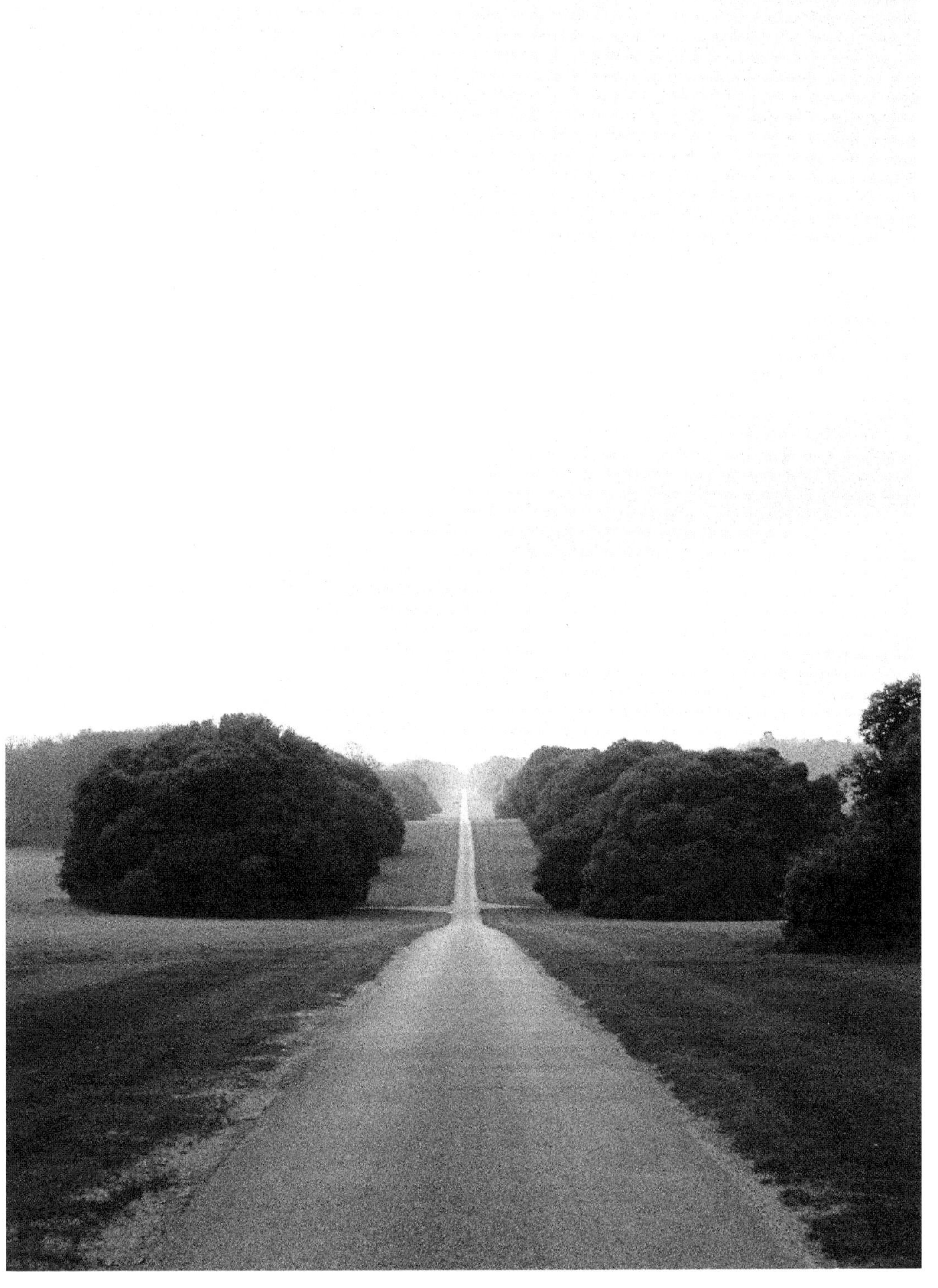

BUILDING A STORY

By this point we have rated and applied colour labels to the catalogue, helping us to quickly retrieve images based on shot type. We've also colour graded the photos. Next comes the final edit, which is where everything comes together and we use a combination of different shot types working as a whole to tell our story.

From the outset, we knew where we were going to go with the story, we had a plot. We had a location, we had a character, and from a combination of those two things, we could create our event. Our character's ultimate desire is to reach the perfect surf spot, to find the ideal beach. The location is Portugal, and the obstacle to him reaching his goal is accessibility. Accessibility is where we bring the client and their product in, which is a Cool & Vintage Land Rover. From that we can create our structure: our beginning, middle and end.

BEGINNING

The opening scene is our surfer in his board-shaping room. This introduces our character and also the lifestyle that he's associated with. The lifestyle isn't explicitly obvious, but there are clues here.

Next, we move in closer and connect our audience to our character and the process of hand-shaping a surfboard. I love the pile of offcuts in the corner.

Moving into the resin room, the lighting conditions change pretty radically, but that makes for a good connecting sequence between the artificially lit board room and the naturally lit middle sequences, on the following page.

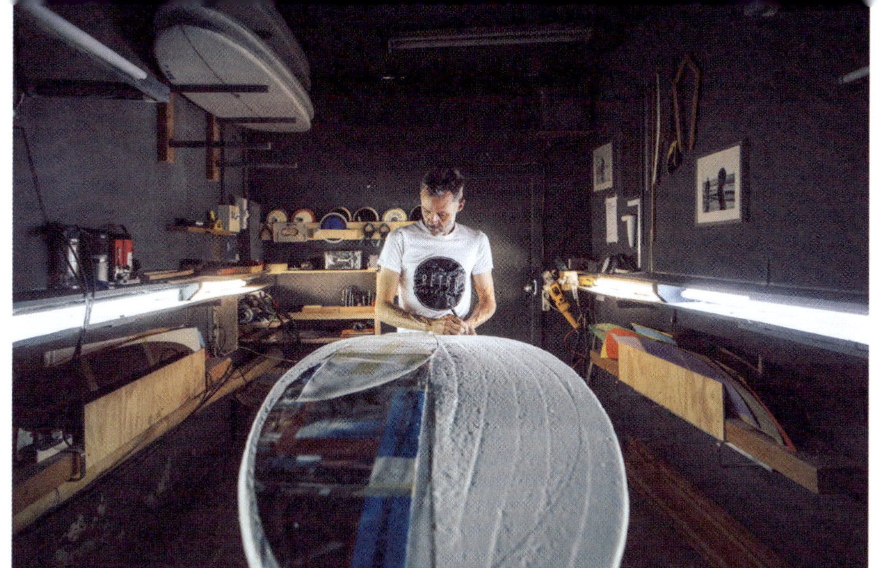

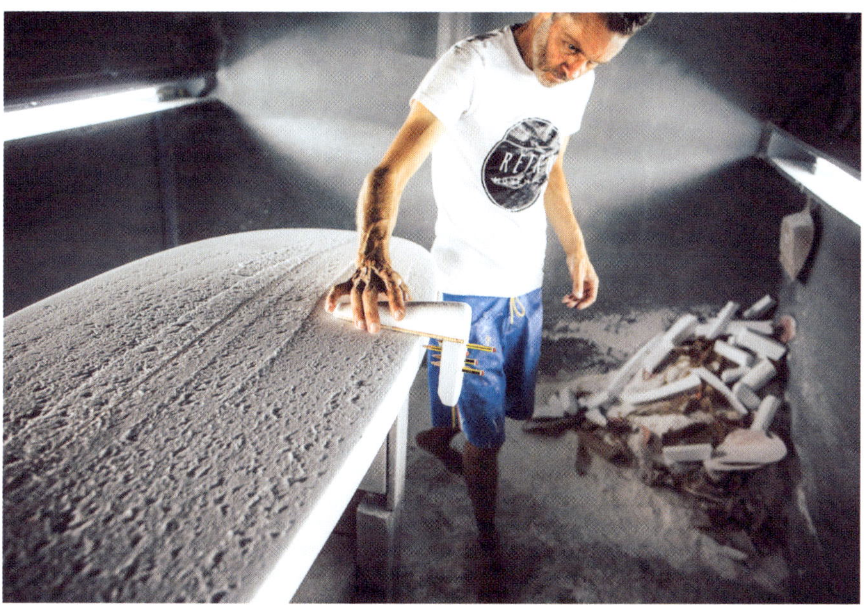

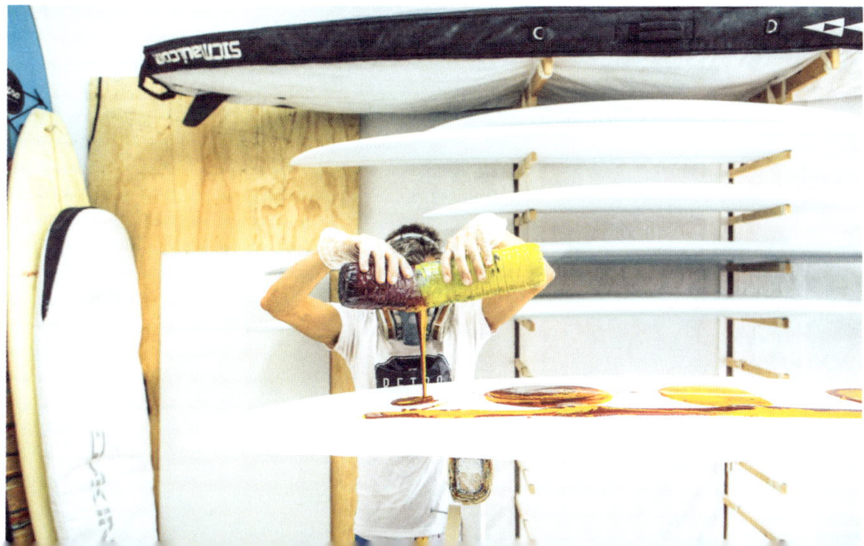

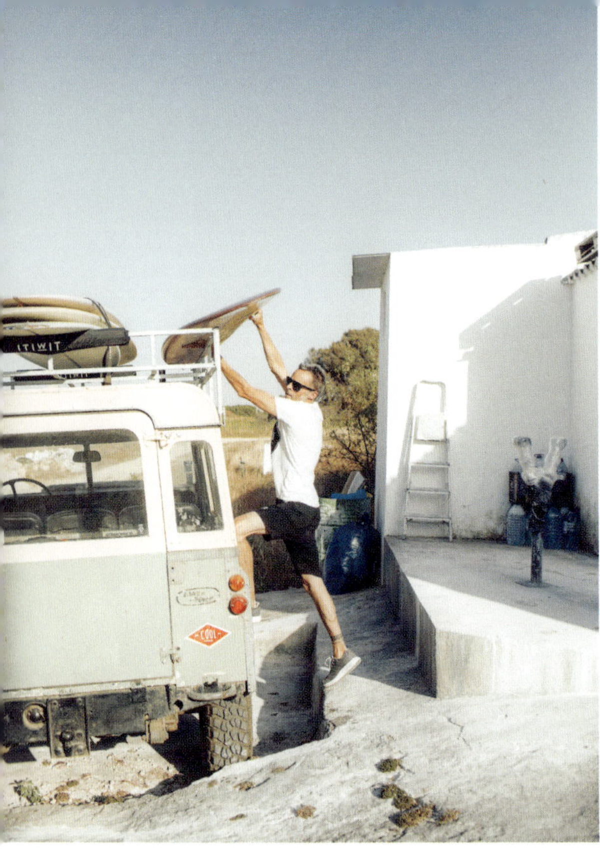

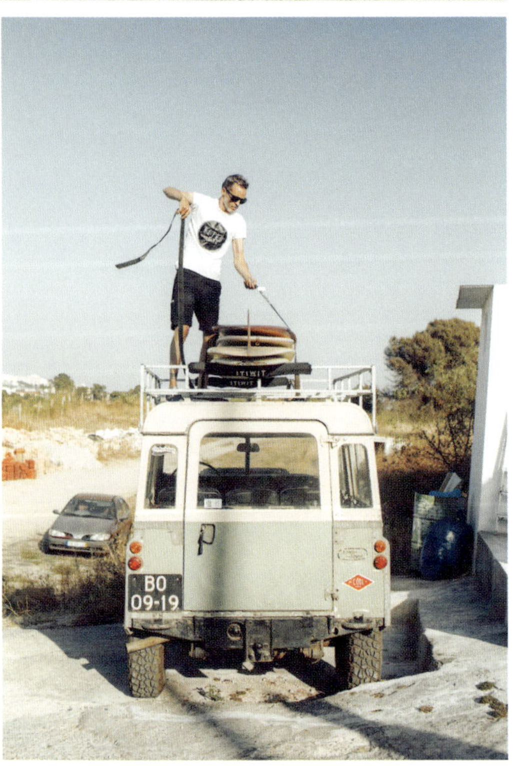

Next, we need to move our character to the beach, and this is where we introduce the Land Rover – the enabler of his lifestyle. I could have cut straight to a beauty shot of the Land Rover on the road, but I directed Dan to carry his board to the truck so I could keep the story flowing and connect the board room to the Land Rover.

A couple of interior images put the audience inside the car.

A tracking shot adds a sense of urgency. You can see the motion blur, so you know he's moving quickly. I converted this into black and white to further emphasise the sense of urgency. This might seem an odd decision amid a sequence of colour shots, but it means the audience will notice it and register that time is of the essence.

A drone shot introduces the landscape as a whole and connects our Land Rover to the ocean.

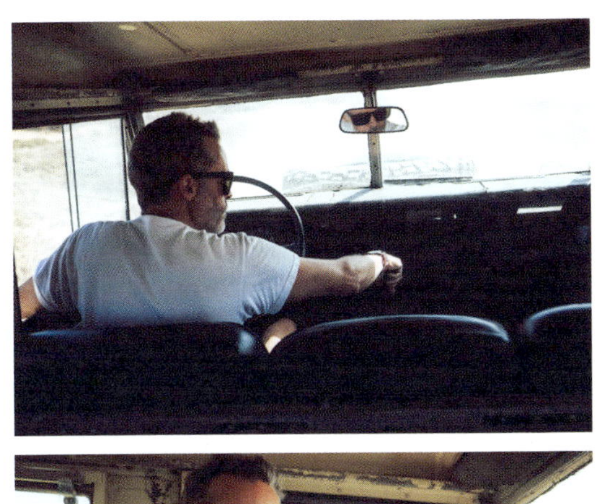
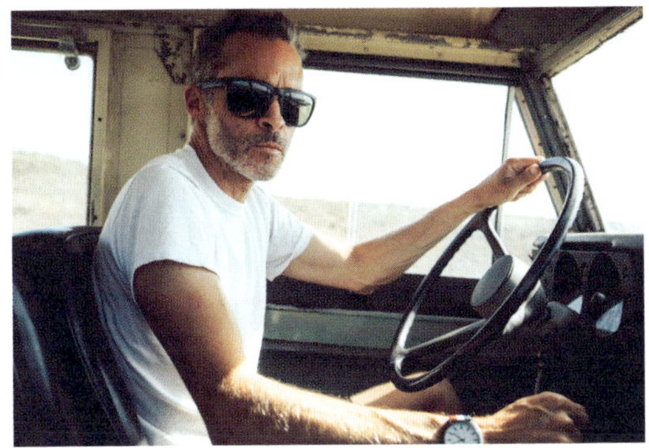
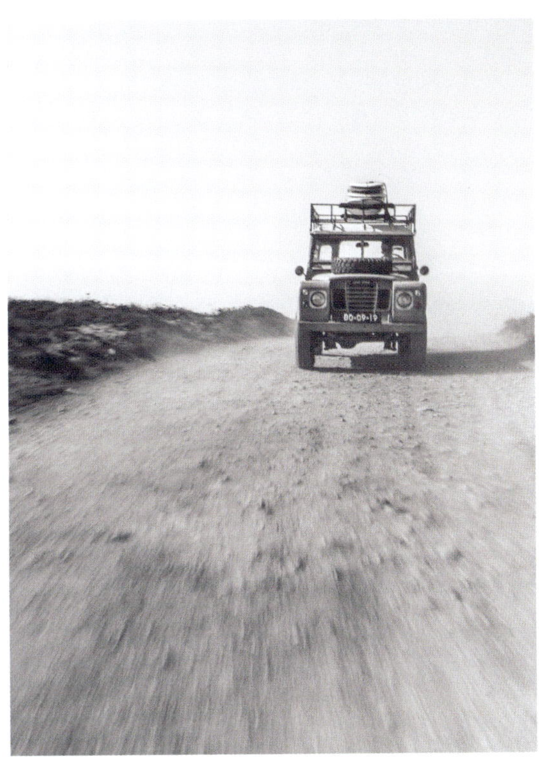

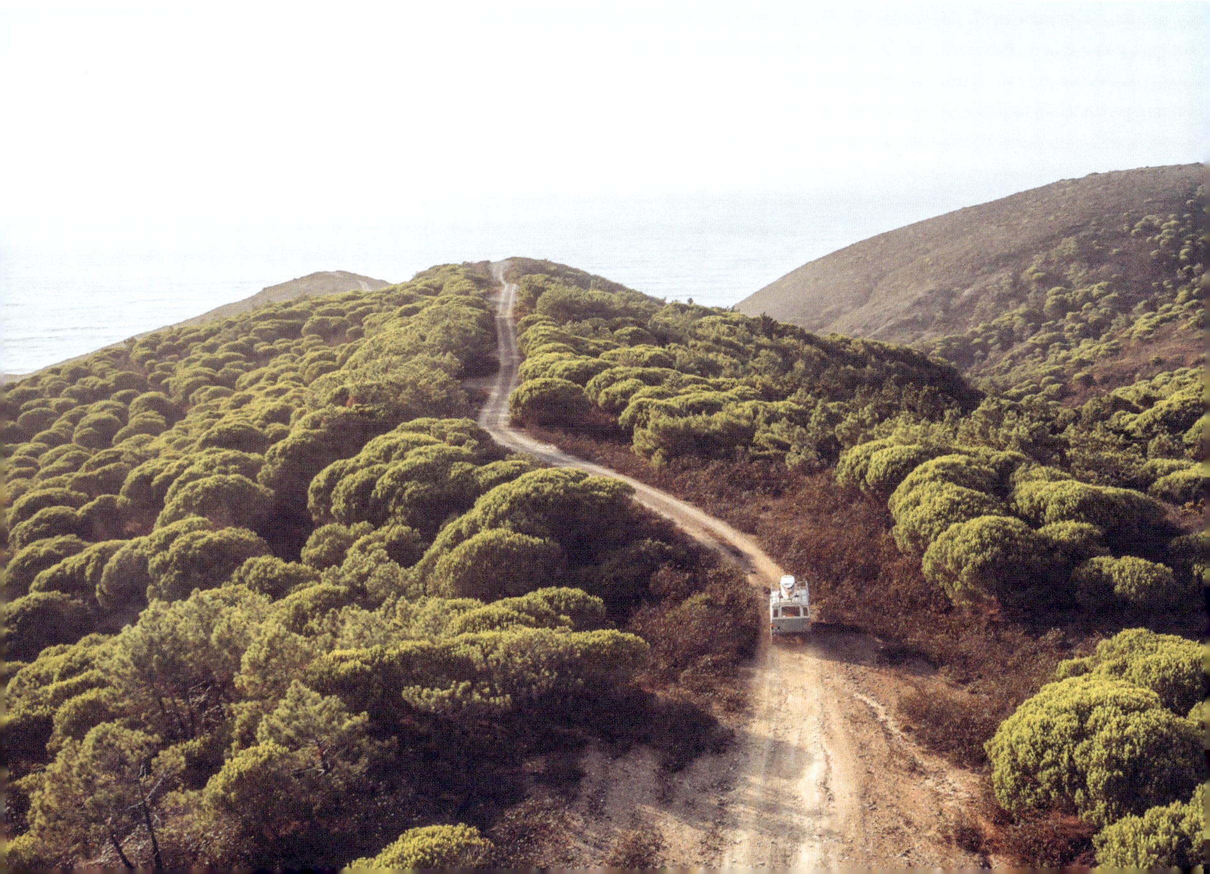

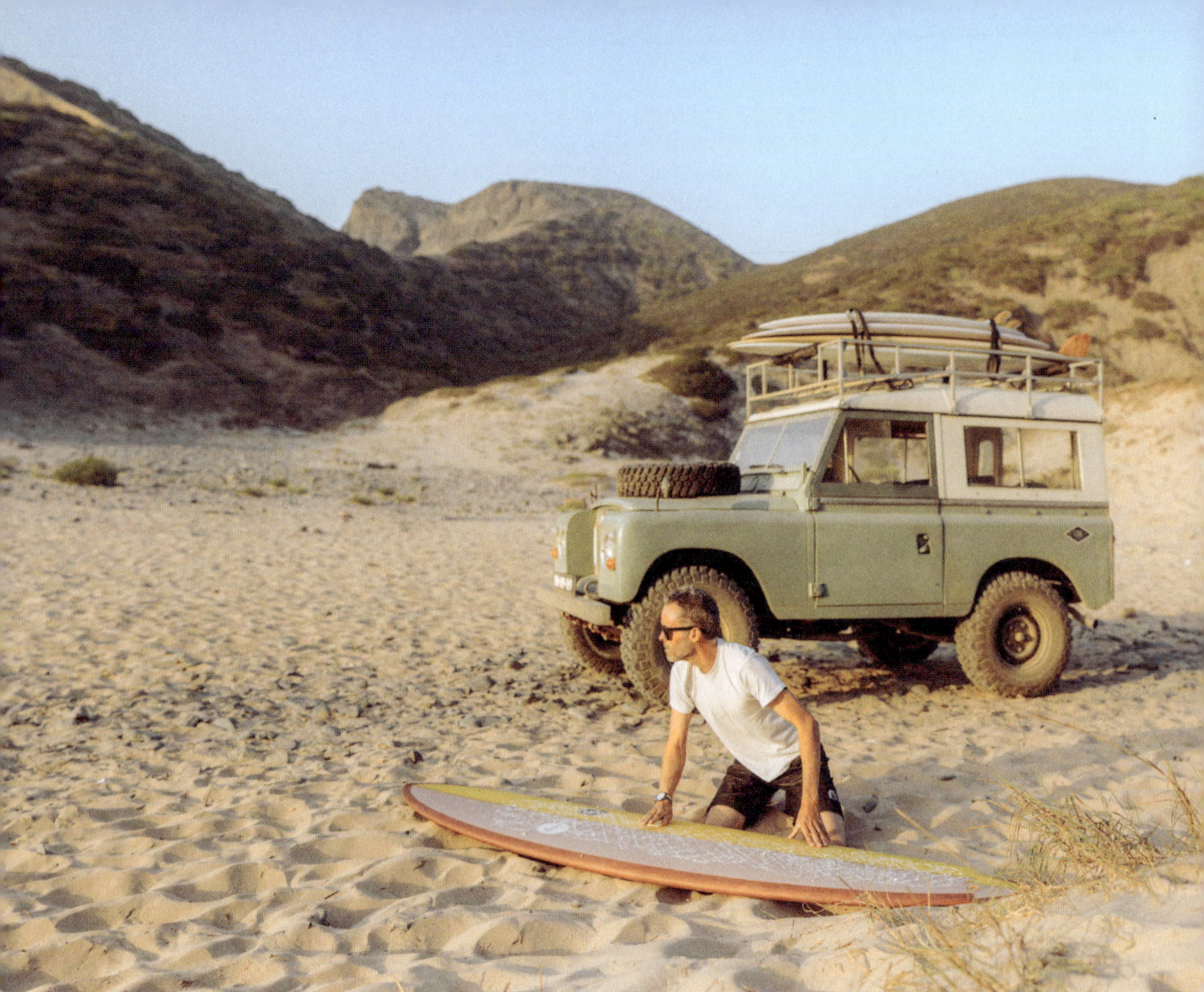

We're moving into the ending here, cutting away from our character to the beach. This stitched image helps orient the audience. I like Dan's pose, looking out towards the sun. It feels a little urgent, like he's keen to make the most of the conditions.

The image of him waxing his board was shot from inside the Land Rover. Paired with an exterior shot of him walking towards the ocean, these connecting sequences help to join the dots between scenes.

Now a beautiful surf image shot at golden hour (see page 103). He made it in time and his ultimate desire has been granted. The colour tone across the image is orange and pink which brings a soothing feeling and this contrasts nicely against the rush of the journey. It evokes a sense of fun, joy and fulfilment.

The final scene depicts Dan back at the truck, looking out at the ocean and reflecting on the day we just followed. Photographed at blue hour (see page 103) the colour tone switches back to the blue tones we began with in the board room; the ending should hold the hand of the beginning, remember? These tones also deliver a feeling of reflection and calm… the end to a perfect day.

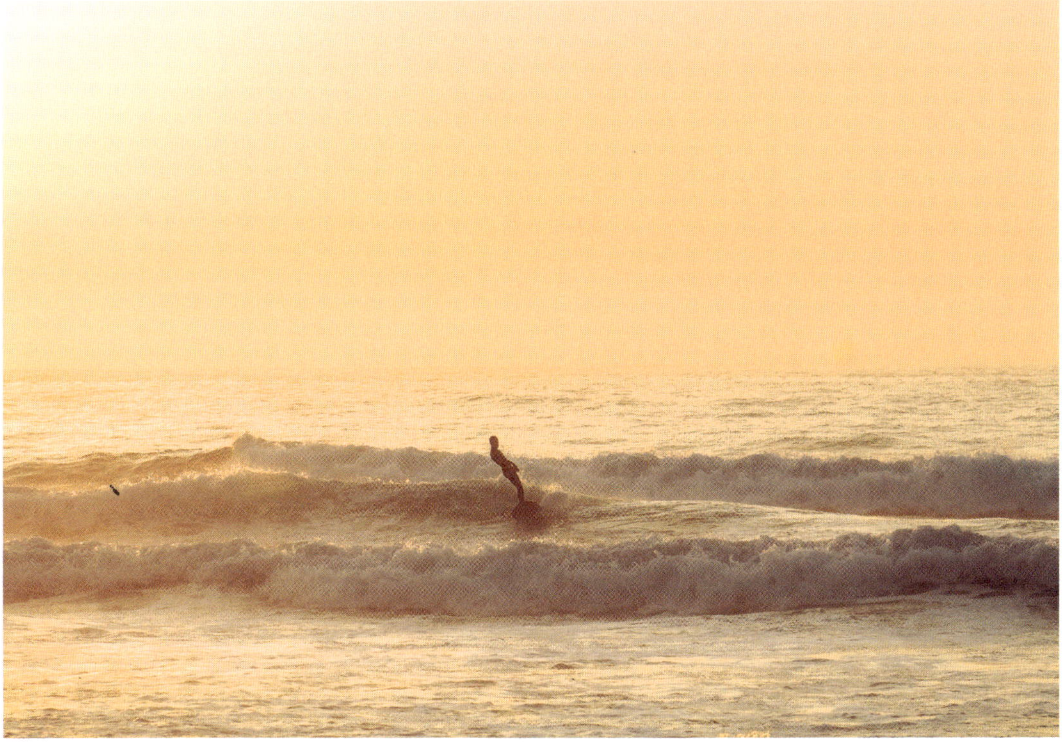

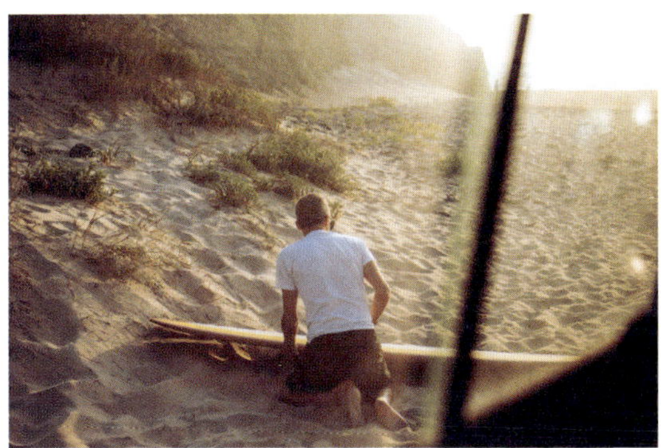
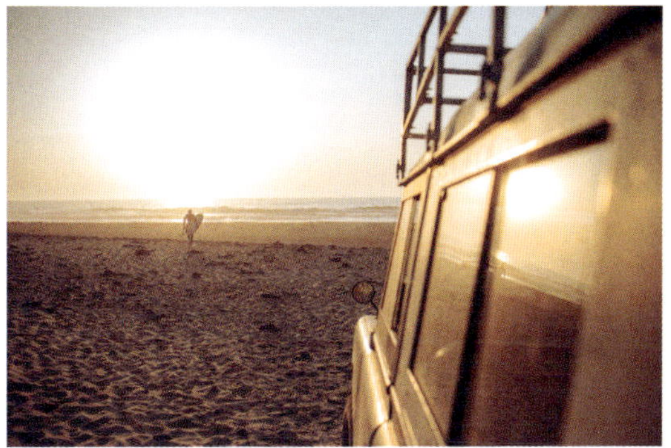
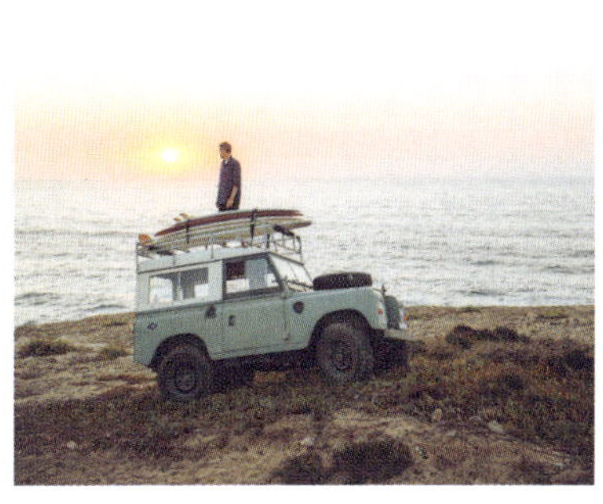
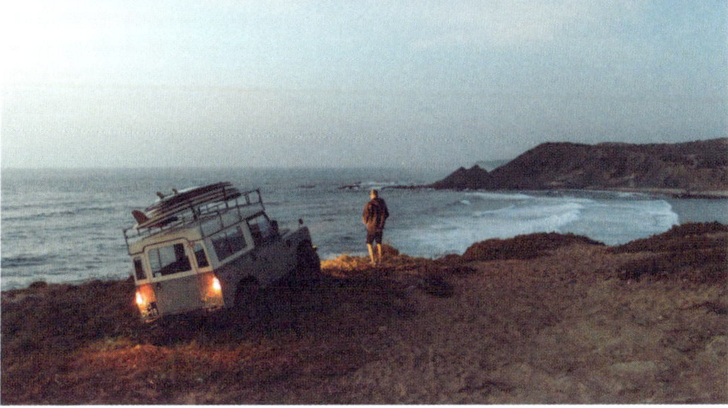

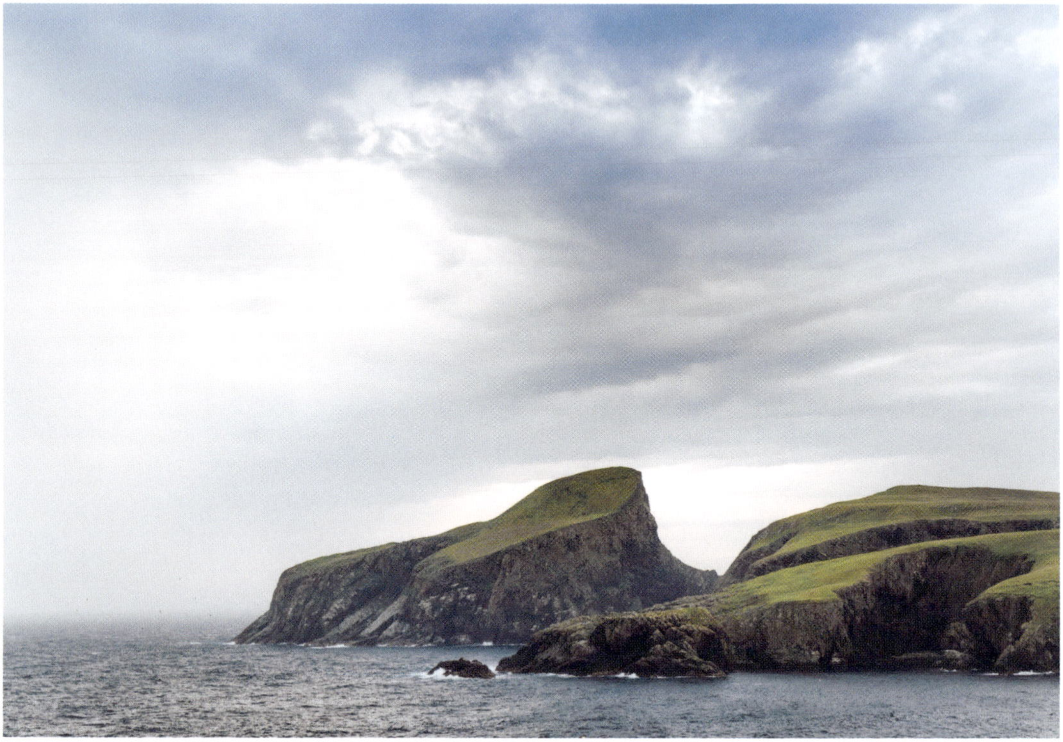

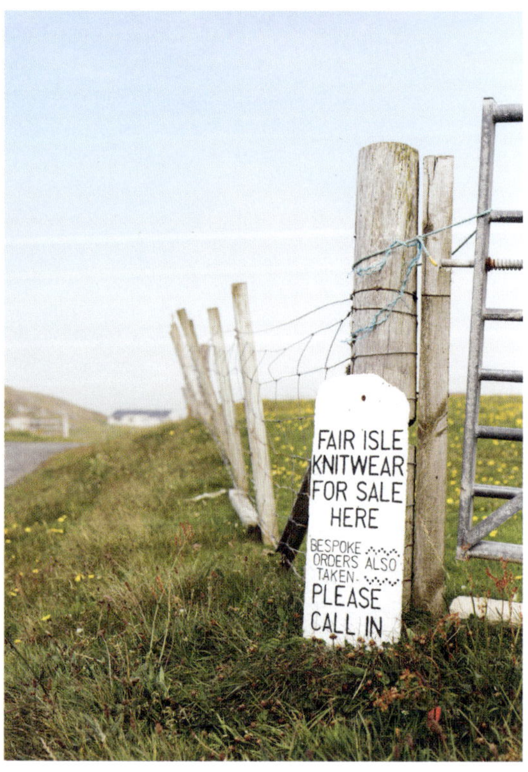
FAIR ISLE
KNITWEAR
FOR SALE
HERE

BESPOKE
ORDERS ALSO
TAKEN.
PLEASE
CALL IN

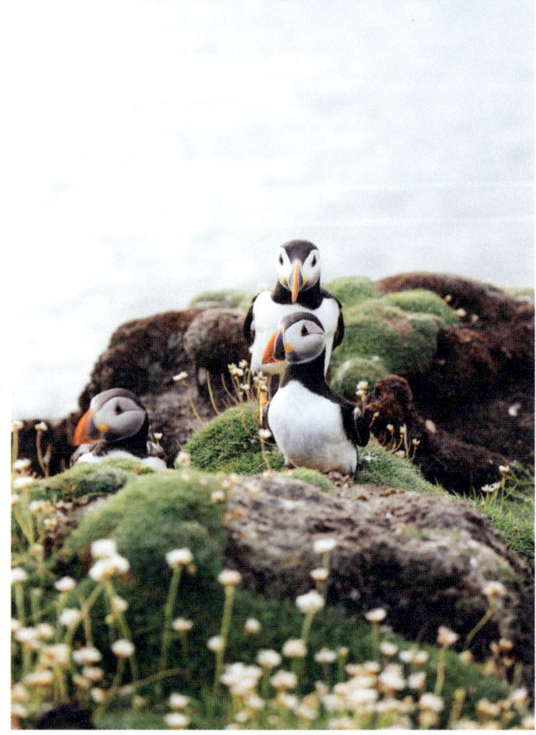

BACKUP, BACKUP, BACKUP

When it comes to digital photography there are those who have lost data and those who will lose data. It's one of those simple facts of life.

However, it's not just backing up photos that causes anxiety and stress, it's the ongoing management of thousands and thousands of digital files usually across multiple machines and locations. This section details my backup process refined over the years using a combination of NAS drives, Amazon's Cloud service and Dropbox. Backups take place automatically across three separate locations, and the subsequent file store allows me to quickly retrieve images from my archive wherever I am working. I'm not saying this will suit your working methods perfectly, but I'm confident there will be elements of this system that you can add to your own workflow.

PREREQUISITES

I have four primary requirements from a data management perspective:

- Storage across three separate locations. It might seem like overkill, but even if you have a shoot backed up on multiple hard drives at home and your house burns down or gets robbed, you're in trouble.
- Automated backup. I don't want to have to remember to backup across these three locations. I want a system that does it for me.
- Instant access to photos, as if they were on my hard drive whether I'm working from my home, the office or on location.
- Automated synchronisation of files between home and office. Changes made at one location need to be reflected at the other.

DEFINE YOUR HABITS

Sitting down and understanding how you like to work is key to developing a process that will fit you. It's hard to change working practices and habits you have formed over several years. It's much easier to formulate a system around the way you work.

My typical shoot day can be broken down into the following steps:

- **Travel to location**
- **Shoot day 1** – Backup at the end of the day
- **Shoot day 2** – Backup at the end of the day
- **Travel home** – Begin edit on my laptop
- **Head to office** – Transfer files from my laptop to my desktop and continue edit on my desktop
- **Head home** – Continue edit on my laptop
- **Submit files to the client**
- **Archive shoot**

From the list above you can see I'm dealing with three key locations: shoot location, office, home. I'm also working across two workstations (laptop and desktop), so across the life of the edit I need to keep my files in sync in all locations and across both machines.

CATALOGUE

As previously discussed, I use Adobe Lightroom for editing and file management. I create a new catalogue for each shoot and save it to Dropbox, which keeps it in sync regardless of which computer or location I'm working from. Any changes made on my desktop at the office will sync to my laptop at home because the catalogue is stored in the Cloud.

BACKUP WORKFLOW ON LOCATION

While on location I stick to the following storage/backup workflow:

- **Location Backup 1**
  Shoot to Compact Flash using a separate card for each day

- **Location Backup 2**
  Return to hotel and download files to laptop hard drive

- **Location Backup 3**
  Make secondary copy onto a SSD HD

This temporary backup process is all well and good on the road, but it doesn't cut it in a studio/archival environment. I have tried manually working with multiple hard drives in the past, but you soon run out of space and need to buy new ones. I forget to maintain numerous backups, and as a result, they fall out of sync with each other. It also makes the retrieval of images further down the line a pain.

Quick retrieval of images from an ever-expanding archive is as important as backing up – remember, time is money.

BACKUP WORKFLOW AT HOME

I use NAS (Network Attached Storage) to store files both at home and in my office. NAS is basically a high-capacity hard drive attached to a network and the internet. It is semi-intelligent in that it can perform basic operations, such as backing up files, without any input from a human. Once given a task, it just cracks on with it – even if you shut down your computer. Since the NAS is attached to a network (via my Wi-Fi router), I can access it over my Wi-Fi connection. It acts just like a hard drive but without the wires!

Another difference from a standard external hard drive is that a NAS is comprised of multiple hard drives working together as a RAID (Redundant Array of Independent Disks). For example, my 16 TB NAS in the office is made up of 4 x 4TB hard drives. The RAID always makes sure your discs are replicated so if one fails, data is saved on the others. It's like a backup within a backup, if you like.

This is my backup workflow when working from home:

- **Home Backup 1**
  Home NAS – Manual

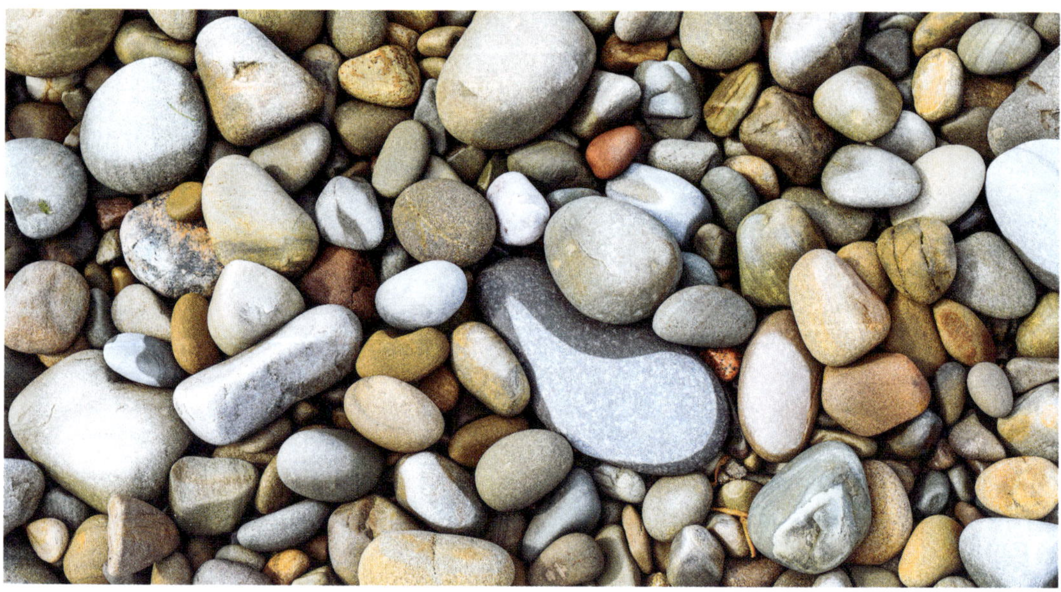

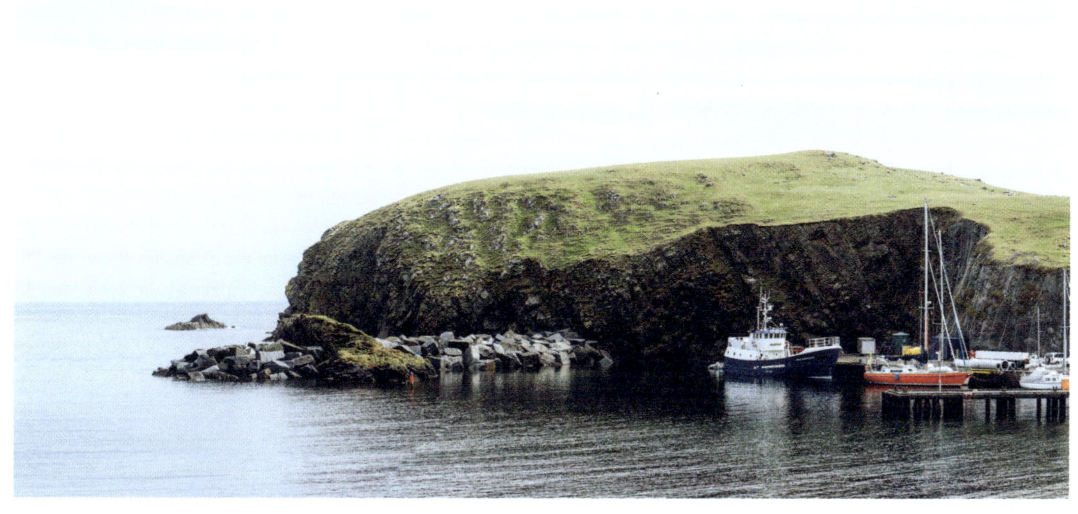

As soon as I return home from a shoot I copy files from my laptop to my home NAS, much like you would an external hard drive, although the NAS is accessible across my Wi-Fi network so I don't need to plug anything into my laptop. It just pops up in my Finder and I drag the folder across.

- **Home Backup 2**
  Cloud – Automatic
  As soon as the files have copied across to the NAS, it detects their presence and immediately begins uploading them to my Cloud storage account using a fast fibre connection. For Cloud storage, I use Amazon Prime Photos since it offers unlimited storage for images.

- **Home Backup 3**
  Office NAS – Automatic
  A second process kicks in overnight. The home NAS copies the new files down to my office NAS ready for me to access when I get there in the morning.

Since I work between two locations (home and office), I need my data stores at both locations to stay in sync. Files modified after a day in the office need to be reflected at home, and vice versa, so I can seamlessly work between both locations and on both computers.

Both my home NAS and my office NAS talk to each other over the internet. My home NAS compares date/time stamps of its own files with those on the office NAS and synchronises whichever machine needs updating with the newer versions. This is called two-way sync and means I can work across both locations, making changes to files and the NAS drives automatically update themselves.

<table>
<tr><td rowspan="4" style="writing-mode: vertical-rl;">REQUIREMENTS</td><td>/</td><td>2 x 16TB NAS
(for two locations; office and home)</td></tr>
<tr><td>/</td><td>1 x subscription to Amazon Prime</td></tr>
<tr><td>/</td><td>1 x subscription to Dropbox</td></tr>
<tr><td>/</td><td>Adobe Lightroom for cataloguing and managing assets</td></tr>
</table>

Step 5: Deliver

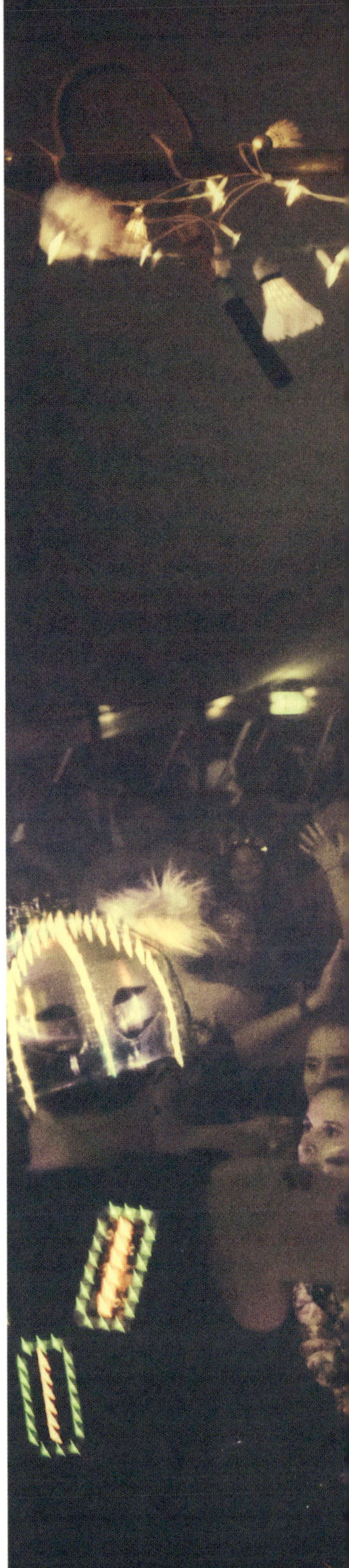

Congratulations – you're nearly there and your wrap party awaits! Long-standing relationships and repeat clients are the goals for a freelancer, so it pays to make every interaction you have with a client as professional as possible. Don't fall at this final hurdle. Delivering photographs to a client in a timely, efficient manner will stand you in good stead for future work. In this chapter, we'll look at file types, colour profiles, sharpening images and a slick web-based image-delivery system.

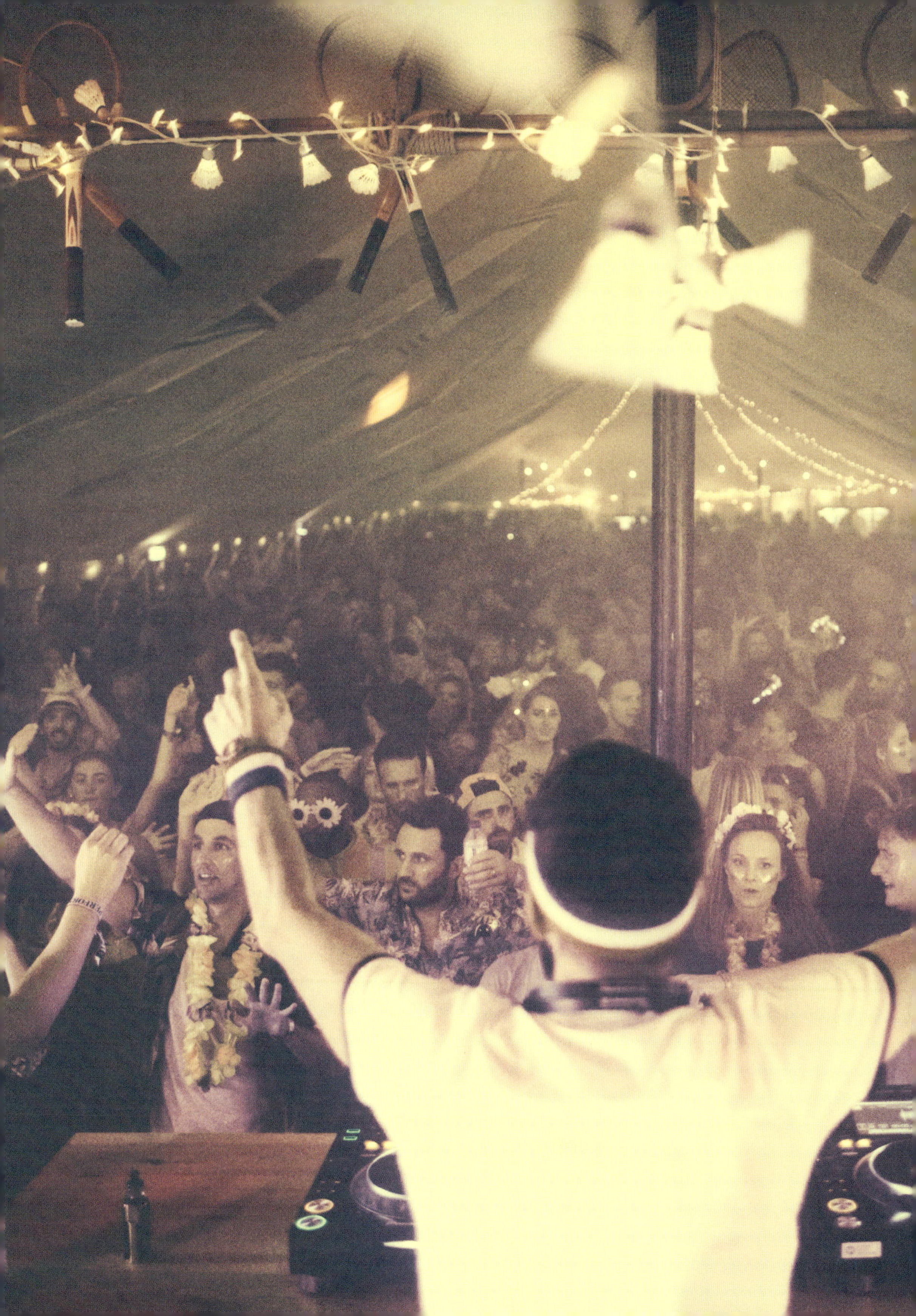

FILE FORMATS

There are three main file types to consider: lossless formats such as Raw and TIFF and a lossy format called JPEG. Let's run through each one in a little more detail and expand on the lossless/lossy concept.

Essentially, lossy compression permanently degrades a file to make it smaller. Sounds undesirable, right? In reality, compression technology is pretty smart and can reduce file sizes significantly before degradation is noticeable.

If you shoot in JPEG, your camera will use lossy compression to make the image smaller so that it can fit more pictures on the card. Raw and TIFF files, on the other hand, are lossless. All of the data is recorded, and therefore, the file is much larger. But that means you have more leeway when it comes to editing the file. There is more room for error because you have more data to work with.

JPEG

The standard file format for digital images, JPEGs were developed explicitly for sharing photographs over the internet. When a camera or an image-editing programme like Photoshop creates a JPEG, it uses lossy compression to generate a smaller file. The lower the file size, the quicker the image loads on a web page. The compression makes a JPEG significantly smaller than other image formats such as Raw or TIFF. However, there is a trade-off: the more you compress an image, the more detail you lose.

Use the JPEG format for displaying images on web pages and social media, but keep in mind that lossy means loss. If you shoot an image in the JPEG format and then edit and save it as a JPEG, it means your picture will have been compressed twice. Once by the

camera and again by Photoshop or Lightroom. Once image data has been thrown away, you can't retrieve it. Multiple saves of the same JPEG file will begin to degrade the photo, as more and more detail is dumped by the compression algorithm – see opposite.

TIFF

TIFF or 'Tagged Image File Format' is the standard format used throughout the printing and publishing industry. Significantly larger than JPEGs (far too big for web pages), TIFF files are an archival format and are used to preserve all of the data in a photograph. I use this format when submitting files to magazines or publishers for printing. Indeed, all of the images in this book were supplied to my publisher in TIFF format. Use them where quality is paramount, although not on a website!

RAW

Think of Raw files like the digital equivalent of a negative in film photography. The Raw file is generated by your camera and is the format used to create JPEGs and TIFFs – just as you would develop prints from negatives. Image adjustments (Brightness, Contrast, Saturation and so on) made to a Raw file using a programme such as Lightroom are never fixed, so you can always go back and re-edit them if necessary.

RECAP

/ Shoot and maintain an archive in a lossless format such as Raw.

/ Use JPEG files when saving images for use on the web/social media, and TIFF files for printing.

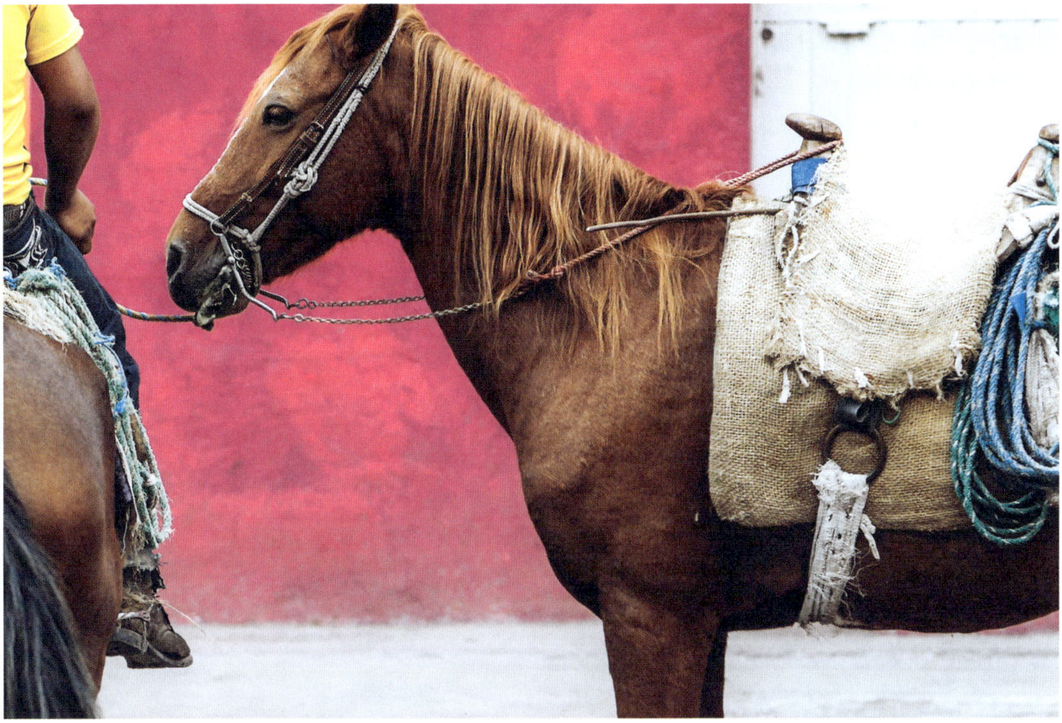

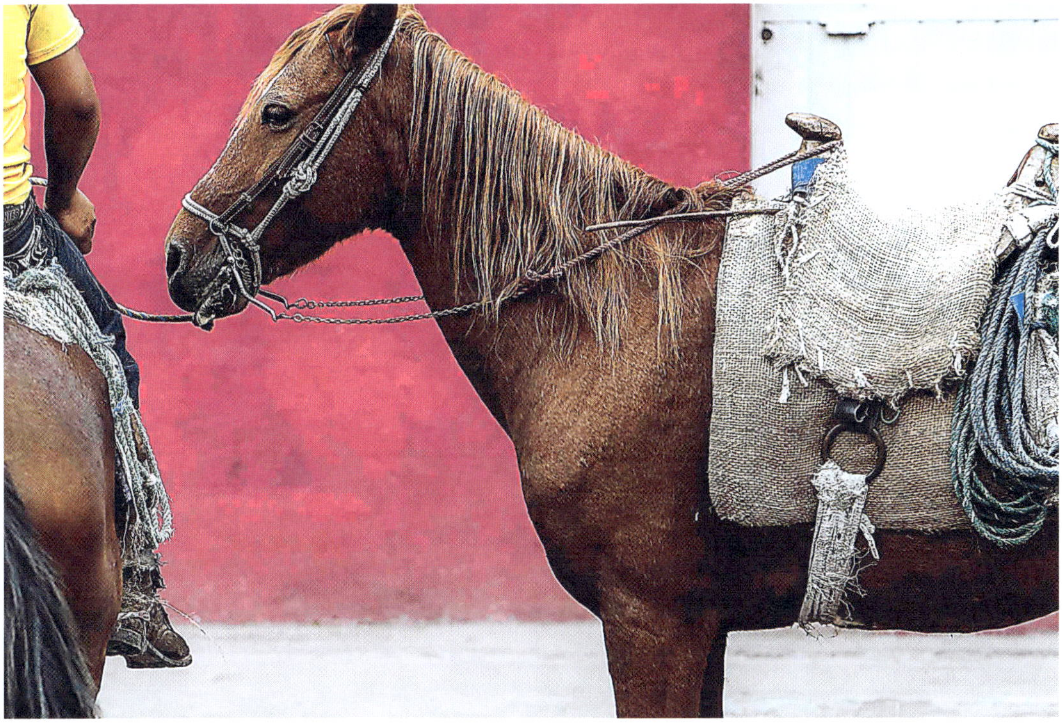

Top image: Original file / Bottom image: JPEG file saved too many times. Detail lost and ugly artefacts present.

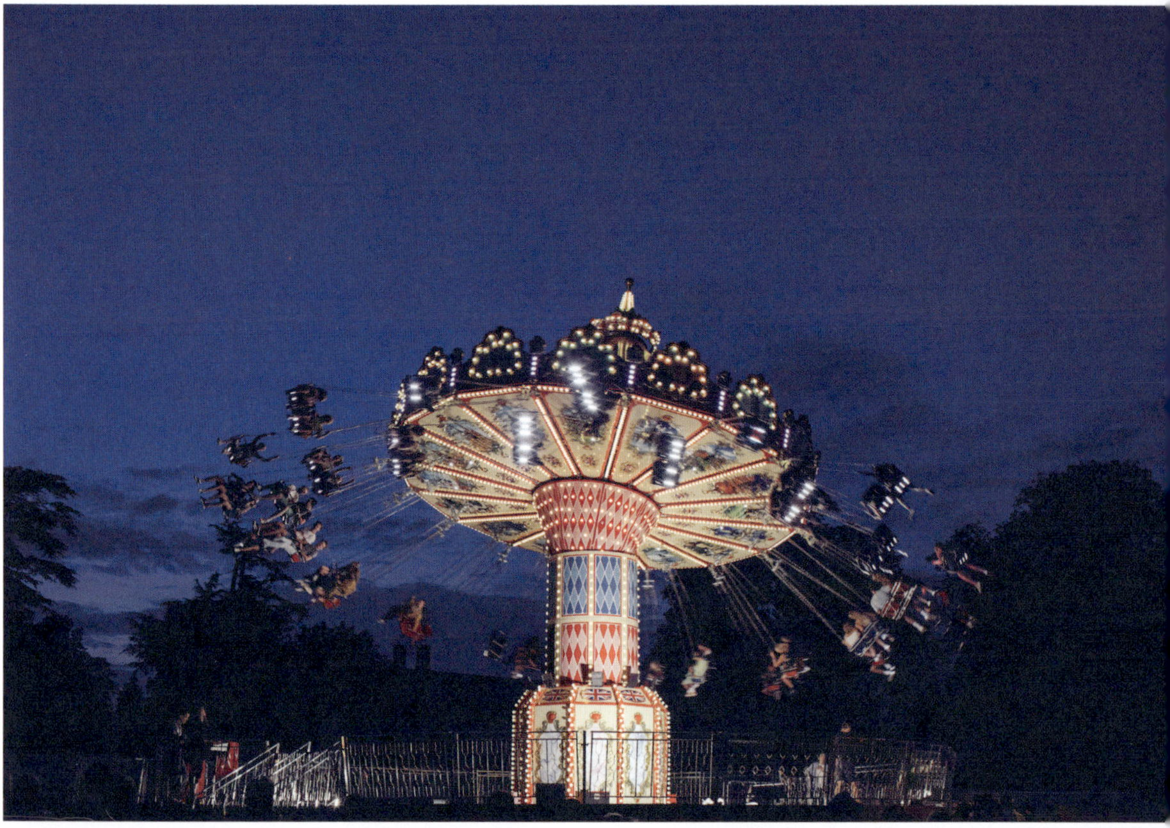

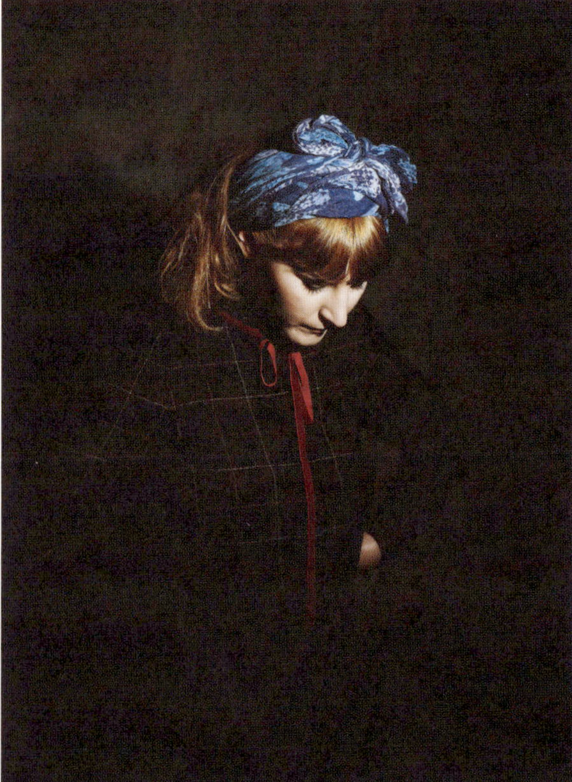
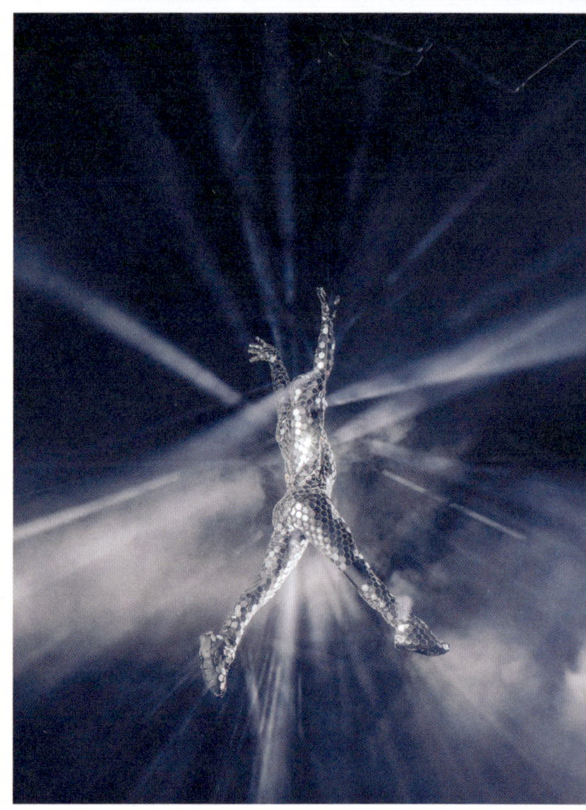

SHARPENING

Sharpening is a critical part of image processing, but it is often misunderstood and applied at random throughout the editing process. I've touched on this in the Edit chapter but 'output sharpening' should be the last modification made to a photo before saving and delivering files.

However, the full process should, in fact, be broken into three distinct areas:

1   Input sharpening is used to eliminate the blur that is inherent in all Raw files. It is applied when you import images from your camera.

2   Creative sharpening is a more manual process, which is used to sharpen specific areas of a picture and direct the viewer's eye.

3   Output sharpening is applied according to the final reproduction size of the image.

INPUT SHARPENING

Although Raw files are in many ways superior to a JPEG, they do come out of the camera a little soft. Input sharpening is a reasonably straightforward process, applied with Lightroom's sharpening slider. Depending on the size of the Raw file and the ISO, I simply tweak the sharpness amount to between 50–70 and leave more involved sharpening to the second stage.

CREATIVE SHARPENING

Creative sharpening is made to specific areas of an image, as opposed to the entire frame. Human eyes are attracted to contrast, and we are therefore drawn to the sharpest details in a photograph. Use creative or selective sharpening to enhance the focal point of your image.

Select the 'Adjustment Brush' in Lightroom and bump the Sharpness slider to 30 and the Clarity slider to 10. Paint over the areas you want to draw focus to in your image, such as the eyes in a portrait or the foreground in a landscape to help lead your viewer's eyes into the scene.

OUTPUT SHARPENING

We live in a multi-platform world, which means your images can be repurposed across a number of different mediums – magazines, websites, social media and so on. Each one has different image size requirements, and every time you resize a digital image, the level of sharpness will change. You can account for this using output sharpening.

Lightroom offers a fairly crude method via its export screen, but I'd suggest using Photoshop for a little more control. Try something like this:

- Filter > Sharpen > Unsharp Mask
- Amount: 65%
- Radius: 0.5 pixels
- Threshold: 0 levels

Turn this into a Photoshop 'Action' so you can apply the process at the click of the button, multiple times on the same image. The sharpening effect is subtle but gradually increases the more you apply it. Working in this way allows you to visualise the level of sharpness required. Remember, this should be the last modification you make before saving your image.

Project /
Finalising Your File

BRIEF

+ Prepare your photo for use on the
  web or as a physical print. Integrate
  a structured sharpening method into
  your workflow and save the file using
  the right format and colour space.

REQUIREMENTS

+ Raw file.

+ Adobe Lightroom.

+ Adobe Photoshop.

OBJECTIVE

+ Improve the quality of your images.

+ Direct a viewer's eye towards the
  focal point of an image.

+ Speed up image processing
  by creating sharpening presets
  in Lightroom.

All digital images need sharpening before they
go into production, but it's important to note
there is no 'correct' level of sharpening. It's a
subjective process and some photographers
will push an image more than others. Think of
it as part of developing your style. Experiment
with the techniques laid out in this exercise and
decide for yourself the best level of sharpness
for you and your work.

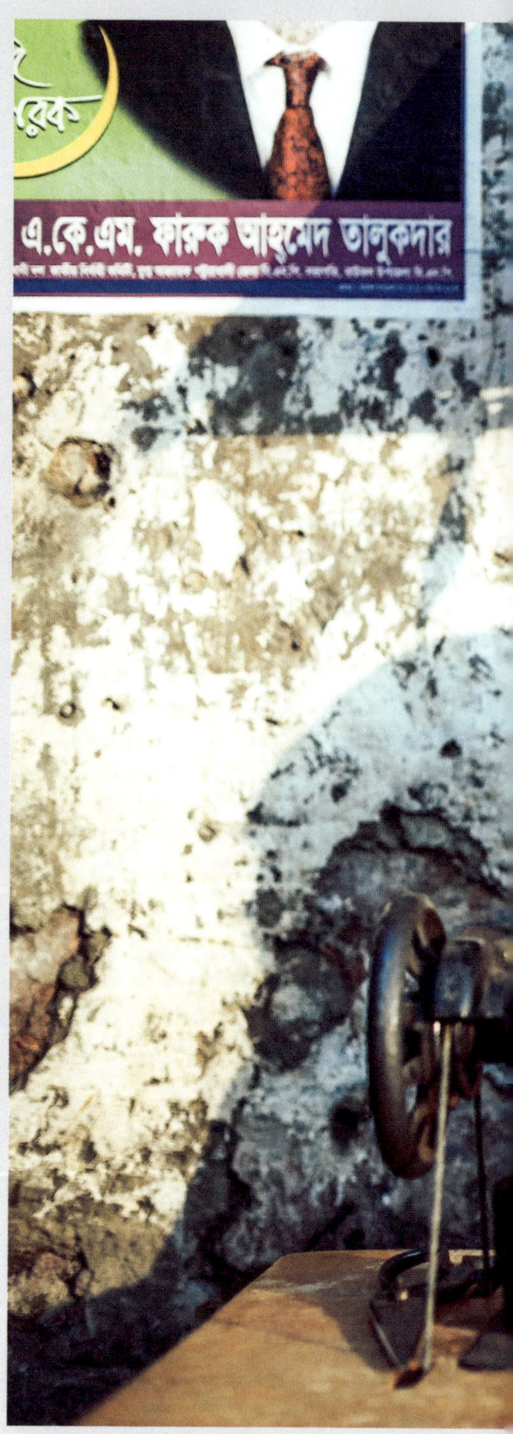

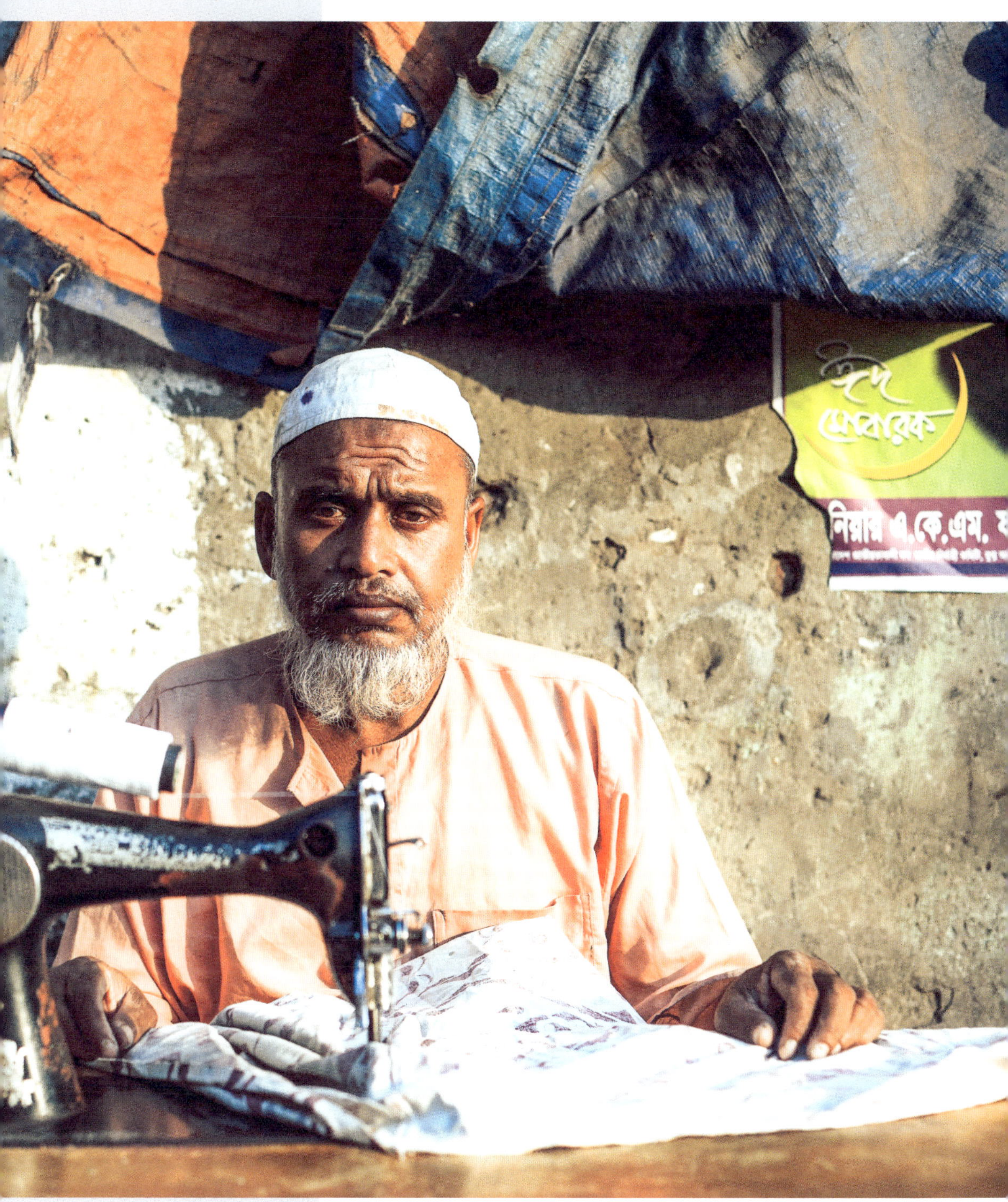

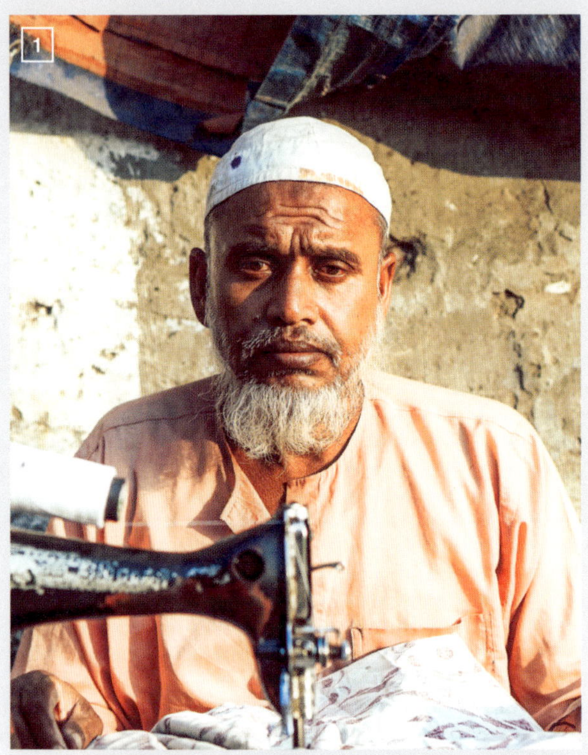

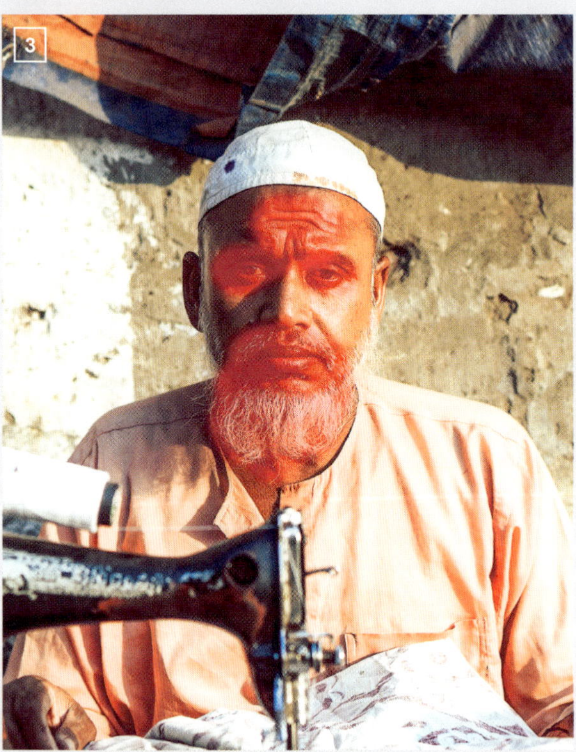

STEP 1 / **INPUT SHARPENING**
Select a Raw photo in Lightroom and scroll down to the Sharpening panel in the Develop module. Boost the amount to around 50.

STEP 2 / **MAKE A PRESET**
Create a simple preset in Lightroom so that you can apply the previous edit to all of your images at the click of a button. Choose:

Develop > Create Preset.

Select only the 'Sharpening' checkbox on the screen that pops up and save it using the name 'Input Sharpening'.

STEP 3 / **CREATIVE SHARPENING**
Choose the Adjustment Brush and boost only the Sharpness slider. Try something like 25 to start with. Paint over areas of the image that you'd like to emphasise – eyes, lips and teeth if a portrait, or the focal point in a landscape scene. You can see the areas I have painted in the image opposite, indicated in red.

STEP 4 / **RESIZE IN PHOTOSHOP**
Open your image in Photoshop and resize according to the end use of your image.

For example:
Website   2500px longest edge
Print   4000px longest edge

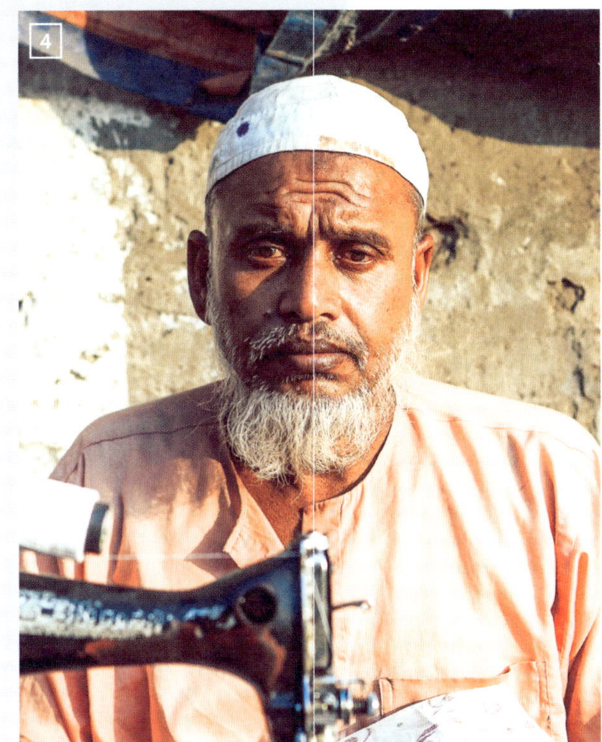

STEP 5 / **OUTPUT SHARPENING**

Duplicate the layer and sharpen again:
Filter > Sharpen > Unsharp Mask.

Amount	65%
Radius	0.5 pixels
Threshold	0 levels

Repeat this step and consider the effect. Make sure you are viewing the image at 100%. Delete a layer if you think you have sharpened too much, alternatively, repeat the step again.

STEP 6 / **SAVE**

Save your image in the appropriate format.

For web use save as a JPEG at 75% quality in the sRGB colour space.

For printing use save as a TIFF in the ProPhoto RGB colour space.

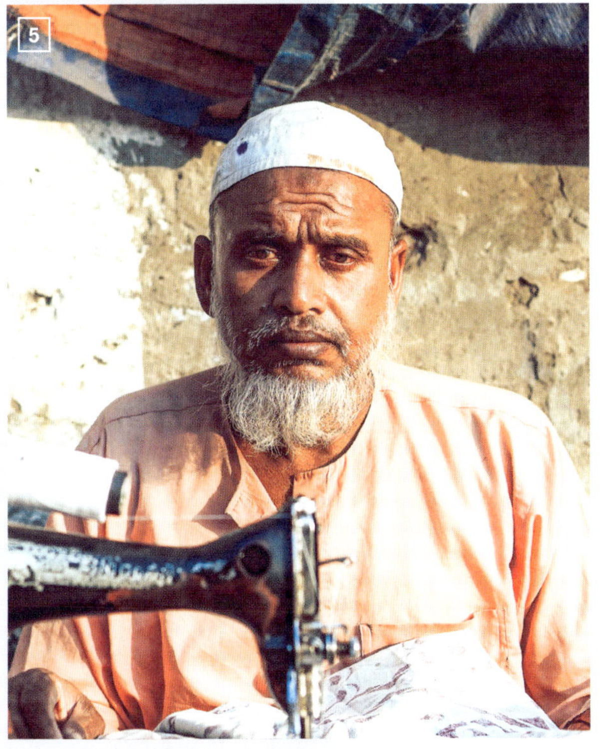

TIP / The output sharpening process referenced in Step 5 is also worth turning into a preset or an 'action', as Photoshop calls them. Using presets and actions for repetitive tasks greatly increases the speed of your workflow. The faster you work, the more you can earn!

DELIVERING YOUR SELECTS

Considering most interaction with your client after the shoot day will be conducted online, it's useful to have a robust, easy-to-use method for getting finalised files across to them.

If shooting digitally, you will likely capture multiple images of the same scene, so you might have an array of different angles or facial expressions if shooting people. You'll narrow these down in the edit, of course, but you still need to 'select' the final image, or as I like to do, ask your client to make the final choice. I think this works in your favour as it gives the client a degree of ownership over the shoot they have commissioned. It puts them back in control.

However, there is a bit of a process involved with a client 'making selects,' especially when working remotely, so it pays to make it as easy as possible for them, as well as yourself. Here follows my workflow for easing the process:

DON'T MAKE PEOPLE WAIT
Export your JPEGs at 2500 pixels in size and at a quality of 75%. This is a low-resolution setting. High resolution means big files, which means longer loading times – something to avoid. Think of these images as preview files – they don't need to be super high quality, as your client is simply choosing their favourites from the shoot at this stage.

EVERYONE LIKES A LIKE BUTTON
Upload your low-resolution files to a web-based gallery for your client to review. I use something called Pixieset, primarily because it allows my clients to 'favourite' images using a simple heart icon, similar to the 'like' button on Facebook. Everyone knows how to 'like' something nowadays, so the process feels easy and intuitive – no need for lengthy explanations

from myself. Pixieset notifies me when a favourites list has been made, and tells me who has made it.

FINALISE THE FAVOURITES
Pixieset can generate a 'Lightroom Copy List' which makes the process of finding your client's favourites super easy. Copy and paste the list into Lightroom's Library search field and Lightroom will filter the full library accordingly, so you will see only see the images your client has selected. This is a good stage to create a Lightroom Collection for easy retrieval in the future. Now you have a list of chosen files, spend a bit more time on the grade. Retouch where necessary and apply output sharpening. These images have now moved from 'previews' to 'production' files. These are the photos your client will end up using so you want them to look the best they possibly can.

FORMAT ACCORDING TO USE
Export your finalised images using settings appropriate for their usage.

COLOUR PROFILE
Ensure the embedded colour profile is correct. It's easy to overlook, but it plays a vital part in maintaining colour accuracy when your images are viewed across different devices. If the images are to be displayed on a screen, choose sRGB, and if they are destined for print, choose ProPhoto RGB.

SEND HIGH RES USING DROPBOX
Export your finalised files to a folder in Dropbox or WeTransfer and send the link to your client.

CONGRATULATIONS, THAT'S A WRAP!

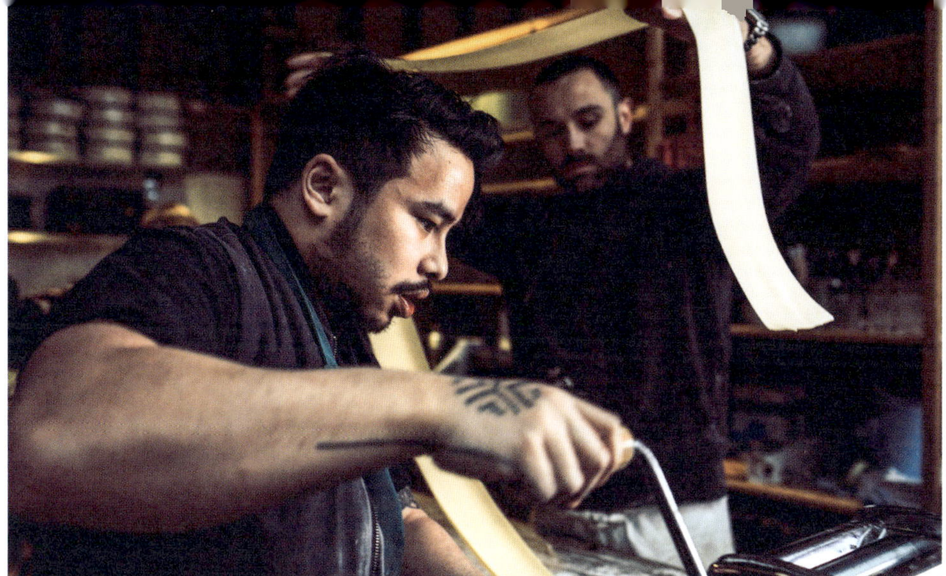

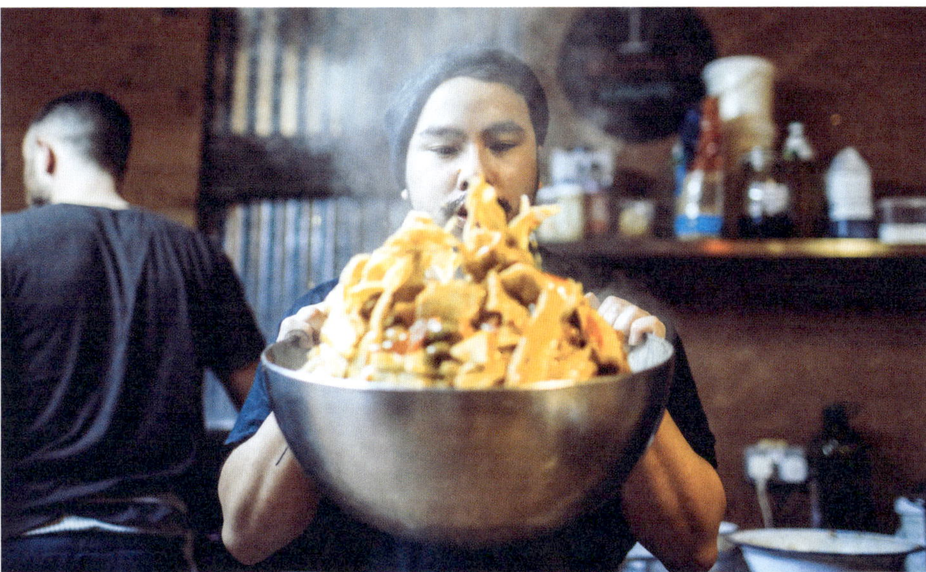

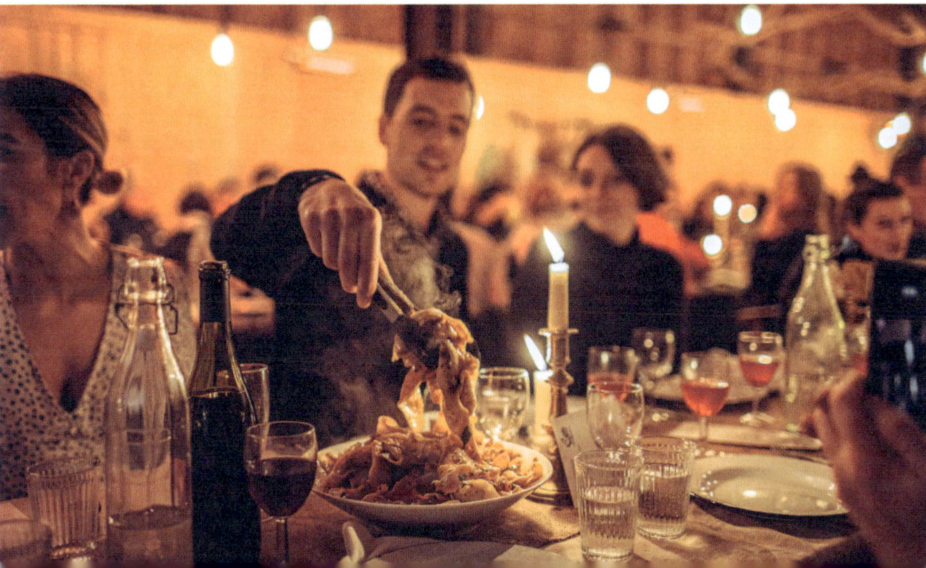

INDEX

A

8mm app 20
50 & stitch technique 118–119, 156
Adams, Ansel 21
Afterlight 2 app 20
aperture 108
    Shutter Priority mode 122, 125
apps 17, 20
atmosphere
    hazing 128–129
    lighting and 100–101, 114–115
    in storytelling 25
Atmosphere Aerosol 128

B

background
    motion blur 120–125, 126
    sharpness 108, 118
backing-up images 139, 159–161
backlighting 104–107
ball head 18
batteries 17, 18
biography 71
bird's-eye views 54–55
blue hour 102–103, 156
branding consistency 58, 61, 68, 71
Brenizer method 118–119, 156
burning 21

C

Cadrage app 20
call sheets 92–95
camera bags 18–19
camera settings
    aperture 108
    auto-focus 108
    f-stop 108
    image format 108
    ISO 108
    release shutter without card 108
    shutter speed 108
    Single Point focusing 108
    Zone Focusing 108
cameras 17, 18
Canon EOS 5D Mark IV 18
Capa, Robert 26
Cargo Collective 58
cataloguing images 139, 159–161
catchlights 116–117
Chambers, Jared 63
character and narrative 25, 28–29, 34, 152

casting 28–29
clothing and styling 28, 94
desire 28, 29
environmental portraiture 32–37
chromatic aberration 110
cinematic shooting technique 128–133
client expectations, managing 78
close-ups 26, 27, 44–45, 53
Cloud storage 159–161
collaborative relationships 62–63
Collections 142–143
colour
    averaging 86–87
    chromatic aberration 110
    combining colour palettes 84–85
    complementary colours 144–145
    editing 86–89
    hue 146
    luminance 146
    mood-boarding for 80–83, 86
    pairing unrelated images by 50–51
    photo story and 144–145
    profile 172
    psychological properties 80–85, 87, 88–89
    saturation 146
    split-toning 147
    target audience and 84–87
colour grading 71, 144–149
    choosing colour palette 86–89
colour palette 71
competitor brands 65
Continual app 20
Continuous mode 125
Costa, Dan 98–99
creative calls 66–67
creative fees 72, 74
creative sharpening 167–171
creative specifications 64
cutaways/details 38–39, 44–45, 54

D

Dabene, Andrea 63
Daroowala, Rishad 63
depth of field 40–41, 108, 110, 118
Designspiration 78, 86
dirty foreground 134–135
Display Purposes 62
distortion 110
dodging 21
domain name 58
drama, adding 31
drone 17

Dropbox 159, 172
DSLR camera 17, 18
    metering point 106

E

editing
    adding light leaks 150
    burning 21
    creating a body of work 50
    dodging 21
    grading 71, 86–89, 144–149
    HSL 146
    introducing grain 150–151
    objectivity 50
    organising your images 139
    pricing into estimate 73
    S-curve 146
    selects 140–143
    sharpening 166–167
    on a smartphone 21
    software 17, 20
    split-toning 147
    tone curve 146
email address 58
emotion, relating to 13
    colour 80–85, 87, 88–89
    portraiture 116–117
    researching target audience 84–86
engaging the viewer 11, 13, 54
equipment 17–19
    pricing into estimate 72, 74
establishing shots 38–39, 40–41
estimating a price 65, 67, 72–75
    negotiating your estimate 73, 74–75
event, storytelling 25, 30–31
everyday cinematic 52–55
example imagery 64, 92
exclusivity terms 65
exposure 108
    dodging and burning 21
Exposure plugin 17, 150–151

F

f-stop 108
file formats 164–165
film, shooting with film to influence grade 148–149
film emulation apps 20
focal point, directing viewer's eye to 168–171
focus
    fixed focal length 110
    panning shots 120–125
    Single Point 108
    Zone 108
Format 58
Franklin, Benjamin 72, 76

G

geotags 62
Getty's Usage Calculator 74, 75
golden hour 100, 102–103
GPS tracking 62
grain 108, 150–151

H

hashtags 62
hazing 128–129, 133
highlight clipping 145
histogram 145
HSL 145, 146
Hyperlapse app 20

I

image grading 71, 144–149
    developing colour palette for 86–87
imagination
    viewer's 11, 13
input sharpening 167–171
Instagram 58, 60–63, 64
intrigue, creating 40–41, 52
intuition 11, 14
ISO 108

J

JPEG files 108, 164–165

L

landscapes 18
layout apps 20–21
lens flare 130–133
lens hood 132
lenses 17, 18
    35mm 42
    50mm 43, 44, 118
    prime 110–111
    telephoto 40, 44, 110, 118
    zoom 18, 110, 130–133
licensing fees 72, 74–75
light leak effects 150
lighting
    backlighting 104–107
    camera aperture 108
    catchlights 114, 116–117
    developing a signature style 101
    diffused 102–103
    environmental portraiture 36
    fill light 116
    golden hour 100
    iPhone portrait mode 112–113
    ISO 108
    lens flare 130–133
    location and atmosphere 100–101

prime lenses 110
reflector 17
Rembrandt lighting 114–115
shooting silhouettes 104–107
shutter speed 108
spot metering 106
Sun Surveyor app 20
timing 100
Lightroom 17, 139, 159
    Capture folder 140
    Collections feature 142–143
    copy list 172
    Develop mode 144–151
    grain slider 150–151
    Library module 139
    Loupe mode 140
    Photo Merge tool 119
    sharpening with 167–171
local story-telling 14
location 152
    environmental portraiture
        32–37
    fees and permits 72
    lighting and 100–101
    and narrative 25, 26–27, 32–37
    recce/scouting 71, 90–91
logo 68, 71
long shots 40–41
lossless format files 164
luminance 146

M

memories, preserving 13
memory cards 18
mood boards 64, 68, 71
    colour 80–83, 86
    examples 79
    personal projects 78
    sources for 78
    unrelated subjects 78
motion blur 108, 120–125
movement
    panning shots 120–125
    tracking shots 126–127
mystery, capturing 104–107

N

narrative, viewer's imagination
    11, 13
NAS (Network Attached Storage)
    160–161
ND (neutral-density) filter 122,
    125
negotiating an estimate 73, 74–75
noise 108
nostalgia 26, 28

O

objectivity when editing 50
opposite colour 44

organising your images 139
output sharpening 167–171

P

panning shots 120–125
period details 26
Photopills app 20
Photoshop 17, 71, 139
    adding light leaks 150
    Dropper tool 86
    resizing in 170
    sharpening with 167–171
Pircher, Julian 63
pitching your work 56–75
    questioning clients 64–65
Pixieset 172
planning apps 20
plot 25, 27, 152
portfolio coherence 58, 61
portraiture 18
    catchlights 116–117
    environmental 32–37
    iPhone portrait mode 112–113
    medium close shots 43
    relating to your subject 98–99
    Rembrandt lighting 114–115
    shaping emotions through
        116–117
    symbolism 33
pre-production days 72
prep 76–91
pricing see estimating a price
projects and exercises
    develop a treatment 68–71
    edit like a painter 88–89
    environmental portraiture
        34–37
    everyday cinematic 52–55
    experimenting with catchlights
        117
    finalising your file 168–171
    lens flare 130–133
    making collections 143
    motion blur 122–125
    one subject, ten ways 46–49
    panning with a smartphone 121
    Rembrandt lighting 15
    shoot with film to influence
        grade 148–149
    shooting silhouettes 104–107
    stitching 119
    tracking 127
props 28
    portraiture 33, 34, 36
    shot lists/call sheets 92–95
punchline 31

R

RAID (Redundant Array of
    Independent Disks) 160–161

Raw files 108, 164–165, 167
reflector 17
relating to your subject 98–99
Rembrandt lighting 114–115
resizing 170
retouching 71
    pricing into estimate 73
reveal 38–39

S

S-curve 146
scene setting 26–27
SCRL app 20
selects 140–143
    delivering 172
shadow 102–103
    dodging and burning 21
    Rembrandt lighting
        114–115
sharpening 166–171
shoot processing 74
shot lists 20, 64, 92–95
shot types
    bird's-eye views 54–55
    cinematic 128–133
    close-ups 44–45, 53
    cutaways/details 38–39,
        44–45, 54
    dirty foreground 134–135
    establishing shots 20–21,
        38–39, 41
    extreme long 40, 53
    long 41
    medium 42–43, 53
    one subject, ten ways 46–49
    panning shots 120–125
    reveals 38–39
    shot from character's point of
        view 54
    shot lists 92–95
    tracking shots 126–127
    transition shots 38–39, 44–45
    using variety of 52–53
Shutter Priority mode 122, 125
shutter speed 108, 120, 122, 125
    tracking shots 127
signature style, developing 101
silhouettes, shooting 104–107
simplicity in storytelling 25,
    31, 34
Single Point focusing 108
SLR 18–19
smartphones
    apps 17, 20
    cameras 17, 18
    image editing on 21
    iPhone portrait mode
        112–113
    panning shots 121
Snapseed app 20, 21

software 17
split-toning 145, 147
Squarespace 58
stitching 118–119, 156
storytelling
    see also character and narrative;
        location
    building a story 22, 25,
        152–157
    plot 25, 27, 152
    shot types 38–48
    story endings 31, 39, 40,
        52, 55
Strohl, Alex 63
structure, importance in
    storytelling 25
subject matter 14
Sun Surveyor app 20
surprise, writing in 31
suspense 31
symbolism 33

T

target audience, researching
    84–87
theme, importance in storytelling
    25
Tice, George 14
TIFF (Tagged Image File Format)
    164
timelapse footage 20
timelines, work 64
tone curve 145, 146
tone and mood 147
Touchretouch app 20, 21
tracking shots 126–127
transition shots 38–39, 44–45
treatments 68–71
tripod 18, 108

U

Unfold app 20
usage fees 72
    Getty's Usage Calculator 74,
        75
usage period 64–65, 75
usage terms 64–65

V

videos, splitting 20
VSCO app 20

W

website portfolio 58–59
wide-angle photography
    118–119

Z

Zone Focusing 108
zoom lens 18, 110, 130–133

THERE IS NO FINISH LINE

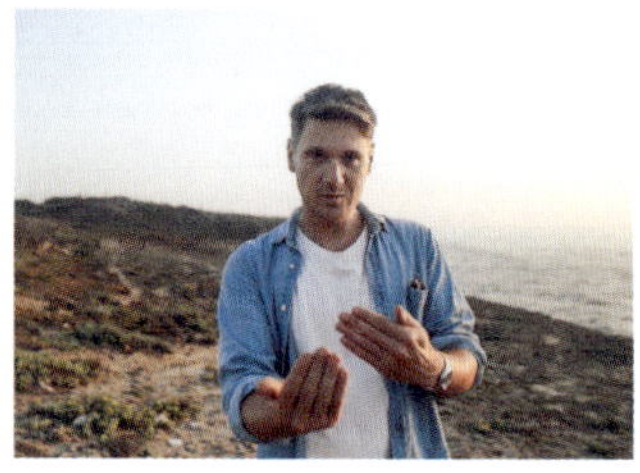

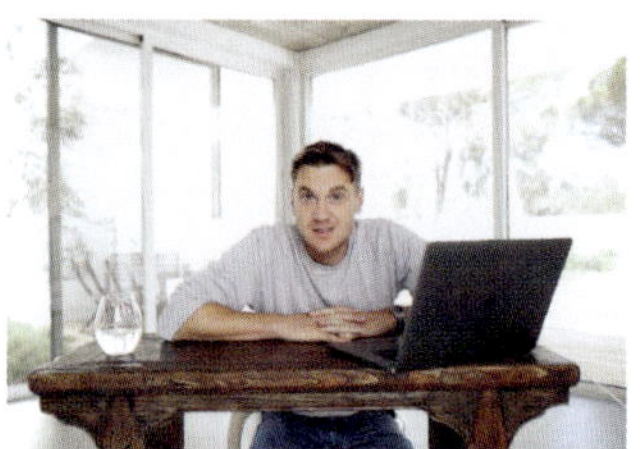

Well done! You've made it to the end. Personally, I don't think there is a finish line. Whatever our experience level, there is always more to learn. If you are still hungry for more, do check out the online video version of this workshop at the following link: **www.madebyfinn.com/workshop**

I describe the processes laid out in this book and prepare, shoot and edit for my client Cool & Vintage. It features:

- 6 hrs of streaming video content
- 9 in-the-field episodes
- 6 interview episodes
- 6 editing episodes

THANKS AGAIN, AND KEEP SHOOTING!

ACKNOWLEDGEMENTS

Thank you to all of the team at Quarto Books. My ever-patient editors Ellie Wilson and Charlotte Frost, designer Isabel Eeles and of course Zara Anvari for commissioning me to write this book in the first place.

Special thanks to my good friend Alex Strohl for asking me to create the online video workshop this book is based on. I had never considered teaching before you approached me, and the resulting journey has been hugely rewarding. I'm so glad we met all those years ago via that little app called Instagram.

Speaking of Instagram, thank you to everyone who follows my account @finn. I have made so many happy connections through the app over the years. Many of you are now good friends, whereas others I am still to meet. Here's hoping we connect for real someday!

Thank you to everyone who appears in this book, especially Dan Costa, the surfboard shaper who let me follow him for a week and Stathis and Christianna for revealing their magical corner of Greece called Pelion.

Huge thanks to all of my clients who trust me with their assignments. Especially the team at Northstar and Audi for sending me on some mad crazy trips – 'sure, I'll hang from a helicopter over an erupting volcano' – long may they last! I greatly appreciate your belief in my abilities. Thank also to friends Sian, James, Jackson and the rest of the team at Fforest, Rosa & Rich at Cereal, Seth Carnill, Kate Hayward, Dan Rubin, Greg Annandale, Jesse Miller, Peter Florence and everyone else who have helped me on this journey.

Thanks to my agents: Biddy, Holly, Kirsty, Charles and Sarah for watching my back. You guys rule.

Lots of love to my lovely Mum and 'wish-you-were-still-here' Dad, and my Grandad: Charlie Thwaites, who gave me my first lesson in photography. I have never forgotten it.

Last but not least, BIG love to my long-suffering family Clare, Harlan, Seren and Otto. You are beyond patient with my happy-snapping, 'just-one-more', camera antics. I hope it doesn't ever wear thin because the pictures I make with you guys are truly the most precious. x